INTANGIBALL

THE SUBTLE THINGS THAT WIN BASEBALL GAMES

LONNIE WHEELER

SIMON & SCHUSTER

NEW YORK   LONDON   TORONTO   SYDNEY   NEW DELHI

Simon & Schuster
1230 Avenue of the Americas
New York, NY 10020

First Simon & Schuster hardcover edition August 2015

SIMON & SCHUSTER and colophon are
registered trademarks of Simon & Schuster, Inc.

For information about special discounts for bulk purchases,
please contact Simon & Schuster Special Sales at
1-866-506-1949 or business@simonandschuster.com.

The Simon & Schuster Speakers Bureau can bring authors to your live event.
For more information or to book an event, contact the Simon & Schuster Speakers
Bureau at 1-866-248-3049 or visit our website at www.simonspeakers.com.

Interior design by Ruth Lee-Mui

Manufactured in the United States of America

1   3   5   7   9   10   8   6   4   2

Library of Congress Cataloging-in-Publication Data

Wheeler, Lonnie.
Intangiball : the subtle things that win baseball games / Lonnie Wheeler.
pages   cm
1. Baseball—Miscellanea.   I. Title.
GV873.W48   2015
796.357—dc23
2015004128

ISBN 978-1-4516-9602-8
ISBN 978-1-4516-9604-2 (ebook)

To Abby, Clark, and Emily

CONTENTS

That which material sense calls intangible,
is found to be substance.

—MARY BAKER EDDY

INTRODUCTION

IT WAS DURING THE SUMMER OF 2008 THAT I BECAME A BASEBALL FAN AGAIN. THE OLD newspaper I'd written for, the doomed *Cincinnati Post,* had bowed out on the final day of the year before, and while its demise put a crimp in my prospects, it did liberate my rooting interest, which was no longer muted by objectivity's shushing index finger. At the same time, our twentysomething daughter was between jobs and hanging at home for a little while—long enough, anyway, to catch some ball games on the basic cable package. She was relatively new to that diversion, and while she was not caught up in the statistical subplots that captivate so many modern-age fans, her enchantment soon became keen enough to take her to the ballpark on a frequent basis. She would also, when necessary, receive automated updates by text messages. Mostly, she got a kick out of the characters—the good-natured grief that Jay Bruce took from the veterans, the eloquent facemaking of Johnny Cueto, the squatty switch-hitting of Javy Valentin, the Mountielike manhood of Joey Votto, Laynce Nix's resemblance to a komodo dragon, and so on. My wife, whose interest in the games had traditionally taken her up to bedtime but never postponed it, began to linger longer in the late innings. Baseball became, for the first time, a family thing. Watching it in that light, unencumbered by twenty inches of editorial burden to follow, was downright pleasant.

The local team had something to do with that. For the better part of a decade, the Reds had slogged to the beat of their big-swinging sluggers, Adam Dunn and Ken Griffey, Jr., successful, likable fellows who had the misfortune of outranking the rest of the clubhouse. Dunn, a six-foot-six, self-deprecating country boy, wielded a humor so potent that less accomplished players didn't want it hurled in their direction. Meanwhile, to many of the rank and file, Griffey had once been the poster on the wall next to the bed. The two of them, with no such intention, established the tone in Cincinnati's clubhouse, and while it was not disagreeable, neither was it particularly inspiring. Griffey's failing legs had filched his former sizzle, and Dunn's passion, while not entirely absent, was concealed somewhere between the edge of his deadpan and the preponderance of his 285 pounds. Both players struck out a lot with men on base, of which there was a shortage to start with. The club had losing records for eight straight seasons. As theater, it wasn't much.

When first Griffey and then Dunn were traded for younger players late in the 2008 season, the Reds began to morph. The floor recognized Votto and Bruce. The clearing of the shadows revealed the sparkle in Brandon Phillips's smile. Pitchers prospered. And through it all there escaped a teamwide enthusiasm—even an efficiency—that was simply nice to see. The new crew made you look. All the while, the organization, for the first time in a generation, was raising highly regarded players on its farm clubs in substantial numbers, and there was a compelling constant among the prospects. Almost to a kid, they were diamond rats. They were backers-up of throws and runners-out of ground balls, hard-trying athletes whose want-its and work ethics were all a partisan could ask for. They had me.

Sensitized in such a way, I began to notice, as the 2009 season approached, short and lengthy articles about a subtle change in the way

Major-League franchises were fashioning their rosters. One column, written by Buster Olney of espn.com, observed that "increasingly, it seems, makeup is regarded as a pivotal factor on whether a player is acquired or dumped—and this might be part of a broader evolution in Major League Baseball." Olney quoted a manager and a club official about the benefits of removing smug, downbeat individuals from their teams and constructing teams, instead, out of players willing to pull hard in the same direction. Another story, posted on Insidethebook.com, went so far as to assign a dollar value to a player's leadership qualities. It did so by noting that the San Diego Padres had signed weathered outfielder Cliff Floyd for $750,000, in spite of the fact that Floyd, diminished by his battle scars, was expected to play very little and offered nothing more, statistically, than would a minimum-salary rookie who could be had for $400,000. San Diego general manager Kevin Towers acknowledged that Floyd had been acquired mostly for his intangibles, and it required only a short reach to conclude that the Padres had paid an extra $350,000 for those.

The previous year, Floyd had been a valued member of the Tampa Bay Rays, who had soared to the American League championship by virtue of a remade roster emphasizing, in addition to defense, a team-first mentality. Under the progressive stewardship of manager Joe Maddon and general manager Andrew Friedman, the Rays set up their breakout season with gutsy personnel decisions, trading a pair of supremely talented young outfielders, Delmon Young and Elijah Dukes, in part for their exchange rates and in part because of their demeanors, which were perceived as detrimental to the esprit de clubhouse. When all was said and redone, the Rays, coming off three straight last-place finishes, and in spite of a payroll that left them financially dwarfed by such division rivals as the Red Sox and Yankees, had assembled a team that mussed the hair and reddened the faces of the redoubtable AL East.

Hardly coincidentally, they had, at the same time, become an outfit that Maddon could do his thing with. "We believed that we stayed pretty much status quo talentwise," he observed in retrospect, "but there was a quantum leap in regard to personality, character, and interaction inside the clubhouse. I'd like to believe that teams are looking more at character these days in making their decisions."

Of course, it wasn't as simple or idealistic as all that. The Rays were required to flash some killer glove work. A skillful new starting pitcher, Matt Garza, needed a shove from his catcher, a long talk from Maddon, and a visit with the club psychologist. A gifted young outfielder, B. J. Upton, was handed a benching for lack of hustle. As it happened, Charlie Manuel, the manager of the Philadelphia Phillies—the team that ultimately would defeat the Rays in the World Series—made similar moves during the course of the season, twice sitting down Jimmy Rollins for conduct unbecoming an All-Star shortstop. Old school, it seemed, was back in session.

The development of the Phillies was not as sudden as Tampa Bay's and, designwise, not as tangibly intangible, but forensics revealed the same chemical traces at the scenes. There was a heartening circumstance here: The game and some of its more traditional admirers had come together at a crossing of common interests. Pluck, soundness, and winning spirit had, at last, in this advanced and exhaustively quantified stage of the sport's evolution, been acknowledged, even embraced, as strategically vital. The day—or the season, as it were—had been won by the respectful, enthusiastic observance of the so-called little things.

I can't speak for every baseball watcher out there, but I can affirm that here in the hills and humidity of Cincinnati, where the professional game got its start and Pete Rose is still revered in spite of it all, the folks like players who like to play, who like to play *right*. Not entirely or deliberately but methodically, since the end-of-day sports shows became so tediously preoccupied with long flies arcing over pinched-in fences . . . since steroids stepped up to the plate . . . the sport had rendered increasingly rare the Roses, the Cobbs, the Jackie Robinsons (as if they're plural), the Pepper Martins, the Phil Rizzutos, the Luis Aparicios, and the gritty grinders of lesser stripe but fundamental excellence and irreproachable heart. Maybe the steroid scandal was like a stock-market correction. Maybe baseball's bloated muscles simply burst. Maybe the great game so indulged its excesses, so distorted the natural order, that it just had to crash.

One manager, in Olney's column, remarked that we were witnessing a major change in the game, right before our eyes.

Might the national pastime have, perhaps unwittingly, but in its own interest, rediscovered its innate, endearing essence? Could this be a purification that we were witnessing, a renaissance of the noblest, winningest qualities that sports can bring to public attention?

As a captivated fan once again, I was compelled to look into that.

ONE

THE FIRST ORDER OF BUSINESS

THE CINCINNATI REDS HAD REASON TO BELIEVE THAT THE TWENTY-FIRST CENTURY WOULD, at the outset, belong to them. Their brassy general manager, Jim Bowden, certainly felt that way, and never more justifiably than on the ceremonial winter night when, in testament to his talent for bodacious deal-making, it was announced that the Reds, for center fielder Mike Cameron, pitcher Brett Tomko, and two minor leaguers, had acquired the official Player of the Decade, the only man ever to receive six million All-Star votes, the youngest hitter to reach 350 home runs, the action figure in the backward ball cap, The Kid himself.

"February 10, 2000," Bowden declared that evening in the crowded Crosley Room of Cinergy Field, "will go down in Reds history and baseball history as the night when one of the biggest trades in the history of our sport took place, when the Michael Jordan of baseball came home to Cincinnati. This is a GM's dream."

Not only was Ken Griffey, Jr., returning to the town where he grew up, where his swift, handsome father batted between Pete Rose and Joe

Morgan on the epic team the city still clings to, where he drank red pop out of the same cooler as Johnny Bench and Tony Perez, but, having conquered most of the modern world in Seattle, he was now joining a conspicuously rising Cincinnati club that, out of nowhere, had won ninety-six games in 1999, an outfit so unforeseeably successful that it was described as "the first harbinger of change in the influence of cash on results."[1] What's more, he was joining the only team he was willing to join, and doing it for the considerable but decidedly reasonable sum—generally referred to as discounted—of $112.5 million for nine years.

"This," said Griffey, flanked by family, beaming Reds honchos, and a phalanx of local politicos, "is the moment I've been waiting for."

The subsequent season, as it turned out, was only mildly successful— a winning one, but ten games short of the St. Louis Cardinals in the Central Division of the National League—in spite of Griffey's forty home runs and 118 runs batted in. The Reds were still managed by Jack McKeon and their lineup carried over the likes of Barry Larkin and Sean Casey, but the pitching dropped off and the general atmosphere, it was widely believed, sorely missed the strong-armed, single-minded leadership of departed outfielder Greg Vaughn, to say nothing of his forty-five homers. "Best influence I ever saw," said Marty Brennaman, the longtime Cincinnati broadcaster, of Vaughn. "He would chew guys out right in the dugout if they were loafing or didn't use their head." Vaughn was a free agent after the '99 season, and the conservatively budgeted Reds couldn't accommodate him and Griffey both.

It was in September 2000 that Griffey began to hear from his left hamstring, an injury that permitted him to come to the plate only three times over the season's final three weeks. Late in spring training of 2001, the hamstring still tender, he went ahead and tore it rounding third base and was reduced to pinch-hitting for most of April, until he was finally placed on the disabled list near the end of the month. His first start of the season came in the Reds' sixty-fifth game. All the while, the ballclub's void in power was not being taken up. In only 364 at-bats that year, Griffey still led Cincinnati in home runs, with twenty-two. It should be noted, though, that when the final results were in, Junior, in fact, was not the Red most likely to whack the ball out of the premises. That distinction applied to rookie outfielder Adam Dunn, who stepped into the lineup even later in the season—July 20—than Griffey.

By then, Dunn, a jocular former quarterback from the University of Texas, had already hit twelve home runs in Chattanooga (AA ball) and another twenty in Louisville (AAA). He had also batted a combined .334 in those stops, and arrived in the Major Leagues as a dynamic presence at the plate. I recall, soon after Dunn's promotion, looking on from the Cinergy press box and turning to Jamie Ramsey, a young media relations assistant for the Reds, to say something like, "You know, Dunn's the only guy on the ballclub who makes me stop what I'm doing and watch when he comes to bat." I also recall Ramsey agreeing readily. Dunn finished 2001 with nineteen home runs for Cincinnati, completing a total of fifty-one for the year.

Nevertheless, the Reds' season—the first for manager Bob Boone, who had replaced McKeon—could, at 66–96, be safely described as a disaster. The other noted hometowner on the roster, thirty-seven-year-old Larkin, a shortstop whom thrifty owner Carl Lindner had sentimentally and unexpectedly signed for three more years and $27 million, was limited to forty-five games by a sports hernia. Between them, Griffey and Larkin, with their 602 plate appearances, occupied 44 percent of the franchise's payroll.

For the Reds, the bad news was only picking up steam. The losing that began in 2001 persisted doggedly. It was unremitting and deeply dispiriting, considering that, for years, since long before Griffey's arrival, the front office had touted 2003, the year that Great American Ball Park was due to open, as the target date for the club's rebirth. Great American was constructed with friendly fences all around, most notably in right field, which so auspiciously matched up with the left-handed longballing of Griffey and Dunn.

The dreary failure (69–93) of 2003 precipitated bloodletting that started three days before the trading deadline, with the firings of Boone and Bowden. Jose Guillen, the team's leading hitter at the time, was packed off to Oakland. Scott Williamson, a force in the bullpen, was traded to Boston. Aaron Boone, third baseman and son of the canned skipper, departed tearfully for the Yankees. In its showcase season, the ballclub was grotesquely depleted. Griffey didn't play after he injured his ankle on July 17. Dunn didn't play after injuring his thumb on August 15. Larkin, coming back from a calf problem, didn't play after August 22 because of an injured ring finger. Over the three years of Larkin's controversial contract, he and Griffey, combined, sat out 478 games.

And on it went. After some messy nonnegotiations, the Reds, at a substantially reduced rate, signed Larkin for one more time around in 2004, and he bounced back nicely in a downsized role. Dunn crushed forty-six home runs that year, one of them, in early August, coming to rest on a piece of driftwood in the Ohio River. The next day, Griffey, returning to the lineup after missing four weeks with a tear of the *right* hamstring, made a sliding catch and ripped the thing off the bone altogether. The ensuing surgery involved three screws.

The Reds' new manager, Dave Miley, promoted from the Triple-A club at Louisville, never had a chance. Dan O'Brien, hired in '04 as the general manager—since booting Bowden, the team had gotten by with a pair of interims—understood his role as a rebuilder and got to work on the organization's player development system. It was a major project. As Dunn clubbed picturesque homers and Griffey, regaining his health if not his magic, had his years and moments, the losing seasons proceeded to pile up. In the middle of 2005, Miley was replaced by Jerry Narron. Early in 2006, O'Brien was replaced by Wayne Krivsky. In 2007, Narron was replaced for half a season by Pete Mackanin, who was replaced in October by Dusty Baker. And just over three weeks into the 2008 season, with the club sitting at 9-12, Krivsky was abruptly fired in favor of fifty-seven-year-old Walt Jocketty.

OWING TO THE GRASSROOTS EFFORTS OF HIS TWO MOST RECENT PREDECESSORS, Jocketty took over a baseball operation that was in better shape than it appeared. There was, by that time, talent at both the major- and minor-league levels. But the sobering truth that the benefits hadn't shown up in Cincinnati—hadn't even stopped by—was problematic for Bob Castellini, the club's relatively new owner.

To Castellini, a produce magnate and lifelong Cincinnatian, it was a matter not merely of impatience but also of integrity. Two years before, when addressing his proud city for the first time after acquiring the club from Lindner, Castellini had stated his agenda with characteristic earnestness. "We didn't get involved with the Reds to wallow in mediocrity," declared the soft-spoken businessman who had given up his luxury box at Great American for the simple reason that the ballclub stunk. "If that's all we've got, we shouldn't be hanging around. We're buying the Reds to win. Anything else is unacceptable.

"I want to make a promise today to Reds fans, wherever you are; a promise from one fan to another. We will bring championship baseball to Cincinnati. From this moment forward, we will work toward that dream and will not rest until we exceed the expectations of our fans. We will bring championship baseball to Cincinnati."

He was not foreign to the concept. For the previous ten years, following stints in the ownership groups of the Reds, Baltimore Orioles, and Texas Rangers, Castellini had held a financial stake in the Cardinals, who in 2004 had won the National League pennant before succumbing to Boston in the World Series. In St. Louis he became acquainted and impressed with Jocketty, whose thirteen years as the Cardinals' general manager involved six division titles and culminated in the World Series championship of 2006. When Jocketty was surprisingly excused by St. Louis following the 2007 season, Castellini wasted little time in bringing him to Cincinnati as a special adviser and, three months later, in dismissing Krivsky in favor of the more tested, familiar alternative now in house. The hiring of a GM of Jocketty's stripe seemed to signal that Castellini was, indeed, sincere about winning.

Yet the move made no initial difference in the National League standings. Under Jocketty's close scrutiny, the Reds pulled within a game of .500 on the first day of June and were still in the vicinity as the trading deadline approached in late July, but embarked then on a dooming 2-14 stretch, by the end of which their metamorphosis would be well under way.

To begin with, Jocketty's inherited ballclub had evolved a bit from the team Krivsky had fielded the year before. Krivsky, who, in 2006, had brought Brandon Phillips to Cincinnati in a fortuitous trade with Cleveland, had a year later pulled off the audacious acquisition of minor leaguer Josh Hamilton,[2] the former number one overall draft pick who had missed more than three years of baseball while suspended for, and reeling from, a drug and alcohol habit. Hamilton produced immediately for the Reds, flashing the outrageous ability that three years later would make him the MVP of the American League. But his history of substance abuse necessitated that the Reds monitor him constantly and handle him carefully. It happened that Hamilton, a North Carolinian, was coached as a youth player by Johnny Narron, the brother of the Reds' manager. Sensibly, it seemed, Johnny was placed on Jerry Narron's staff with the responsibility of looking after the fragile phenom. However, as Hamilton's dramatic story made him a media sensation, the rhythms of the Reds' clubhouse were subtly disturbed. Jealousy may have been a factor. Players murmured about preferential treatment. Meanwhile, the organization, already mindful of the perils that challenge a recovering addict, took note of Hamilton's tendency toward injury. The upshot was that the following winter, Krivsky, in pursuit of sorely needed pitching, swapped Hamilton to the Texas Rangers for Edinson Volquez, a gifted but unpredictable right-hander, and tiny reliever Daniel Ray Herrera.

As Hamilton took off in Texas, where he would immediately lead the American League in RBIs and total bases, Volquez swiftly emerged as the ace of a Cincinnati rotation that also included a rookie, twenty-two-year-old Johnny Cueto. At the same time, newcomers were making their marks in the Reds' everyday lineup. Jay Bruce, a twenty-one-year-old outfielder rated by some as the top prospect in all the minor leagues, came up in late May and looked the part. Joey Votto, taking over at first base, would place second in the 2008 Rookie of the Year balloting, behind Geovany Soto of the Cubs. Not lacking power, the Reds ranked fourth in the league (out of sixteen teams) in homers; and yet, their run total lagged far behind at twelfth. Something was amiss.

There was no shortage of obvious problems to point to. The club got little out of the shortstop and catcher positions. In his first Cincinnati season, Baker—who was Krivsky's appointment, with Castellini's enthusiastic blessing—could never settle on a leadoff batter, rolling through ten of them, starting with center fielder Corey Patterson, who, in thirty-five starts at the top of the order, responded with a sickly .217 on-base percentage. An unholy collaboration of shallow pitching and second-rate fielding left the Reds' overall defense thirteenth in the NL in runs allowed.

Jocketty, a team-culture advocate whose departure from the Cardinals was related to his reluctance to abandon traditional ideals for a more fashionable, predominantly numbers-based method of management, saw deeper issues. That was why, on July 31, with an eighth straight losing season all but assured, he traded the Player of the (previous) Decade, the future Hall of Famer who the night before had delivered the six-hundred-eighth home run of his magnificent career, to the Chicago White Sox. In exchange for Griffey, the Reds received relief pitcher Nick Masset and minor-league infielder Danny Richar. Less than two weeks later, Jocketty dealt a perennial forty-home-run hitter—2008 would be the fourth straight season Dunn hit *exactly* that many—to the Arizona Diamondbacks for pitcher Micah Owings, minor-league pitcher Dallas Buck, and minor-league utility man Wilkin Castillo.

"It's a delicate thing," Jocketty remarked in retrospect. "I don't want to be quoted as saying those two were . . . they weren't really a problem. They were terrific guys, and individually performed well. But, you know, their approach may have not been what we eventually wanted here."

What he sought was the model he had worked with in Oakland— where he was director of minor-league operations, and where his baseball sensibilities were strongly influenced by general manager Sandy Alderson and managers Billy Martin and Tony La Russa—and carried to St. Louis. Jocketty wanted a ballclub built upon not only power, pitching, and physical wherewithal, but the ethic that would put it all into play. He sought a merging of body and spirit, of talent and purpose, held together by leaders who would beneficially imprint not just the lineup, but the collective consciousness.

"I mentioned in the press conference when I got hired that the first order of business was to change the culture," the GM continued. "We'd gotten so used to losing. You've got to get people believing in themselves and the team and the organization, that you can be winners. If you don't think that way, you're not going to play that way. You've got to have a strong foundation in your organization."

The efficacious teaming of personalities is an amorphous, inherently subjective exercise, following no particular formula from clubhouse to clubhouse. On a more established, less impressionable ballclub than the Reds—say, the Yankees of Derek Jeter, Andy Pettitte, Paul O'Neill, and so on, or the Red Sox with David Ortiz, Jason Varitek, and Kevin Millar—the manufacture of humor and home runs may have represented bountiful, winning contributions from Griffey and Dunn. In Cincinnati, however, the culture was in question. The general manager was on a mission to re-create it. And Griffey and Dunn, as the best-paid, best-known, most decorated players on the team, *were* the culture.

"Being with Adam and Ken, they're two of my favorite people ever," Bruce said to Jayson Stark of espn.com. "They're unbelievable guys, and extraordinary at what they do on a baseball field. But they kind of ran the show, even without running the show. They didn't really have to say anything. They still were like the leaders. They were kind of just—I don't know—a little more, uhhh, veterany." [3]

Of course, as far as the setting of a tone is concerned, not all veterans are created equal. In Major-League society, eminence matters. Big seasons accumulate cachet. Big reputations build up clout in the clubhouse.

Stature engenders influence. Envy, perhaps. Even fear, if a guy's rebuke is sharp enough.

"You know," observed workhorse pitcher Bronson Arroyo, a member of the world champion Red Sox of 2004, "based on what you do in the game, regardless of your personality, if you are a big enough player you demand respect, no matter what. I saw it in Curt Schilling. Schilling could say something and somebody else could make the exact same statement, but more people would believe Curt because it was him. Griffey was kind of in the same boat. Griffey has done so well in his career, and done so many unbelievable things in the game, that people look to him as a leader. Regardless of what he did, whether he came into the locker room and was just quiet, didn't put on his uniform until thirty minutes before the game, people were still going to look to him as their leader. Adam came up under his leadership and kind of followed along with that."

For the Reds, this scenario was not without its benefits. Griffey played a highly intelligent brand of baseball, taking expert angles in the outfield and running the bases with nearly impeccable judgment of when his duct-taped legs could be coaxed to the next station. He risked his health in pursuit of fly balls. He persevered through debilitating injuries to a knee, an ankle, a shoulder, a hip, a quad, both hamstrings, and tendons up and down his chassis. He enjoyed the game. He oozed success. For the sake of the organization, he deferred a lot of money on his contract. And, in an age when home run hitters were routinely linked to artificial performance enhancement, Griffey, while rising to fifth all-time in that pantheon—fourth among the unaccused—remained above reproach. Dunn, for his part, brought to the sport a football mentality. He hit hard and played hurt; he played whole *seasons* hurt. Over a period of seven years, he played in more games than anyone else in the National League. At the plate, meanwhile, he demonstrated consistent, remarkable discipline; his vital annual numbers (home runs and walks) were practically givens. Dunn was also stone-faced hilarious, and his low-key comedy was turned on himself frequently enough to put ego in perspective.

However, theirs happened not to be an energizing, elevating, example-setting form of leadership. That's neither an indictment nor a failing. It was simply their styles. Griffey, for instance, wasn't one to school the youngsters on how to train for a season or prepare for a ball-game. Even when nursing another of his hamstring problems, he was often not to be seen among his teammates doing their late-afternoon stretching—an issue that he was compelled to address. "They say, 'He doesn't stretch.' I stretch all the time," Junior explained one day in the Cincinnati clubhouse. "I stretch when I get up. I stretch during the game in the outfield. I stretch on the rail when I'm in the on-deck circle. When the team stretches, I've already stretched. I stretch before you guys [the media] get in the locker room. I do a lot more than you guys know. I'll go out and ride my bike fifteen or twenty miles at three in the morning. I try to keep what I do secretive."

All of that, of course, was his prerogative. It was probably not, how-ever, the best face to put on for struggling young teammates with wide eyes fixed upon the Michael Jordan of baseball. What was good for The Kid, they may well have figured, ought to be good for *this* kid.[4]

A thornier if not uncommon matter was Griffey's tendency to run at significantly reduced speed on ground balls almost certain to result in outs. While the perfunctory trot was viscerally displeasing, was it a lack of hustle, or actually a prudent hedge against his fragile hamstrings?

"I didn't read anything into the way he played," said Bruce, perhaps the most ardent of Junior's admirers in the Cincinnati camp. (As a nine-year-old, Bruce had picked up a telephone in east Texas and attempted to call Griffey in the Mariners' clubhouse.) "His body only allowed him to play so hard. I think that mentally, Ken gave everything he had without becoming reinjured."

The symbolic artifact of Griffey's clubhouse presence was a leather massage chair parked next to his locker. Dunn had one, too. These were in addition to the couches where various Reds watched television and various others might indulge now and then in pregame catnaps. On the cue of *Cincinnati Enquirer* columnist Paul Daugherty, the recliners became a cause célèbre for the local message boards and media. Ultimately, the Reds (Dave Miley was the manager at the time) had them removed, at which point the story went national.

Reclinergate provoked from Dunn a spate of grousing about Miley and whatever else came to mind, followed by the announcement that his chair wished to be traded. Dunn's country candor made him incapable of disingenuousness. At the trade deadline a year in advance of when he was actually swapped, he *expected* to be, and team sources said he responded with open irritation when he saw his name on the lineup card and had to pull on his uniform.

Dunn was a leading practitioner of laid-back, and his lumbering style of left-fielding (owing, at least in part, to an unpublicized meniscus tear in his right knee that went unrepaired for two years) contributed further to an image of a guy who ran on low batteries. Joe Posnanski, the estimable baseball writer, once posted a blog on Dunn that was entitled "The Least Exciting Player Ever." More damning was the common assumption that the Big Donkey, as he was called, simply didn't care all that much. That was largely untrue, but the perception was so prevailing that it circulated within the industry. To wit, there was the infamous Toronto radio interview of June 2008, two months before Dunn was traded, with Blue Jays general manager J. P. Ricciardi, who, in reply to the suggestion that he acquire Cincinnati's imposing fly swatter, said, "Do you know the guy doesn't really like baseball all that much . . . ? We've done our homework on guys like Adam Dunn and there's a reason why we don't want Adam Dunn."[5]

Ricciardi's remarks spoke dramatically to the value that at least some front offices place on a player's vibe. And yet, even among the team builders who put great store in, for instance, an athlete's character, there's little consensus as to what traits most plainly and favorably constitute it. To wit, Baker, well known for his sensitivity in the interpersonal aspects of managing, held Dunn in high regard (he told *Sports*

Illustrated [6] that the large outfielder was "probably one of the best guys I've ever managed"), as he did Griffey. The feeling was similar among the Cincinnati players, who took it a step further. Observing the natural order, they ceded to Griffey and Dunn a role that the big guys weren't particularly interested in.

Johnny Bench, the Hall of Fame catcher who was frequently around the team, saw that dynamic clearly. "See, they weren't leaders," Bench said. "They didn't *want* to be. And that's okay, you don't have to be. But everybody *made* them leaders."

The Reds' pitching staff, however, was not lacking veteran and willing role models. Arroyo's perspective was broadened by his rich experience in Boston. Aaron Harang, an accomplished but struggling starter, never rubbed anybody any way but right. The closer, Francisco Cordero, acquired as a free agent, dispensed wisdom in the bullpen. And journeyman David Weathers was considered by at least a few teammates to be the leading leader of the entire ballclub, quite a distinction for a relief pitcher. Among the Cincinnati regulars, second baseman Brandon Phillips, a gifted, charismatic player, had openly expressed his interest in leadership. Phillips, however, while using his sparkling smile to win over Reds watchers (especially the women), came up a little short in the way of example setting. Brash and flashy—as a kid in Atlanta, his favorite athlete was Deion Sanders—he was, at the same time, sensitive about his reputation and easily upset by perceived slights. While his work in the infield was creative, quick-witted, and occasionally downright brilliant—a couple of times a week, it seemed, he would cause my wife to hurry in from the kitchen to catch the replay of his latest sleight-of-glove stunt—Phillips had also run afoul of his fans and manager (Baker had fined him more than once) with periodic lapses of concentration and of hustle while running (or *not* running) the bases. That left the Reds without a looming, on-field, follow-me presence among them.

"We've got a bunch of young or pretty average guys in this locker room," said Arroyo. "And for that reason, we're all in the same boat, we all feel like we're pulling on the same rope. It gives everybody a little more sense of ownership, no doubt. I definitely think the turnover in our clubhouse has changed the environment in here."

The leadership vacancies lured in younger, more fervid players. Inhibitions were peeled away. Votto could now freely assert the quiet intensity that characterized his approach. Among peers and other newbies, rookie infielder Adam Rosales, upon hitting a ball over a fence, could sprint around the bases without feeling silly. In the freshened, unjaded atmosphere, rookie catcher Ryan Hanigan, an undrafted New Englander brought up from the minors in August, found the self-assurance to commit his considerable diligence to the calling of a game. Bruce, not feeling so little brotherish anymore, stepped up in the pecking order. Without the star power of Griffey and Dunn, the difference in the Reds was hardly discernible in the standings and that, of itself, was a commentary, an encouragement.

For Jocketty, the sweeping task of culture change was just beginning. Meanwhile, as he noted the progress of Votto and Bruce and Volquez and Cueto and Hanigan, and as he sensed the fervency with which business was now being conducted at Great American Ball Park, it was not lost on him that the same sort of dynamic was at work—as it happened, a little further along—in Philadelphia, where the Phillies were making a spirited run at the World Series.

TWO

IT REALLY IS A TEAM SPORT

THE CASE I'LL MAKE CANNOT BE CLINICALLY PROVED. NOR, TO ANY TENABLE EXTENT, CAN it be demonstrated or popularized by statistical persuasion. In that respect, mathematics has me at a disadvantage. The algorithmic study of baseball known as *sabermetrics* (the name coined in reference to SABR, the Society for American Baseball Research) has illuminated the sport in spectacular detail, and my attentions elsewhere should by no means reflect a lack of awe for those advances. It's just that the numbers can only go so far. That's *far,* mind you, much farther than even a trained, straining eye could have made out even at the tail end of the twentieth century. Between fingertip access and the ingenious, inexhaustible parsing of performance and play-by-play, the fetching of information has become practically preternatural. In less time than it takes to write this sentence, and in spite of the fact that such records weren't kept when, say, Ken Boyer played for the St. Louis Cardinals in the fifties and sixties, one can easily find, for Boyer's whole career and any particular year, the very number of theoretical wins that he was responsible for, both offensively and defensively, in comparison to a replacement-level player (his WAR); the number of runs his work at third base was worth; the number of runs per game a team would have scored if every batter in the lineup was him; the number of times he advanced from first to third on a single; the number of times he reached on an error against a finesse pitcher; the number of double plays he grounded into while batting fourth in the order; the number of runners he tagged out; the percentage of his team's strikeouts he was responsible for; his batting average with the score tied; his batting average from the seventh inning to the ninth; his batting average when he was facing a starting pitcher for the third time in a game; his batting average on balls he put in play (BABIP) with two outs in the inning; his on-base percentage (OBP) with one out and runners at first and second; and his on-base-plus-slugging percentage (OPS) against Bob Purkey and Johnny Podres.

No doubt, Branch Rickey, the groundbreaking executive who, almost a half-century since his passing, remains the game's guiding light, would show a high regard for the sabermetric beast now crashing about the industry. He did, after all, author an enduring avant-garde article on the subject—before it had acquired the contemporary name—for *Life* magazine in 1954,[1] introducing a lengthy equation that subtracted defensive yield from offensive output to arrive at team efficiency. A similar exercise, Rickey pointed out, could also measure individual production. The futuristic piece spoke of such presently popular concepts as isolated power (as differentiated from slugging percentage, which, as a product of total bases, includes singles) and the overrating of the RBI. He was also, in 1947, the first general manager to hire a statistician, in spite of his skepticism when Allan Roth first walked into the Brooklyn Dodgers' offices with page upon page of cryptic computing.[2]

However, notwithstanding his manifest appreciation for baseball's inherent math, Rickey never compromised the premium he placed on the qualities he referred to as intangibles. To wit:

- "Statistics, of course, cannot tell the whole story. They fall short of bridging the gap between human expectancy and fulfillment. They cannot measure such intangibles as intelligence, courage, disposition, effort."[3]
- "Rickey," wrote biographer Lee Lowenfish, "was trying to build the spirit of teamwork in his professional players. Turning a squad of individuals into a *team* of players was always his primary goal as a coach and manager."[4]

The man who embodied all of the above, Rickey believed, was the great first baseman George Sisler, whom he coached at the University of Michigan, signed and managed for the St. Louis Browns, and hired as a scout in Brooklyn. "George Sisler," he wrote in *The American Diamond,* "was fortified with the ideal temperament for a baseball player, for his will to win was not a savage, uncontrolled emotion. . . . His intelligent daring, versatility, contagious spirit in contests, his refusal to condone mistakes which were controllable in advance, his brief yet effective words of instruction, and above all, his marvelous aptitude made him a nonpareil. . . . More than any player I ever knew, George was able by example more than words to bring his teammates to a unified and insatiable desire to win."[5]

As to modern sabermetrics, my guess is that Branch Rickey would ride that worthy steed to the edge of pennants, hop off, and thank it for its meritorious service. The journey's anchor leg he knew to be a necessarily human endeavor. As he once put it, "The greatest single thing that makes a championship player is his desire to be one. The greatest single quality of a championship club is a collective, dominating urge to win."[6]

The discussion to follow is about *that* part of the game—the part about the heart, the will, and all the collaborating assets that elude digitizing. It's about the subtle, unselfish, professional, instructive, inspirational, unrecorded, and generally helpful things a baseball player can do for the betterment of his team. It's about the competitive value of those commonly extolled but abidingly fuzzy attributes that are still called what Rickey called them: *intangibles*.

"Paying attention to every little thing—that's what intangibles mean," said Derek Jeter, the man they call Mr. Intangible because, well, he sort of is. "It all comes down to the little things that are important to winning. You can't focus on one thing; you have to focus on *everything*. No matter what you're trying to accomplish—not just playing sports—you have to pay attention to detail."

An important clarification here: Intangibles occupy a vast territory. They can be perpetrated and felt in countless ways and myriad settings. For baseball purposes, we'll organize them into two basic types.

- First, and most conspicuously, there are the minor feats of fundamental execution that, when persistently observed, add up to playing the game properly. These are *situational* intangibles. This category takes in the traditional batting stuff, for instance, that, say, the prototypical two-hole hitter is supposed to do, like taking a strike, if he must, to allow the leadoff guy to steal second, or making certain that when he grounds out he does so in such a fashion that the runner scurries along in the process. For outfielders, there's hitting the relay man and having each other's backs and somehow, through hustle and dispatch, holding successful batters a base short of where they would have ended up had a less diligent player been on duty. For an infielder, there's keeping the runners close to their bases, lining up properly for relays, and, by various devices, such as blocking a bad throw or digging a ball out of the dirt, saving teammates from what would otherwise go down as errors. For a catcher, there's putting up targets, framing pitches, signaling pickoffs, blocking the plate, and hollering at the cutoff men. For all those folks, there's prudent, opportunistic, full-out baserunning. Situational intangibles are largely untallied but direct and perceptible and, in the main, immediate in their implications.

- And then, of an altogether different stripe, there are the less visible, more abstract *environmental* intangibles. These are the undocumented deeds by which players make other players better, a
  sort of baseball variation of the Golden Rule: Doing for the other
  guys what you would have each of *them* do for the other guys, as
  well. Environmental intangibles are the socially transmitted acts
  of being a good teammate, in whatever anecdotal form: a piece of
  advice here, a word of encouragement there, a timely gag, a stern
  look, a slap on the shoulder, a lesson passed along, an example well
  set. They're the ambient reflection of qualities that do a clubhouse
  good: confidence, accountability, enthusiasm, intensity, respect,
  consideration, commitment. They're wisdom shared, inspiration
  provided, and professionalism demonstrated.

None of the above would actually be intangible if it could be quantified with any measure of mainstream acceptance. The most meticulous
recordkeeping may track such discernible gains as runners advanced
during a player's at-bats, but *finding* that information is another matter, and its consideration in the fellow's statistical profile is still another.
Meanwhile, Carl Crawford is awarded no popular data point when he
busts his tail to cut off a ball deep in the left-center-field gap before it
can bounce to the wall, halting the batter at second base and the runner
at third; but the play could make his *pitcher* a little bit better, according
to the numbers; and his team, according to the standings. Chase Utley
is not rewarded metrically for having maximized his secondary lead (the
extra steps taken when the pitch is delivered to home plate) and foiled a
double play by reaching the next base in short order.[7] The environmental
contributions—the simple acts of helping out—are even further beyond
the pale of detection and tally. However, parties associated with the extraordinary Tampa Bay Rays of 2008 attest that, in ways that had nothing to do with his twenty home runs or pedestrian .247 batting average,
veteran Eric Hinske made a decidedly better player of Evan Longoria,
the Rookie of the Year in the American League, and a decidedly better

ballclub of Tampa Bay. This assertion can't be reasonably denied any more than it can be empirically validated. Believing it, though, requires that we trust the manager and players who say it was so, and our intuition, as well.

While the influence of Hinske—and all the beneficent teammates like him—can be credited only anecdotally, to dismiss it altogether is to snub the game's soul and disavow an enchanting element of its mystery. In the same spirit, to pooh-pooh the power of a single-minded, *e pluribus unum* partnership is to believe that Joe Torre, the manager of the 1998 Yankee team (Jeter, Pettitte, O'Neill, Bernie Williams, Scott Brosius, David Cone, and company) that won 114 games in the regular season and rolled through the playoffs and World Series, was full of beans when he said, "I think it was the intangibles that set us apart. My players embodied all the keys needed for success as team players—self-knowledge; fairness, trust, and respect; communication; serenity; optimism; intuition; steadiness; sacrifice, and the three C's (caring, conviction, commitment). Bring together a group like that, and you have the opportunity to accomplish things you never dreamed possible."[8]

To slough off the significance of character is to suppose it merely happenstance that, in 2004, when at least four of the preeminent heart-and-soul guys of the generation—Millar, Varitek, Ortiz, and Curt Schilling—banded together in Boston, the accursed Red Sox won their first World Series in eighty-six years, then won another (with Dustin Pedroia swapping, existentially, for Millar) three years later.

To contend that players can't prosper from the company they keep is to presume that Bronson Arroyo—who was there when the Red Sox were down to Torre's club three games to none in the 2004 American League Championship Series, and Millar prophetically warned his teammates before game four that the Yankees better not let them win one— was off his rocker when he said, "Kevin Millar, to me, brings so much to the table in the locker room, above and beyond anyone I've ever played with, that if he could never play in a game I would pay the guy two million bucks to sit on the bench." . . . And that Mike Schmidt, the great third baseman whose only world championship came a year after Pete Rose signed with Philadelphia, was blowing smoke when he said, "I'm not sure that I would have ever risen to Hall of Fame stature, or that my career would have been catapulted to where it was starting in 1979 and '80, if Pete hadn't chosen to come to the Phillies."[9] . . . And that the former slugger Jack Clark was simply blabbering when he said, "Every player should be lucky enough to play one year with Joe Morgan, and he'd be a better player for having done so."[10]

To insist that intrasquad support and cooperation don't amount to much is to disregard Morgan (which many sabermetrics enthusiasts strongly advise, by the way) when he claims[11] that his penchant for drawing walks had roots in the counsel of a minor-league manager, Billy Goodman, who, passing down advice from an old teammate, Ted Williams, stressed to Little Joe the importance of looking at a lot of pitches; and that Nellie Fox, a much older Houston Astro and second baseman, mentored him on numerous details, including his footwork for double plays and his style of fielding glove; and that, in Cincinnati with the Big Red Machine, he benefited substantially from Johnny Bench's understanding of hitting mechanics; and that, in turn, Bench prospered from Morgan's talent for deciphering and relaying catchers' signs when he was on base, a principal example being a series in Los Angeles during which Morgan consistently reached first, managed leadoffs long enough to get a good view of Joe Ferguson's signals, passed them along to Bench with an arranged twitch of some sort, and his grateful teammate went eight for ten; and that, before a playoff series against Pittsburgh in 1975, he gathered Ken Griffey, Dave Concepcion, and George Foster to show them tapes of the pickoff moves of the Pirates' pitchers, after which those four Reds stole seven bases in game two without being thrown out and, in the clinching game three, Griffey forced a ninth-inning balk that led to the winning run.

To neglect tone setting is to suggest that Kirk Gibson had no effect on the Los Angeles Dodgers when he came over from Detroit as a free agent in 1988 and, during spring training, went off on his teammates after one of them put eye black in his hat, letting the fellows know in unsparing terms that he hadn't signed on for giggles, but to kick some National League backside. It is to presume that the voters got it wrong when they selected Gibson as MVP that year, even though he led the National League in nothing official and wasn't really close in most of the major categories. It is to imply that the other Dodgers were unmoved when Gibson, not expected to play in the World Series against the heavily favored Oakland A's because of a knee injury in one leg and a hamstring problem in the other, hobbled up to the plate with two outs in the bottom of the ninth inning of game one, his team down a run, and somehow willed a two-run, walkoff home run against the great closer, Dennis Eckersley.

To maintain that sharing doesn't matter much is to call it coincidence that Ty Cobb loved to talk about hitting with his Detroit Tiger teammates and after he'd won fifteen batting titles, the players on the receiving end of his wisdom, both before and after he added managing to his duties, went on to secure another eleven (the first of them going to Harry Heilmann, who actually edged out Cobb himself).[12]

To reject the relevance of group dynamics is to imply that players-only meetings, alleged to be points of origin for so many surges toward so many pennants, in fact have no competitive consequence and never did.

To gloss over the game's symbiotic nature is to consider it a bunch of hooey that catchers actually inform, guide, calm, encourage, or generally handle pitchers, even though Varitek, at one point considered by baseball people to be the best at getting the best out of a battery mate,[13] won championships at virtually every level and somehow caught a record four no-hitters; reliever Jeff Brantley declared that one of his catchers, Bob Brenly, taught him as much about pitching as anyone; Bob Gibson traced his record-setting performance in 1968 (earned run average of 1.12) to an early season suggestion from Tim McCarver that he mix in more backdoor sliders;[14] Steve Carlton, for a while there, would throw only to McCarver; a study published in *Baseball Prospectus* concluded that a catcher who works uncommonly well with his pitching staff can, comparatively, save in excess of thirty runs over the course of a season;[15] and Tom Seaver, taking a moment in his Hall of Fame induction speech to explain how he was able to win 311 games, put it this way: "All you have to do is look at the individuals that were sixty feet, six inches away from me . . . Jerry Grote . . . Carlton Fisk . . . Johnny Bench."

To make light of the matter of makeup is to wave off what Whitey Herzog had to say about the transition between his first year managing in St. Louis, which was the strike-blunted 1981 season (when the Cardinals put up an excellent record with a few players whose deportment Herzog didn't particularly care for),[16] and his second, when the club won the World Series with several carefully chosen acquisitions he had made in his additional role as general manager. "We'd cleaned house, gotten the speed, relief pitching and catching we needed," the White Rat wrote in *White Rat*. "More importantly, we had twenty-five good guys on the club, no more drag-asses, no more prima donnas. It was a club that I could win a pennant with."[17]

To trivialize intangibles is to insist that the seemingly inexplicable performance of the Baltimore Orioles in 2012—literally turning around their record from 69–93 to 93–69 in spite of outscoring their opponents by a mere seven runs (which, according to the sabermetric algorithm known as the Pythagorean Theory, should have fetched them only eighty-two victories), establishing the highest winning percentage in modern baseball for one-run games (.763, at 29–9), and going an unfathomable 16-2 in extra-inning affairs, in the process making the postseason for the first time in fifteen years—was largely attributable to luck, and perhaps a bit of excellent managing by Buck Showalter.

NOW A CAVEAT. THERE ARE NUMEROUS INTANGIBLES—WORK ETHIC, FOR EXAMPLE—THAT contribute directly, if not conspicuously, to a player's statistical résumé. When Jeter resolved early in his career to move to Tampa so that he could train at the Yankees' spring facility during the off-season, the results probably showed up in his 203 hits in 1998 and his .989 OPS in 1999.

These chapters, however, will not dwell on the ways in which, through good graces of character, a player improves *himself*. That wouldn't add to the conversation. Jeter's work ethic, kneaded into the dough and manifesting itself in the leavening of his metric loaf, has already nourished the dossier with which his contracts are negotiated. Voters have used that information to place him on fourteen All-Star teams. They'll take another look at it before electing him to the Hall of Fame.

The subject we're talking about involves whatever it is that makes a player better—and sometimes worse—than his slash lines (batting average/on-base percentage/slugging percentage), or even the dizzying decimals tucked behind the bonus tabs of his baseball-reference.com page. This book is dedicated not to the wellspring of personal production, but to deepening the understanding of what a player truly brings to a *team*, besides that which is so abundantly, visibly, and increasingly asserted by elaborate accounting. The point of interest is not the considerable individual advantage that Jeter has gained through his irreproachable professionalism, but the effect that his winning habits may have had on the likes of Posada, Pettitte, Robinson Cano, and Mariano Rivera, to name a few; not what moving to Tampa did for Jeter, but the difference it might have made for the teammates who followed him there.

While the discussion will, for the most part, steer clear of the stampede of stats, there is no ignoring the buffalo in the base path. And the feelings are mutual. In their quest to assign an arithmetic value to virtually every microevent that alters the landscape of an inning, the number crunchers are keeping a curious eye on this subject.[18] Bill James himself, the most iconic of baseball quantifiers, has studied what he refers to as baseball IQ, but categorizes as Percentage Player Index (in which the all-time champ is Joe Morgan).[19] The underlying question provoking this research is reasonable enough: If Jeter's or Hinske's or Varitek's intangibles have any practical worth in a ballgame, shouldn't there be corroborating evidence? The answer is *yes*, indeed there should. And there *is*, though it's not discernible on spreadsheets, for the most part. If you're willing, however, to peek in unconventional places, and if you don't insist on precise empirical validation for every actuality, you can, in fact, catch glimpses of a player's effect on those around him, crudely approximated in the numbers. The thing is, those numbers don't show up in the columns of the player himself; they show up in those of teammates. I call them *second-level statistics*.

They're the batting-average points that Ralph Garr tacks on when Hank Aaron shows him what to eat, who to listen to, and when to get to bed; the extra slugging percentage that David Ortiz acquires when he starts working out with Manny Ramirez; the saves that David Weathers grinds out when he latches onto John Franco's advice, and slows himself down in crucial situations; the runs that Bob Friend is spared because opponents are fearful of Roberto Clemente's arm; the RBIs that David Wright comes into because Jose Reyes makes the task ninety feet easier; the strikeouts that Gary Nolan racks up when Johnny Bench insists on certain pitches in certain spots; the homer that rookie Chris Getz hits, the first of his career, after venerable Jim Thome—is it simply coincidence?—assures him that tonight will be the night.

Second-level statistics are the encrypted messages of the intangibles champ. They're too misty to pinpoint and plain impossible to compute, but their chief producers—the league leaders in making other people better—are presumably okay with that, because it's what being a teammate is all about. It's about doing things, large or small, that will count toward your personal credit only in the eyes of the truly informed.

Interestingly, we have no difficulty recognizing, even celebrating, the uncountable, humdrum deeds in other sports. In basketball, appreciation is heaped upon the worker bees who screen for Michael Jordan and clear out for Kobe Bryant, who guard, hustle, pick, roll, help, switch, communicate, see the floor, and move without the ball, which, after all, they have in their hands for only a fleeting fraction of a game. A good team doesn't even *want* more than two or three players who specialize in scoring. The headliners require their enablers, the humble teammates who, embracing their roles, are content to give up the rock and glory. In a fluid, five-man, geometric, interdependent game played in a comparatively small space with a rather large ball, all of the above is apparent enough. In football, meanwhile, the money stats are reserved for the relative few. It's the offensive tackle's job to see that the quarterback is free and clear to sling his forty-two-yard touchdown pass to the preening receiver; the right guard's to ensure that the franchise running back produces another three-figure rushing day; the nose tackle's to collapse the pocket so the cornerback can swoop in and pick-six the hurried throw to the flanker; the defensive end's to occupy the blockers so the linebacker can slam down the ball carrier. The football center, unlike a point guard, has no chance of getting the ball back after passing it along. Needless to say, soccer and hockey are games of perceptible synergy, a player's every turn and tack sending signals to a close associate. That's what team sports are *supposed* to be. Even baseball, in its own understated style.

But the sport is not universally viewed that way. Its codependence is steeply discounted, and the mushrooming statistical profiles, increasingly isolating every player from his surroundings, only encourage it. "Baseball is an individual sport," wrote Joshua Fisher in *Hardball Times*. "This is perhaps the most important concept a person can understand about baseball. Once one accepts that baseball is an individual sport, all of the context-dependent noise goes away. Pitching wins, runs batted in and even errors can be tossed aside."[20]

Notwithstanding that popular school of thought, perhaps the most important concept a person can understand about baseball is that, in spite of its one-on-one, batter-by-batter nature, it is *not* an individual sport. Context is not merely noise; it's the very framework of the game. It's the compound circumstance that defines the challenge before player and team. Were that not the case, there would, for instance, be no strategic advantage to the intentional walk, seeing as how it guarantees that the batter will accomplish the ostensibly single most important thing (getting on base) he can. However, in the context of runners in scoring position, a base on balls is productive to the offense only if (in most cases) one among the batters who follow is up to the task of delivering the run-scoring blow that the walked man was denied. It all revolves around the mutable, unrelenting, altogether pertinent, *context*—not only the score, the inning, the outs, the park, and perhaps the weather, but who's up, who's on, who's next, who's available, who's pitching, and what's in everybody's head. To evaluate a ballplayer by filtering out the context is, among other things, to ignore how closely a teammate is tethered to his teammates. It is to miss the point that, yes, baseball, too, is a team sport.

"The classic case is the guy who gives himself up by hitting behind the runner," remarked John Schuerholz, the vastly successful former general manager of the Atlanta Braves. "It's a hitter who can work counts, make the pitcher exert himself in the early innings. The bullpen guy who has pitched two days in row and goes into the manager's office and says, 'If you need me today, I can go an inning or so.'

"Statistics talk about how productive a player has been and you can expect he will be. Modern stats do that more effectively than traditional statistical bases. But, no matter how deeply you core into them, they don't tell you anything about the character of the man, the winning spirit of the player, the God-given ability of that individual to impact others by his example, his work ethic, his commitment, his determination, his reliability, his consistency. Those are not statistical fields of measurement. They are observations and intuitive and instinctive fields of measure. It's more subtle in our game."

IT WASN'T THE INTENTION OF THE TRUE SABERMETRIC VISIONARIES—BILL JAMES AND Pete Palmer, for instance—to overwhelm baseball's selfless, soulful side. James, in fact, has paid homage to what he labels *undocumented skills.*[21] Nevertheless, their data-based revelations have animated not only the persuaded sportswriter but also the emboldened fan who saw, suddenly, that a demonstrable grasp of the game was no longer exclusive to the good old boys who played it at the professional level. Through educated tracking, he, too, could now be an authority of sorts, and could even flaunt his knowledge in his fantasy league.

If exception is periodically taken here to the fashionable mantras promulgated on sabermetrics-friendly platforms, the disagreement, for the most part, is not with the pacesetters and thought changers in the field of statistical analysis. The perspective was well stated by Sheldon Hirsch or Alan Hirsch or both in their book, *The Beauty of Short Hops*:[22]

> Bill James is no Jamesian. Throughout his voluminous works, he sprinkles recognition that much in baseball can't be quantified, that his formulae should be seen only as imperfect tools to guide understanding, that the game cannot be reduced to a social science, and that its greatness lies beyond the numbers. But many of James's acolytes are less discerning. Endless harm is done by those who misunderstand and misappropriate the spirit of a revolution.

With the glorification of such mathematically compelling and alphabetically soupy items as isolated power (ISO), equivalent average (EqA), defense-independent pitching statistics (DIPS), pitcher abuse points (PAP), value over replacement player (VORP), and player empirical comparison and optimization algorithm (PECOTA), there has developed, in turn, an unmistakable and perhaps accidental neglect of the national pastime's human virtues. Are we, however, quite all right with quantities overshadowing qualities?[23] Is the antiquation of character an evolutionary phase of baseball that we truly believe has arrived?

It's certainly not what Joe Torre believes. He said as much to his general manager in 2006, after seeing the Yankees reduced from a makeup-based ballclub to one that performed best on paper. "Do yourself a favor," he told Brian Cashman. "Never forget there is a heartbeat in this game."[24] Torre elaborated on that sentiment one afternoon late in 2009, from his customary pregame perch atop the back of the bench in the dugout of the Los Angeles Dodgers, the team he had moved on to manage.

"I think we've gotten a little too technical, as far as statistics," he explained. "A lot of decisions may be based on numbers, and that's what made me tell Brian that there's a place for statistics in this game, but don't forget there's a heartbeat. There's a certain thing that, if you're looking at numbers and something doesn't make sense, you have to trust the player more than that. I'm convinced that those things show up in the standings.[25] You can trick the media, you can trick the fans, but you can't trick your teammates. Integrity is the thing."

Torre, it should be noted, was considered a players' manager, a self-assured, steady-handed juggler of egos. Tony La Russa was a different sort, an intense, studious skipper whose attention to statistical intelligence fostered a reputation as the most prepared, cerebral, and, for a while, sabermetrically inclined in his field. That was why, with the Cardinals' mastermind across from me one day in the visitors' quarters at Great American Ball Park, I started out with, "My premise is that the numbers can take you a long way—maybe ninety or ninety-five percent of the way—but . . ." And that was as far as I got.

"I don't think the stats and sabermetrics and all that stuff goes a long way," La Russa interrupted. "It goes a *little* way. I think there is a distinct issue—problem—with overrating how useful that information is."

It was two hours before the game. La Russa had just returned to his office from a long run, and he was speaking deliberately, sifting through the word choices, with a golf tournament on his television and a Jack Higgins novel on his desk. "My opinion is that it's been way overexaggerated. It gives you a certain basis of information—it's a nice and useful tool—but it has a lot of limitations, mostly because these are *people*, they're *individuals*, they're not machines. So, I think you pay a lot of attention to the person. It's a team, so a lot counts to how he contributes to the team feeling, and how he cares about the team. Organizations have different philosophies, and some stress character more than others. The guys who play for us, they have to display and demonstrate the qualities that have a lot more to do with their contribution to the team than something you can produce from a computer."

If it was the populist appeal—and, yes, the good sense that it all makes—that gave wing to sabermetrics, shouldn't the same sort of grass-roots enthusiasm rally the plucky, timeless intangible to the high office it once occupied? Not many of us can relate to Ichiro's speed, Prince Fielder's power, Joe Mauer's stroke, or Justin Verlander's stuff, but with just a little wishful thinking we can see ourselves as David Eckstein, Craig Counsell, Bill Hall, Aaron Hill, Ryan Theriot, Marco Scutaro, DeWayne Wise, Jose Altuve, or Darwin Barney. Maybe even, on a particularly good day, Kevin Youkilis, Marlon Byrd, Barry Zito, Michael Cuddyer, Jamie Moyer, Placido Polanco, or Dustin Pedroia. Who in his hardball dreams, with some added arm strength and just a tad more bat speed, couldn't at least be a backup catcher? A utility infielder—Jamey Carroll—for sure. The will, the moxie, the crease in the cap, the natural *feel* for playing ball—it's all there, right? And those things—those baseball senses, embedded in the bones—they're part of the package, aren't they? If they weren't, if that deep-seated affinity of ours were somehow of no account, by what impulse, what primal tug, could we possibly love the game as we always have?

Don't we dearly hope and duly trust that diligence, grit, enterprise, sacrifice, and hard work are still everything they ever were to the institution that over time has so famously reflected our nation? Isn't that what the best of our fanship is largely about? Imagine a sport that makes no room for rectitude, that no longer values values. Could we, in good faith, hold it sacred?

Of course, it doesn't have to be like that. A trust in science needn't preclude a faith in spirit.

THREE

A CRITICAL MASS

PAT GILLICK WAS THE GENERAL MANAGER OF THE TORONTO BLUE JAYS WHEN HIS NOTION of a winning ballplayer took a perceptible turn. A Hall of Fame executive who was described by author Michael Lewis, in the postscript to *Money-ball,*[1] as Grand Poo-Bah of the Raccoon lodge (the lodge being the club of baseball types who flipped out over the counterculture philosophies advanced in Lewis's landmark book),[2] Gillick had come by his traditional views through traditional means. As a left-handed pitcher, he spent five seasons in the farm system of the Baltimore organization, where he was exposed to, and captivated by, the philosophies of Harry Dalton, the Ori-oles' director of scouting and minor-league operations.[3] Dalton, in turn, had inherited the same principles from his predecessor, Jim McLaughlin, who codified Baltimore's emphasis on a player's character—his makeup, in baseball terms—through an emphasis on what he called the *whole ballplayer.* When Gillick's front-office career began with the Houston Astros in the early 1960s and continued with the Yankees in the mid-seventies, and even when he moved on to Toronto in 1977, he preached and practiced makeup. But his appreciation of it didn't fully mature until the Blue Jays were hitting tall cotton in the early 1990s, when they won the World Series back to back.

"Almost fifty years ago, when I started out, at that point I thought that ability was eighty percent of what made a player and intangibles probably twenty percent," Gillick said. In Toronto, those percentages shifted to, he estimated, "forty percent makeup and sixty percent ability." It wasn't merely a subtle rebalancing. Gillick's revised calculations emerged out of a crescendo of experience. The formula finally fell into place when he observed the environmental uptick brought to bear on the Blue Jays with the arrivals of Dave Winfield, David Cone, Jack Morris, Paul Molitor, and their winning ways. "As a player progresses through the system, much more becomes attributable to makeup. You've got to grind it out. The most important thing is passion for the game and a tremendous work ethic. Ability is paramount, don't get me wrong. But if they don't have the desire and passion to be a good teammate, all it does is disrupt the other employees. Those are the things I look for. Putting the team before yourself."

Of course, skeptics could point out that Winfield, Cone, Morris, and Molitor brought a bit more to the table than good manners. Molitor and Winfield are in the Hall of Fame. Cone and Morris, between them, won 448 games in the Major Leagues. Molitor, who was signed as a free agent for the 1993 season—the other three were acquired in 1992—was thirty-six at the time. Winfield was forty, Morris thirty-seven. Ironically, Cone, who was only twenty-nine, turned out to be the only member of the quartet who didn't produce for the Blue Jays on a large scale. Nevertheless, it's evident that, at Toronto and elsewhere, Gillick had a taste for high-end talent.

But that proclivity was not indiscriminate. "Pat really goes out and beats the pavement," said Jamie Moyer, the ancient left-hander whom Gillick traded for in Philadelphia.[4] "It's not just going out and signing people just to sign them. I think he really looks into individuals. It's really easy to say, 'Hey, that guy's a good player.' But what about personality?

Who is he? How can this person help this club, not only on the field but off the field? And Pat really works hard at that." The same considerations naturally apply to the negotiable players on his own roster, and that point was vividly illustrated when, upon assuming the general-manager position for the Seattle Mariners—who, less than two years earlier, had dealt away future Hall of Fame pitcher Randy Johnson at midseason—Gillick was faced with an agonizing decision in regard to another surefire Hall of Famer, his center fielder, the Player of the Decade, Ken Griffey, Jr. It was a call that, tapping into the lessons of Baltimore and Toronto, he was well prepared to make.

"When I went to Seattle in 2000," he recalled, "a guy demanded a trade and had a no-trade clause. There were only like three clubs he could go to: the Mets, Atlanta, and Cincinnati. So we got [in return, Mike] Cameron, and Cameron was a guy who set a tone. We had Jay Buhner, Edgar Martinez, John Olerud, Danny Wilson; we had a good group. They were good baseball players, good human beings, and good teammates." It should be noted that, in reference to the good group with which he was willing to take on the American League, Gillick conspicuously omitted Alex Rodriguez's famous name. There was a reason for that. "I think A-Rod and the other guy were more on a personal agenda. Don't know that they were as team oriented as they should be."

The season following Griffey's departure to Cincinnati, the Mariners increased their victory total from seventy-nine to ninety-one and made the American League playoffs, after which Rodriguez took advantage of his free agency to leave the Northwest and sign a record-setting contract with the Texas Rangers. The *next* summer, prodded by manager Lou Piniella, Seattle's downsized crew, having lost three ostensible Hall of Famers[5] in as many years and applied just 37 percent of its revenue toward player payroll—the lowest percentage in the big leagues[6]— somehow tied the Major-League record for regular-season wins (held by the Chicago Cubs of *1906*) with an astonishing 116.[7]

In 2006, pushing seventy years old, Gillick tried his hand at general managing in the National League for the first time. As he took stock of the Phillies and pondered how to pull them out of the rut they'd been in for going on six seasons, the baseball lifer was eminently mindful of the role modeling that had served his team so well in Toronto, of the climate change that had set Seattle on fire, of the working ideology he'd been refining for nearly half a century.[8]

For most of the Phillies' rut years, the team had been Bobby Abreu's. At thirty-two, Abreu was a powerful, durable, consistent, fan friendly, handsomely paid ($13.6 million, with raises due the next two years) left-handed-hitting outfielder with a batting eye so highly developed and a corresponding walk total so prolific that he had become a very special player to, among others, the on-base-percentage crowd. With Abreu avoiding outs at a stirring clip, teammate Jimmy Rollins recalled the marching orders for other Phillies being, "Get on base for Bobby."[9]

Rollins, however, a proficient hitter, baserunner, and shortstop, had by then been to three All-Star games, and his keystone partner, Chase Utley, had emerged as an annual presence in the Most Valuable Player voting. Through his seasoned eyes, Gillick could see that culture change was waiting at the door. On July 30, 2006, he opened it and pointed Abreu toward New York. The trade sent pitcher Cory Lidle to the Yankees, as well, in exchange for three minor leaguers and a left-handed pitcher, Matt Smith, who had worked a total of twelve Major League innings. The Phillies' record at the time was 48-54. After the trade, they went 37-23.

Rollins and Utley proved eminently ready, in effectively differing ways, for the leadership roles they inherited from Abreu and, to a lesser extent, veteran catcher Mike Lieberthal. Rollins's charisma put a spring in the Phillies' step, and Utley's vehemence added an edge to their intensity. "He'll look a guy in the eye and say, 'We don't do things like that around here. We run balls out. We play hard,'" noted Gillick of Utley. "He's the kind of guy who doesn't stand back and put up with any nonsense."

Abreu's departure also opened an outfield spot for Shane Victorino, a smallish, spirited switch-hitter whose offensive numbers couldn't compare with those of the man he replaced. Utley and mashing first baseman

Ryan Howard, whose breakout season resulted in the National League MVP award, shouldered that load. Victorino, however, was a Gillick kind of guy.

Conveniently, the Philadelphia manager, Charlie Manuel, who arrived a year before Gillick, was an old warhorse who shared his GM's perspective on what it takes to succeed in their industry. For both, the club of choice was a little fresher, a little more single-minded and self-charging, than the one that had been chronically finishing second or third in the NL East. It was a purposefully assembled band of ballplayers with the kind of mettle and heart to, say, win a division by overcoming a seven-game deficit with seventeen to play, which is what the Phillies did at the expense of the New York Mets in 2007.

"When we made these moves, from a chemistry standpoint, man, we became a lot more energetic," said Manuel, nearly three years later. "Jimmy Rollins stepped up and embraced guys like Howard and Utley and Victorino. Utley made us better by the way he plays the game. His heart, his mental toughness, his desire, his preparation. I never told him this, but I give him a lot of credit for Pat Burrell. Once Pat Burrell got married, and some of his buddies left our team, he became real good friends with Chase, and he became a guy who studied his hitting more. Chase plays because he wants to, because he loves it. That rubs off on a lot of people. I think what really makes our team go is the fact that we've got some real good players, first of all, but we also have guys who like to play. It's about being relaxed and focused at the same time. Those things produce confidence, and they produce numbers."

It is, of course, impossible to calculate, in wins or losses or on-base-plus-slugging percentage, the rubbing-off effect of a pro like Utley or the beneficent contagion of a dynamo like Rollins (who was also possessed of sufficient talent to win the 2007 MVP award). The advantages, assuming they exist, are played out anecdotally and reckoned subjectively. But if they're indeed real, and if they truly make a difference, they might well show up in, for example, a team that has what it takes not only to rally down the stretch and overcome a daunting deficit to win a division and snatch a spot in the playoffs, but to do it again the following year. In 2008, with sixteen games to play, the Phillies trailed the Mets by three and a half games in the NL East and the Milwaukee Brewers by four in the wildcard race. They won thirteen of those, including four straight against the Brewers.

Reflecting on the rise of the Phillies, Jayson Stark, a baseball columnist for espn.com with deep ties to Philadelphia, hearkened back to the swapping-out of Abreu.[10] "They sure didn't trade him because they thought the most advanced prospects they got back—C. J. Henry and Matt Smith—were their tickets to a brighter tomorrow. . . . Nope," wrote Stark, "the Phillies traded Bobby Abreu for one basic reason: to get him out of the way. Out of Jimmy Rollins' way. Out of Chase Utley's way. Out of Ryan Howard's way. They became a whole different team that day."

And that, coincidence or not, was the effect Jocketty had in mind when, with the template still warm, he traded Griffey and Dunn to clear the stage for Votto, Bruce, Phillips, and the teammates they would hopefully lead to better things for the Reds.

"If you look closely," continued Stark, "it's not hard to envision a very similar phenomenon erupting in Cincinnati."

IN THE MEANTIME, THE OTHER LEAGUE WAS ALSO BEING WON IN A FASHION THAT CELebrated the subtleties and spirit of the game.

The only time in their ten-year history that the Tampa Bay Rays— actually, the *Devil* Rays for that duration—had struggled out of the cellar in the AL East, they still trailed the Yankees by thirty and a half games. For the Devil Rays, last place was a way of life. "When I first got here [in 2006]," said Joe Maddon, the club's famously open-minded manager, "God, it was so evident within five minutes, three minutes, *two* minutes, that we needed a culture change. It was probably the worst situation I've ever seen on any professional level. If they didn't win, it didn't really matter. 'We're in Tampa Bay, it's no big deal.' It was a place without any accountability."

Maddon's full effect was not immediate, but he was joined in the struggle by allies from the office above, who were so intent upon transforming the franchise that, prior to the 2008 season, they changed its name (exorcising the *Devil*) and color scheme. More meaningful to Maddon was that he and general manager Andrew Friedman shared one very pertinent fascination: Branch Rickey. Friedman was a former Tulane outfielder whom the Rays spirited away from MidMark Capital (a private equity investment firm) at the age of twenty-six to take over as their director of baseball development. Two years later he was promoted to GM, in which position he hired Maddon and, at thirty-one, was recognized by *The Sporting News* as Executive of the Year for 2008. "A lot of what we do stems from Branch Rickey," Friedman stated plainly. "I've read so much of him that I can't separate what I've read anymore from what's just in my head."

Maddon and Friedman were fully aware, of course, that Rickey was an early, ardent advocate of sophisticated statistical study. They also understood that he was much more than that, because *baseball* was—is— much more than that. It consequently occurred to the Rays' main men that wisdom such as Rickey's is never outdated and, furthermore, that their bottom-feeding ballclub was disconcertingly short on the stuff that he held in such high regard. And so, with precious raw materials (Evan Longoria, Carl Crawford, B. J. Upton, James Shields, David Price, etc.) piled up from years of high draft choices hard earned by all those dismal records, Tampa Bay began to negotiate for just the right complements.

The reconstruction of the Rays got under way unassumingly. In 2007, Carlos Pena, a conscientious but underachieving (and therefore economical) first baseman, signed on as a free agent by way of Boston, and infielder Akinori Iwamura crossed over from the Yakult Swallows. At the midseason trade deadline, pushing for run prevention, Friedman traded for relief pitchers Grant Balfour and Dan Wheeler, the latter acquired from Houston for burly infielder Ty Wigginton, an offensive specialist. At that point, the Rays had a purpose but not much of a prayer. When all was said and done, their defense was still horrid, their string of dysfunctional seasons was still intact, and Tampa Bay had produced the game's worst record for the second year in a row.

Many will contend that the club's roster moves for 2008 were made primarily in the interest of getting outs, and Friedman himself is among them, but Cliff Floyd, a bad-legged, been-around designated hitter with a reputation as a first-rate teammate, was not brought in for defense. Nor was Eric Hinske, an outfielder seldom mistaken for Willie Mays but widely respected for how he swung the bat and went about his business. In addition to Floyd and Hinske, new yeomen willing to row with the flow included veteran reliever Troy Percival and, in a trade with the Minnesota Twins, two youthful players prized foremost for what they offered when the other team was up to bat: shortstop Jason Bartlett and starter Matt Garza. Bartlett would supplant Brendan Harris, a hit-first infielder sent to the Twins in the same deal, along with outfielder Delmon Young. The inclusion of Young was an attention getter, considering that he had driven in 93 runs at the age of twenty-one, finishing second in the Rookie of the Year voting. When Elijah Dukes, another young, talented outfielder, was traded to the Washington Nationals five days later, a common theme, in addition to the defensive considerations, was evident: Young and Dukes both had histories of behavioral issues, and both manned their oars with splashy, brazen strokes out of sync with the rest of the crew.

"In order to really elicit change, you have to be willing to change personnel," Maddon reflected on a May afternoon, from the visiting manager's office in Cleveland. "But you can't treat it like a fantasy baseball team, because personalities do matter. We deliberately brought people in not only to contribute on the field, but we thought they could have a great impact in the locker room."

The pursuit of impact personalities might not have been so paramount had the Rays not been so young and unaccustomed to diligence. "They don't even know how to act sometimes," the skipper said. "Who's going to teach them? You're not even going to *get* to on-base percentage if you don't know how to act on a Major-League level."

Maddon's principal exhibit involved Evan Longoria, the Rays' vital young third baseman, and Hinske, who'd begun his big-league career as Rookie of the Year in Toronto but more recently had been relegated to reserve duty with the Blue Jays and Red Sox. By addressing his job professionally with Longoria close at hand and paying attention, Hinske was able to mentor his impressionable teammate on the structure of a baseball day, weight training, studying video, batting approach, situational challenges, mental preparation, and the general rigors of readiness.[11] Maddon studied this dynamic from a distance, understanding as he did that the scuffling veteran—at the outset, Hinske was not even assured a spot on the Rays' roster—was reaching a rising star in a way that a manager couldn't. "All of a sudden," observed Maddon, his eyes beaming behind his stylish, retro eyeglass frames, "Longo combines this extraordinary talent with the wisdom of an Eric Hinske.

"I believe in support. It can come from a coach or manager, yes, but we don't have the same relationship that they're going to have in the locker room sitting next to each other or going out together for a beer. There are those moments you just can't infiltrate as a coach or manager. I believe in the character within the group. We always talk about the word *makeup*. Enthusiasm comes into it, but I don't think it's as important as the work ethic, the ability to interact with groups, and the accountability factor. I think you can only get so many enthusiasts, and they can pretty much infiltrate the rest of the group. I believe in accountability. If you get a bunch of guys who are accountable and don't dissemble, now you've got something. It's all about balance."

Balance, in fact, is a concept that courses through Maddon's operating principles. Intensity and fun. Knowledge and yearning. The physical and the abstract. Numbers and intangibles: "We're into the sabermetrics, absolutely. I want to see pitches per plate appearance, two-strike batting averages, fly-ball batting averages. My point is, why can't you have it all? A lot of times I would hear that, well, if he hits thirty or forty home runs, we can live with everything else; but a lot of times, if you look back, those thirty or forty home runs never won the World Series."

Maddon, who, at age fifty-one, was chosen by the Rays to replace Lou Piniella, spent thirty-one years in the Anaheim organization, the final dozen as a bench coach, the last half dozen working with manager Mike Scioscia, a firm advocate of fundamentals and especially aggressive baserunning. Carrying those inclinations to Florida, Maddon also brought along his balancing act, which included a penchant for the unconventional—he once ordered Josh Hamilton intentionally walked with the bases loaded—and a gift for interpersonal relations. "Even when we were playing poorly, which was a lot of the time, he stayed positive the entire time," said outfielder Rocco Baldelli, whose six years with Tampa Bay were evenly divided between Piniella's stewardship and Maddon's. "He makes you feel like great things are about to happen, even when great things weren't happening at all. When you expect to win games, you win more games, I think. I'm not saying this stuff happens overnight. It took a while for people to buy into it. But the atmosphere in Tampa started with Joe Maddon."

Twice the age of most of his players, Maddon was somehow able to stride over the generation gap (or maybe jump it on the bicycle he frequently pedaled to work). He'd been lugging around a laptop before the bulk of his lineup was in grade school. He used it for spray charts and stats of personal interest, many of them hustle plays in which an opportunistic runner would grab an extra base or a sprint-to-first hitter would avoid a 6-4-3 or an outfielder would dutifully back up another to prevent an error. "Little things." Situational baseball.

While a stickler for playing the game the right way, as the cliché goes, the Rays' manager chooses not to be the rules police. One of the many signs he has posted in the clubhouse is a quote from former Federal Reserve chairman Alan Greenspan: "Rules cannot take the place of character." Maddon is a character guy. He's a people guy. A family guy. He grew up in an apartment over his father's plumbing business in blue-collar Hazleton, Pennsylvania, where, on the local football and baseball teams, Maddon was typically the captain, official or de facto.[12] That distinction was the fruit of his intuitive calming, encouraging effect on others. The same sensibilities drew him to the well-rounded, highly intelligent, uncommonly social (among *themselves,* that is) championship Cardinal teams with Bob Gibson, Steve Carlton, Curt Flood, Lou Brock, Tim McCarver, Bill White, Dick Groat, Roger Maris, and Orlando Cepeda;[13] and also to their rivals, the low-scoring, high-winning Dodgers of Sandy Koufax, Don Drysdale, Maury Wills, Tommy Davis, John Roseboro, and tough-minded manager Walter Alston. "I really believe we can reflect the old Dodgers or the old Cardinals," Maddon said that day in Cleveland. "That's my goal." Fundamental, situational, little-thing, grind-it-out, one-for-all, old-school baseball.

It's no accident that Maddon's traditions trace back through those of the Cardinals and Dodgers, which, in turn, traced back to Branch Rickey, whose promotion of team culture was so idealistic, so schmaltzy, some would say, that, in spite of his deep-seated success and station in the game, he was often belittled for it. (Rickey was such a champion of rah-rah that, at spring training, he actually dredged up college cheers from his days at Ohio Wesleyan and Michigan.)[14] When, in 2008, Maddon designed for the Rays a team T-shirt bearing the peculiar motto *9=8* (signifying that nine players working together would lead to a spot among MLB's eight playoff teams), that smacked of Rickey. When he embarked on a crusade against assumptionism—*assuming,* when running out a ground ball, that an infielder is going to make an accurate throw; *assuming,* when picking up a single in the outfield, that the runner moving along to second base will stop there; *assuming* that your lazy fly ball will be caught—he was operating in the Rickey tradition. For Maddon, the Rickey tradition boils down to detail and oneness. It's a commitment to *team,* and all that the term entails.

"Some people would say that chemistry's not the issue, and you always have a good chemistry when you're winning," said Ken Ravizza, a sports psychologist[15] and college professor who worked closely with the Rays. "But, baseball, man, it's every day. It's the duration of the season. It's about building a culture, and part of Joe's culture building is the chemistry issue."

In that regard, a manager's challenge is to get all the young guys and old guys, the stars and the subs, the pitchers and the hitters, to prioritize the common purpose and appreciate what they can do for each other; in a way, to simply appreciate each other. It's to identify the leaders and urge them in that capacity; to summon the assembled muscle of his roster and bring it all to bear on a single task; to forge a collective, complementary efficacy.

"From the very first day I got here," said Maddon, whose positivity has developed into an art form,[16] "I talked about building relationships. That was the first thing I ever talked about, and I saw that as being the most important thing. I got six or seven of what I perceived to be the more influential players on the team and went over team policy with *them,* in the event that they'd eventually take it to the masses.[17] It met with a lot of resistance. So, it took a while. Some of it was neatly planned—we had an eye on it—and some of it just grew. You just fertilize it and it grows a little bit. You nurture it and work on it every day. You don't let crap slide. If you see something negatively festering [Garza's troublesome temper, Upton's occasional breach of hustle, the drama fostered by Young and Dukes], you've got to get after it right now. By the time [2008] came around, we had all of that internal infrastructure being built. It was just so much better."

So, in turn, was the result. Competing in the game's richest, roughest division, with an uncelebrated roster on which no player earned more than $6 million, the reborn, utterly remarkable Rays, in the face of season-long expectations that their luck would surely run out before autumn arrived, held off the Red Sox and fully embarrassed the Yankees (whose formidable lineup included Bobby Abreu), in the process not only striking a blow for defense—theirs had been upgraded almost inconceivably, starting with Bartlett's work at shortstop—but offering up a smashing example of the melodies that can arise out of good vibrations in the workplace.

As they took over first place on the day after the All-Star break and stayed there the rest of the regular season—all without a top-ten player on the American League's list of batting averages, home runs, OPS (on-base plus slugging percentage), or WAR (wins above replacement level)—the Rays also provided a case study for a theory that I've found generally applicable. Its essence is that a clubhouse becomes a winning asset when its leadership is the province of not one or two powerful personalities but a critical mass of them: five, six, or more respected individuals whose habits and attitudes establish a distinct, dedicated environment. A culture.

A critical mass of character is what Maddon recognized, wittingly or not, in the special St. Louis clubs personified by Gibson, McCarver, Flood, and Cepeda. It's what Rickey's Brooklyn Dodgers developed when they rallied around Jackie Robinson. It's what manager Joe McCarthy insisted upon for his Bronx Bombers, as if Ruth, Gehrig, Dickey, and DiMaggio weren't quite sufficient. It's, in fact, what practically every manager pines for: a firm foundation of makeup that supports a team constitution so resilient that it can't be compromised even by a bad egg or two.

The Braves had it when they were dominating the National League for fifteen years, with John Schuerholz administering, Bobby Cox holding forth in the dugout, and Chipper Jones, Greg Maddux, and Tom Glavine, among others, defining professionalism on the field. The Yankees, with Joe Torre supplying the managerial zen and Derek Jeter making intangibles sexy, had it when they were winning three straight World Series, and playing in six of them over eight seasons. Then the Red Sox had it, in their own inimitable way. Jocketty and skipper Tony La Russa made sure their Cardinals usually had it, too. And in 2008, Jocketty was trying hard to attain it in Cincinnati, where, as in Tampa Bay, it wasn't a simple proposition.

Market realities presented a complication. Inherently, the most influential players in a clubhouse—the components of critical mass—tend to be those with star power, which a small-market franchise is typically hard-pressed to afford. Then there's the difficulty of defining good makeup and, in turn, identifying it. Like beauty and humor, it is a matter of taste. Most would generally agree that a ballplayer's makeup comes down to how he goes about his business, but there's not a template for that, nor a finite number of fashions. Bottom line: The best makeup is the approach that produces the best results on both the individual and the team levels.

"Makeup is an interesting word that we spend a lot of time each organizational meeting discussing," observed Friedman, who transitioned into baseball from Wall Street. "It means different things to different people. Simply said, we have good people that care about the team and put forth the effort to help other people and be a sounding board. All those things are important in how we evaluate a player. [But] it's not always the easiest thing to find, especially in a situation like ours where we're always going to be integrating young players into the environment. Being a smaller revenue team, we can't always get the great teammate with impeccable makeup and great skills. But when you get that critical mass, it's much easier to create upside. That said, if you take the bucket of professional players, the top twenty percent or so are going to be very good players irrespective of their makeup. The twenty percent at the bottom of the bucket, no matter how good their makeup is, they don't have the requisite skills to impact a Major-League team. There's a huge middle group there where there's a fine line between them, and I definitely think makeup is a big separator in that group.

"Our hope is to get to the point where we have a great infrastructure in place, where if we brought somebody in who we felt wasn't necessarily a strong makeup guy or high character guy, we could put him in our infrastructure and have a better chance of having that work. We didn't have that infrastructure in '06 and we definitely didn't in '07. But I think Willie Aybar [a 2008 arrival] is a good example. He had some off-the-field issues that are well documented, but we knew that Carlos Pena had a relationship with him and we knew he [Pena] would be a good influence. It turns out that Willie is a phenomenal teammate. If we were going to start a team tomorrow from scratch, it's hard to know, if you take twenty-five unique individuals and put them together, what the end result would be. Hinske benefited Longoria a lot, but that was a hard thing to forecast because what if the personalities didn't match and they didn't get along? If they're good people individually, we'll take our chances."

Pena, in particular, was an avid customer of the culture that the Rays were crafting. Social by nature, he was always quick to lighten the burden on a teammate, but less effective at doing the same for himself. Realizing that, he sought out Dr. John Eliot, a performance psychologist the Rays had contracted to help young players with their mental conditioning.[18] Eliot advised Pena to let the game be fun again, an approach that Maddon, perhaps the funnest of Major-League managers, certainly encouraged. By letting the fun back in, Pena would be letting the tension out. He would be slipping off the self-imposed constraints that shackled his natural skills. He'd be charged by enthusiasm, and his teammates could plug into the same outlet.

Pena had joined the organization in the second year of the Maddon administration, his sixth season in the league, and, playing in a ballpark not known for outsize offense, he immediately jacked up his home run total to forty-six (previous high: twenty-seven) while increasing his OPS more than 200 points over his prior full-season best. The bump in production was, of course, *very* fun, and so was being a Ray. To Pena, the club just felt right. To him, that salubrious air was at the heart of Tampa Bay's romp to the American League pennant in 2008.

"This is the perfect environment," declared the handsome first baseman in the afterglow (May 2009). "Never in my life have I felt so comfortable about being myself on a baseball team. And the differences in mentality show up on the field. A hitter goes up there fully trusting his ability, trusting that all he has to do is see the ball and keep things simple, *knowing* instead of *hoping* that something good is going to happen. I believe it's because of that aura, that energy, that things started to work out. Talent is the most obvious thing, but talent alone doesn't do it. It *doesn't*. Yes, we are a talented ballclub, no doubt about that. However, that was also true the year before we won, and the year before that. You say, what changed? In my opinion, it was the energy. It was our way of looking at things. I believe the difference in our team last year was our makeup. The culture changed."

From Pena's perspective, there was no mystery concerning the source of that change. In Maddon, he admired a fresh capacity not only to loosen and bring comfort to the ballclub, but to do so while effecting an unflinching raising of the standard, and both of those with the same end in mind: to bring out the best in his players. "That's amazing to me, to have those two things," Pena said. "All of us here know that if we don't go out there and play hard, it's not going to be tolerated. There's a line we can never cross, and that's the line of disrespect for the game. That's a fact. Yet he's never said it. How cool is it that he doesn't have to say it?"

Among those who were close to the Rays in 2008, the consensus was that the club's working camaraderie crystallized in spring training, when the players' not-gonna-take-it-anymore attitude—Tampa Bay had never lost fewer than ninety-one games in a season—manifested itself in a brawl with the Yankees. A Rays reserve, Elliot Johnson, had broken the wrist of New York catcher Francisco Cervelli in a collision at home plate, and the Yankees took exception. The response came when outfielder Shelley Duncan slid into second base with his spikes high enough to gash Iwamura's thigh. That brought the combustible Jonny Gomes roaring in from right field and rushing Duncan. A hard-playing, home-run-hitting outfielder, Gomes had been somewhat marginalized by the Rays' new emphasis on defense, but his heart soldiered on full-time. When he charged the scene at second base, the benches followed—Tampa Bay's in a critical mass that bore significance.

"I don't think the fight *needed* to happen," Gomes explained later, "but it kind of set the attitude tone. It really became a desire to not lose, versus the desire to win. We were sick and tired of losing in that organization. The organization really gave us every opportunity to take the next step. We got a new manager. We got new ownership. They redid the stadium. We got new uniforms. It was just a good opportunity to put all that behind us and start with a clean slate."

In early June, Gomes was at it again, suspended five games for racing onto the field and punching Coco Crisp of the Red Sox after James Shields, in retaliation for Crisp's hard slide into Iwamura the day before, had hit the Boston outfielder with a pitch and Crisp had charged Shields. Worth noting were the facts that, in both instances, Gomes was defending a teammate; both times, the other team involved was a ranking heavyweight from the same division; and in March and again in June, Gomes was joined by virtually the entire Tampa Bay roster.

"Not every team would have reacted the way our team reacted [in the Boston incident] or the way we reacted against the Yankees in spring training," Maddon told Marc Lancaster of the *Tampa Tribune*.[19] "In those circumstances, if you have a team that is not tight, you're not going to see that kind of reaction. That was sincerely aggressive in a good way, and I liked it."

He also liked that the impetus derived from a part-time player who was adding value to his presence, manning an important role on the roster. In filling out his bench, a manager searches for a little something extra that a nonregular might contribute to the cause even when he's not in the lineup. "There are certain guys who just impart courage within a group, just by being there," Maddon elaborated later from the Cleveland clubhouse. "If things don't work out well, they're going to pick them up. Whether good or bad happens, their effort level is always going to be at the highest. Jon Gomes. I think those guys are essential to a roster. You can't have a whole bunch of those guys on your team because you may not be good enough at that point, but if you have one well-chosen guy like that, he can inspire the rest of the group."

Three days after the skirmish with the Red Sox, Gomes's unquantifiable contribution was approximated by catcher Dioner Navarro, when, in the dugout between innings, he called out Garza for losing his composure on the mound. Shouting and jostling ensued, but the message got through. The next day, Garza went to Maddon and asked for help controlling his temper. Maddon put him in touch with Ken Ravizza, and, coincidentally or not—Maddon felt strongly that it wasn't—Garza's ERA for the balance of the season improved by more than a run.

The Garza-Navarro confrontation made the point that effective team chemistry ought not to be confused with constant laughs and lollipops. Rather, it's a matter of players making other players better by whatever means. What Garza needed, for instance, was what Navarro harshly, bluntly, aggressively supplied. Even when expressed as confrontation, symbiotic succor often leads—as it led in this instance, owing to Garza's ultimate willingness to hear out the people who were there to help him— to a more collaborative, supportive, agreeable atmosphere.

Given the sensibilities that Friedman shared with Maddon, it's not surprising that the same sort of climate prevailed in the Rays' front office. Friedman, whose intensity is reflected in the fact that, as an amateur player, he patterned himself after Lenny Dykstra—the gritty former outfielder with the nickname of Nails, which Friedman borrowed—labored long hours in pursuit of what he called "positive arbitrage,"[20] which is essentially Tampa Bay's terminology for the exploitation of market inefficiencies described in *Moneyball* and resourcefully pursued by the Oakland A's general manager, Billy Beane. And yes, the research undertaken by the Rays to attain positive arbitrage included a heavy reliance on advanced statistical analysis.[21] Friedman, however, also saw to it that deskbound employees had a means of breaking away from the pace of the workday. In the interest of a little fun in the off-season, he arranged for the familiar RBI Baseball video game to be moved from the ballpark's Mountain Dew Extreme Zone to the front-office conference room, and on it the GM proceeded to dominate the rank and file.

Meanwhile, at field level, Tampa Bay's merry oneness had become so evident by late season, 2008, that Kevin Millar, who had earned his doctorate in chemistry while a member of the world-champion Red Sox (class of 2004), recognized it right away from the somber dugout of the Baltimore Orioles. On the diverse, individualistic Boston teams, Millar had been the guy who kept the others loose and dangerous, the originator of the "Cowboy Up" identity. In New England, he was an intangibles superhero. Now, gazing across at Maddon, Pena, Longoria, Crawford, Gomes, Hinske, Floyd, and the rest of the high-riding Rays, he was taken back a few years.

"With two weeks to go, we're packing up for the season, and they're over there with their entire team wearing Mohawks," Millar recalled, not without envy. "The manager has a Mohawk and the pitching coach has a Mohawk, and there was a swagger there. You need that swagger. I told our guys to look over there—that's what a *team* is about, right there."

The aging Oriole reflected for a beat. "That's what we had with the Red Sox," he said. "We were regular guys. We weren't the most talented players, but we were a *team*. And *teams* win championships, not players. You play in October, that's *fun*. I told our guys, that's a lot of fun what the Rays are doing. Chemistry is huge. *Huge!*"

BEFORE THE PHILLIES' FIRST PLAYOFF GAME OF 2008, THEIR OLD LEFT-HANDER, JAMIE Moyer, sidled up to their young left-hander, Cole Hamels, and volunteered some veteran advice concerning the important start that Hamels was about to make against the Milwaukee Brewers. It was nothing profound—the usual "be yourself, don't try to do too much" kind of stuff—but, in light of Hamels's postseason defeat the year before, when, by his own admission, he *was* trying to do too much, Moyer's wisely delivered words hit the mark like a cutter on the corner. Hamels proceeded to work eight breezy, scoreless, two-hit, nine-strikeout innings to put the Phils on track toward the National League Championship Series, in which he twice beat the Dodgers.

Going on forty-six, Moyer led Philadelphia that year with sixteen wins, and they were hard capital that he could invest in the clubhouse. As the most seasoned constituent in the team's critical mass of makeup, he had a subtle hand in additional victories that can't be numbered.

Moyer's role on that championship club was described well by Jayson Stark in *Worth the Wait: Tales of the 2008 Phillies.*

> If you watch a Phillies game—any Phillies game—we can almost guarantee that sooner or later, the TV cameras will zero in on the Phillies' dugout. And somebody will be locked in deep conversation with Jamie Moyer. On the art of pitching, on the art of professionalism, or on just about anything in between. He holds a place on his team that's utterly unique—a fascinating cross between Warren Spahn and Gandhi. Jamie Moyer draws teammates to him like a giant magnetic force—to watch and listen.

Of course, not many players compete well enough at forty-five to be in a position to share the perspective that so many sunrises bring. Production talks. "I've seen that sort of thing happen more with pitchers than I would hitters," said Gillick. "[For a position player], you almost have to be a regular and better if you're a star. You have immediate credibility. If you're an All-Star in the field and an All-Star in the clubhouse, that's the whole package."

Jimmy Rollins was an All-Star, and consequently, when he declared before the 2007 and 2008 seasons that the Phillies were the team to beat in the National League East, it was not dismissed by his immediate peers as empty bluster. It was, instead, a call to arms and bats. Rollins's leadership chops might have been lightly compromised when Manuel benched him once for jogging to first base after a pop-up and again for arriving late to Shea Stadium, but on both occasions, the spunky shortstop righted the situation by electing to not only support his skipper but maintain his active membership in their mutual admiration society; to preserve the integrity of the Phillies' critical mass.

The prophecies weren't forgotten when Rollins was ultimately proven right. "No one," he said,[22] "wants to make a statement and put himself out there. So I knew it was going to resonate in this clubhouse.

And that's what I wanted. . . . This was an organization that wasn't used to winning. That's what we had to do—change the way we approached the game, change the way we thought about it. We were always a team with talent. We were always a team that ran the bases well. But I wanted to be known as a team that wins well."

In back-to-back seasons, the Phillies did that most dramatically—historically, in fact—over the climactic weeks of the regular seasons, when it was most essential. Rollins ascribed it to a feeling, a focus, a sense of purpose, an *expectation.* Manuel rolled all that together and said, "I thought, without a doubt, that 2008 had a lot to do with our energy as a team. Even sometimes when we have meetings and I'm critical, I'll stand up and tell them that the things we want to keep are how we go about our business and how we *like to play.* Especially from about the last week of August through the playoffs, we were tight and close and it seemed like winning was just expected."

It was Hamels who started the clinching game five of the NLCS in Los Angeles, and it was Rollins who *actually* started it, with a lead-off home run. But that game wouldn't even have occurred if not for a pair of heroic home runs in the eighth inning the night before, a tying two-run blow by Victorino and another two-run affair off the bat of forty-year-old Matt Stairs, pinch-hitting. Designated for assignment by Toronto—which meant, in effect, that the Blue Jays had no plans to keep him on their roster—Stairs had been acquired by trade in August, one of several role players whom Gillick had brought to Philadelphia for, among other things, veteran presence, much in the same way that Friedman had added Hinske, Floyd, Wheeler, Percival, reliever Trever Miller, and outfielder Gabe Gross to the Rays' mix.

Like the Phillies', though, the Rays' rainmakers were mostly twenty-somethings in their prime or on the ascent, able players suddenly caught up in a culture, caught up *together,* and having a blast with it. In Tampa Bay's triumphant first playoff game against the White Sox (with Griffey manning center field for Chicago), the precocious Longoria, not quite twenty-two, announced himself and his young club with two home runs.

Upton, just turned twenty-four, turned the same trick in the concluding fourth game. Then, while Hamels was winning the MVP award in the NLCS, Garza (both pitchers were twenty-four) was doing the same in the American League finals against the Red Sox. Tampa Bay's place opposite the National League champs was battened down by twenty-two-year-old rookie lefthander David Price, who, with only fourteen innings of regular-season experience behind him, was called upon by Maddon with the bases loaded, two outs, and a 3-1 lead in the eighth inning of game seven. Unencumbered by precedents, the Rays' maverick manager left the kid out there in the ninth for his first professional save.

With no Yankees, Red Sox, Cardinals, Braves, or (presumably) performance-enhancing drugs, what followed was a new-age World Series with old-timey values, a competitive fete of two fresh teams that had purposefully retooled around skills, certainly, but also energy, makeup, and plurality. Yet, for all of its appeal to the baseball purist or the softie for story lines—the Rays were the ultimate underdogs, and the Phillies hadn't won the whole shebang since Mike Schmidt clubbed 48 home runs and Steve Carlton tossed 304 innings in 1980—the matchup was a comparative dud in the television ratings, attracting some of the smallest World Series audiences since the Nielsen authorities starting paying attention forty years earlier.

America was apparently unimpressed when the Rays won the second game, 4-2, with classic little things, bringing in runs on two ground balls and a safety squeeze. Maddon, however, could not be counted among the indifferent. "I can't tell you how happy I was with that," he said. "That's beautiful." [23] In game three, the upstart American Leaguers, at it again, cashed in a couple of groundouts in the seventh and tied the score in the eighth when Upton stole second and third—after leading the AL in stolen bases, Tampa Bay set a postseason record with twenty-three—and trucked home on a throwing error. The Phillies, as if to prove they could play even *smaller* ball, won that one in the bottom of the ninth on a hit batter, two intentional walks, and a dribbling single.

In game five, with Philadelphia poised to clinch, Pena pulled the

Rays even with a two-out single off Hamels in the sixth. Baldelli tied it again in the seventh on a one-out home run. Bartlett then singled, moved to second on a sacrifice, and had every intention of scoring when Iwamura bounced a ball in the vicinity of second base that Utley fielded and began, ostensibly, to throw to first. That enabled the opportunistic Bartlett to steam past third and proceed at top speed toward the go-ahead run, the problem being that Utley had merely *faked* his peg to Howard, instead firing home and surprising Bartlett at the plate to end the inning. For all that, Utley received an ordinary assist, but there was no statistic available for *creating* the critical out.

The Phillies untied the game for good on a double by Burrell and single by Pedro Feliz in the bottom of the seventh. In spite of three home runs by Howard—ringing anomalies in such a base-at-a-time Series—Hamels was again the MVP, which, unofficially, made Moyer the MVM (Most Valuable Mentor) and left Utley as merely the sharpest guy in the park.

Or would that have been Gillick?

FOUR

SCREW YOU, PEREZ

A WORD ON CHEMISTRY. IT IS A TERM ROUNDLY MISUNDERSTOOD IN THE BASEBALL SENSE, often used interchangeably with intangibles and shrugged off as a palsy-walsy sort of thing, the quaint notion of teammates as good buddies. That's surely part of it, but a small part, and perhaps the least significant.

"Can you win with teammates you don't like? Yes, you can," said Chipper Jones, whose ball-playing partners, for all of his nineteen splendid years in the Major Leagues, wore Atlanta Braves uniforms. "But lesser teams will go out and win because of good chemistry. There's a lot to be said for waking up in the morning and looking forward to going to the ballpark instead of playing with guys you loathe."

Everybody getting along, that's the camaraderie concept. An atmosphere of brotherhood and good cheer.[1] Addressing the topic of contentment in the workplace, a series of experiments conducted at Warwick University in England determined, "Positive emotions appear to invigorate human beings, while negative emotions have the opposite effect. . . .

Happier workers, our research found, were 12 percent more productive. Unhappier workers were 10 percent less productive."[2]

While the numbers are useful, most of us, like Jones, would accept the premise without them. Harmony's marvelous. In the context of baseball, however, functional chemistry, to its full and vital extent, pertains less to buddyism than to solidarity toward the common mission; a matter not of amity but of unanimity, or close to it.

A collective sense of purpose.

A cooperative understanding of what each man can do for the next.

A shared vision of winning.

A mutual dedication to whatever it takes.

Of course, if a title of any stripe is won, talent has been heavily involved, and that applies even to the championship teams hailed for their intangible mettle. The Yankees of 1998 had Mariano Rivera, George Steinbrenner's money, and eight players with at least 17 home runs. The Rays of 2008 could pitch and field with the best of them and enjoyed the rewards of the game's most fertile farm system. The Phillies of that year had two recent MVPs (Ryan Howard and Jimmy Rollins) and the best second baseman in the league (Chase Utley). The Giants of 2012 had an MVP catcher in Buster Posey and a starting rotation stellar enough to send a two-time Cy Young Award winner (Tim Lincecum) to the bullpen for the playoffs and World Series. The reconstituted Red Sox of 2013, for all the star power they had traded off (Adrian Gonzalez, Carl Crawford, Josh Beckett, Kevin Youkilis), and for all their bonding through facial hair, still had a former MVP (Dustin Pedroia), an esteemed run producer (David Ortiz) who had been named to eight All-Star teams, an unassailable closer (Koji Uehara), and the most efficient offense in the American League.

The fact is that good chemistry will never trump a club's or player's basic aptitude for playing ball. But it *contributes* to that capacity. When one teammate's answer matches another's question, when one's intensity shames another's indifference, when one's imagination snaps another's tedium, chemistry has occurred. A dimension has been added. Somebody has been enhanced.

Good chemistry is when two squad members cross-pollinate in such a way as to bring out the best in at least one of them. It's when the habits, personality, and general example of Player A have a positive effect on Player B and, better yet, on players B through V. When a team's entire alphabet fits together in that way, giving and taking, mixing and matching to make winning words and lyrical phrases, that's when you've got some poetry going on.

Good chemistry is when a learned veteran (Eric Hinske) meets a receptive rookie (Evan Longoria). When a dead-serious slugger (Kirk Gibson) signs with a club ('88 Dodgers) that could use an adjustment in attitude. When a great player with the gift of compatibility (Tony Perez) keeps things cool between two very important others (Pete Rose and Johnny Bench). When a wacky-dancing, injured closer (Brian Wilson) lightens the dugout and loosens his team ('12 Giants) throughout a hairy, brink-of-elimination postseason. When three guys here and four over there and ultimately all their confederates magnify each other to the point of becoming more than the simple numeric sum of themselves . . . that's the alchemy of champions.

The mixing of the cocktail falls principally upon the general manager, and it's an exercise in the abstract, more finesse than formula. "It depends on receptivity," said John Schuerholz, who built his Atlanta ballclubs with such things in mind. "If you've got a guy with a lot of enthusiasm and surround him with those who have like qualities and receptivity, it's going to have an impact. But if you surround him with a bunch of dolts, it's not." Provided he's been on the job long enough, a thorough GM will always keep a critical mass of character in his shaker. "If you've invited that one person into your organization and didn't care about the first fifty, it's not going to matter a hill of beans."

That said, a player's best attributes might well be squandered if replicated by too many teammates. Twenty-five clubhouse comedians, for instance, each well-equipped for easing tension, are a lot more than a loose room requires. The matching of makeups is an undertaking in balance and synthesis.

"Chemistry is an important ingredient," said Pete Mackanin, a bench coach for the Phillies at the time. "It's a blend of the enthusiasm of the younger players with the competence of the older players. I think that's why, on occasion, you see teams like Tampa Bay, the Twins in '87, all these Cinderella teams—or the few that have come into prominence."

As the fusion of personae, the workings of winning chemistry bear a provocative resemblance to the psychological concept of gestalt, a conceit introduced by German scientists to describe dynamics of visual perception. The term means "unified whole," and the basic idea is that, when we view a design or structure of numerous parts, if those elements are effectively integrated we tend to see them as a singular, autonomous entity. Extrapolated to baseball, gestalt could describe what a general manager is striving for in his conscious attempt to make order out of twenty-five supremely talented, highly charged, characteristically proud, and culturally diverse players.

To achieve gestalt among assembled athletes is to arrange marriages of both physical and social compatibility. "Team balancing is really a study in art," Branch Rickey wrote. "Team balancing is a problem that faces general management constantly and whose proper solution produces championships."[3]

Rickey was referring to the optimization of production, the swapping and acquisition of appropriate players in primarily a hitting, pitching, fielding sense. If your shortstop is blessed with surpassing range, velvety hands, and a lightning release, wouldn't it be wise to employ a second baseman who knows his way around a double play? If the cleanup batter can roll up 350 total bases in a season, shouldn't a premium be placed on out-avoiders for the top of the lineup? If a pitching staff has a penchant for throwing fly balls, swift outfielders would surely be in order. Similarly, if a roster is rife with the potential and vigor of fresh young talents, a savvy old pro or two would seem just the ticket. A brooding ballclub could use a brightener of moods and a timid team might be well served by a secretary of swagger. A tentative one could do with a deputy of been there, done that.

Among skeptics, a prevailing theory has it that chemistry is merely the jaunty product of winning. And, surely, success makes a ballclub feel better about itself. But those vibes, themselves, are not legless. The resonance of winning can help sustain the trend if it functions to swell the players' confidence, amplify their energy, stimulate their enthusiasm, accelerate their intensity, quicken their resolve, or ramp up their commitment. When winning occurs so regularly that it becomes an *expectation*, positivity cuts a wide path across a clubhouse. Inhibiting doubts are diminished. Success is felt, anticipated, visualized. That vision becomes what has been described as "magnetic north," a force of nature that points every player's compass in the same direction.[4]

What if a similar effect could be brought to bear without the hot streak? What if a *player* evoked that type of expectation? A player with his own contagious confidence. A player with championship rings on his fingers. A player who, somehow—by his history, his aspect, his competence, his toughness, whatever—just makes the other players like their chances. Is it merely coincidence that guys such as Orlando Cabrera, Mike Cameron, Jonny Gomes, and Edgar Renteria, while maybe a little short on All-Star appearances, keep turning up in October, from one team to another? Was it simply happenstance that little David Eckstein ("Never lose the belief that every second of your life is worth giving the best that you can. It's all about having heart.")[5] was the leadoff hitter and shortstop for World Series champions from both leagues?

In the chicken-egg cycle of a winning environment, we can say for certain that the environment needn't *follow* the winning. It can precipitate it. It can be—to an extent, *must* be—out front, laying the groundwork.

A ballclub's collaborative disposition may be an intangible proposition, but it's far from indiscernible to one familiar with its look and feel. Whitey Herzog could see in spring training of 1982, seven months before his Cardinals won the World Series, that his radical remake of the roster had produced the desired effect. "I flew back to St. Pete and looked over my team," he recalled in his autobiography. "The thing that impressed me most was that they were the hardest-working bunch of players I'd ever seen."[6]

Joe Torre had a comparable reaction at the Yankees' camp in 1998, identifying different virtues every bit as purposeful: "I've never seen a team develop such strong bonds of love and cooperation, and I'm certain it helped them achieve their goals," he wrote in *Joe Torre's Ground Rules for Winners.* "The atmosphere in spring training was special—a combination of utter determination and looseness unlike any I had seen before."[7]

That kind of gestalt is rarely accidental. Joe Maddon understood, from his first day in Tampa Bay, that the reinvention process would involve the development of not only hitters and pitchers, but a consortium of character, as well. "Everybody always says that winning creates chemistry," remarked the Rays' manager. "But I believe that good chemistry can create winning."

Bill James put it this way: "If you work really hard building a great team but you don't work on your clubhouse, you're wasting your effort."[8]

THAT BRINGS US, NATURALLY, TO THE INFAMOUS OAKLAND TEAMS OF THE EARLY SEVENTIES, the snarling, scuffling, three-straight World Series winners featuring Reggie Jackson, Catfish Hunter, Vida Blue, Sal Bando, Joe Rudi, Blue Moon Odom, Bert Campaneris, Ken Holtzman, Ray Fosse, Gene Tenace, managers Dick Williams and Alvin Dark, and the stingy, carnival-barking owner, Charlie O. Finley. Given their notorious concomitance of contentiousness and championships, it's not uncommon for "Oakland A's" to be a throwaway phrase for those who scoff at any notion of chemistry.

From afar, the A's were Team Antipathy. Odom and Blue tangled after the club clinched a spot in the 1972 World Series. When Mike Andrews made two errors in a loss to the Mets in the '73 Series, Finley removed him from the roster, prompting Andrews to sue. In '74, after Dark had replaced Williams, Bando growled that the new skipper couldn't manage a meat market. Jackson and Billy North went at it that year, and just prior to the first World Series game, Odom and Fingers threw down in Los Angeles, sending Fingers to the hospital for five stitches in his scalp. "Things like that are normal on this team," Bando, the team captain, told reporters. A few minutes later, Hunter announced that he would become a free agent—the first of the modern era—because Finley hadn't made good on half his contract.

If chemistry is about a ballclub abiding in a state of lovey-dovey, the Athletics lacked it in the extreme. Their flagrant example, however, doesn't reveal it to be immaterial. Oakland goes to show, rather, that chemistry's nature has been grossly misrepresented.

"Contrary to popular myth," wrote scientist Peter Senge in *The Fifth Discipline*, "great teams are not characterized by an absence of conflict. . . . In great teams, conflict becomes productive. . . . The free flow of conflicting ideas is critical for creative thinking, for discovering new solutions no one individual would have come to on his own. . . . Conflict becomes, in effect, part of the ongoing dialogue."[9]

So it was with Oakland. "Once the game started," said Fingers, "we played together, and we were going to beat you."[10]

The A's, in fact, fully satisfied the most basic criterion for good chemistry: They made each other better. They were signally proud, intensely competitive, chronically combative players united in their contempt for Finley and their fierce compulsion to outdo the bastard they had just rolled around on the clubhouse floor with. For all their fisticuffs, the A's, to a conspicuous degree, supported and complemented each other for nine innings every day. They took the game seriously and played it properly. They were intelligent enough, even as they fought their teammates, not to fight their *dependency* on them.

"We didn't have all the greatest arms in the outfield," pointed out Tenace, propped against a wall in the visitors' tunnel at Camden Yards in Baltimore, as the batting coach for the Toronto Blue Jays, "but Campaneris had the best arm on the infield and he would go out farther than most shortstops would go to take the relay. He'd bust out there to the spot where he thought Billy North could get it to him. Those are the little intangibles we did as a team. We executed as well as anyone ever played the game as far as moving runners over and getting guys in. We had twenty-five guys with tremendous baseball instincts. Getting bunts down, rundown situations, hitting a cutoff man, reading the ball in the dirt and taking the extra base. That was about as full-package of a club as you could put together. We had guys who enjoyed the competition. From start to finish, it was all about winning. We had no selfishness. I don't know what chemistry really is, but I know that those intangibles are part of the chemistry."

On that point, Jackson can help out. "Chemistry, as they call it, isn't about being chummy and agreeing with each other," he explained in *Sixty Feet, Six Inches,* his book-length dialogue with Bob Gibson. "It's about good people—and a lot of talented players who win. *That's* chemistry.

"We were mad all the time because Charlie Finley was so cheap and we didn't have the amenities that most teams did, even though we were winning championships. We couldn't slug Charlie, so we took it out on each other. Fights were so common in that clubhouse that we'd just deal the cards and keep playing, unless it was your turn to break it up. But everyone made up afterwards. I don't think it ever undermined what we were trying to do on the field."[11]

The St. Louis teams of the sixties—the ones that Maddon admires so much—come to mind when Jackson equates chemistry with quality people: Gibson, Bill White, Tim McCarver, Curt Flood, Lou Brock, Steve Carlton, Mike Shannon, Roger Maris, Dick Groat, Dal Maxvill, Orlando Cepeda . . . not all of them convivial, necessarily, but all companionable and certainly formidable. Regarding the Cardinals' 1964 world championship, won at the expense of the Yankees, Gibson remarked that he and his teammates "knew that our triumph was not a product of hitting and fielding and pitching skills alone, but, in an almost tangible sense, of the mental, social, and spiritual qualities that made the Cardinals unique—of intelligence, courage, brotherhood, and faith. I know that sounds corny as hell, but I honestly can't explain the '64 Cardinals any other way.

That's what and who we were."[12] Joe Torre was traded to St. Louis in 1969 and played there for only six of his eighteen Major-League seasons, but said later that he learned more about the game in his Cardinal years than he had at any other time.[13]

The eminent baseball writer Tom Boswell has expressed a particular appreciation for the alternative school of esprit de corps, admiring teams peopled with lively minds and potent personalities. "My favorite clubhouse," Boswell wrote in *Why Time Begins on Opening Day*, published in 1985, "was that of the '77–'78 Yankees. Those world champs were perhaps the most acid-tongued, thick-skinned, insult-you-to-your-face team that ever spit tobacco juice on a teammate's new Gucci loafers. . . . The heirs to the tradition were the '82 Brewers, led by Cy Young winner Pete Vuckovich."[14]

He was partial, also, to the resourceful, thoughtful groups Earl Weaver consistently won with in Baltimore during the late sixties and well beyond. Boswell portrayed characteristic Orioles as players who embraced fundamentals, avoided cliques, had themselves a fine time, and often signed back with Baltimore for less than they might have made on the open market. The attraction was an organization that "not only shows respect for, but actually encourages intelligence, humor, eccentricity and dissent. . . . The front office considers temperament as well as talent. Perhaps this single commitment has brought the Orioles their consistent excellence."[15]

The Big Red Machine was another cast of characters who thrived on individualism, working together just fine without standing on the likes of common cordiality—in fact, feeding off its opposite. It was the Reds' custom to rag each other ruthlessly. Their manager, Sparky Anderson, was instinctively wary of the jocular cross fire, which had its source in the imposing wills of Pete Rose, Johnny Bench, Tony Perez, and Joe Morgan. At one point, early in 1975, concerned that younger players might be intimidated by the culture of insults, Anderson established a gag rule barring any Red from verbally ripping into another. But it wasn't doing much good. The club was feeling stifled. When its record sank to 18–19 and Morgan's shin was ripped open as he covered second base against the Expos, necessitating fourteen stitches, the soon-to-be MVP had had enough.

The next day, arriving straight and freshly mended from the doctor's office, Morgan swaggered into the locker room with a smile on his face, glanced around, and shouted, "Screw you, Perez. Screw you, Rose. Screw you, Bench. And [looking directly at Sparky] that goes for you, too!" Anderson grinned, the clubhouse cracked up,[16] and the Reds, before winning the World Series, went 90–35 for the rest of the regular season.

WE COULD, AND SOON ENOUGH WILL, GO ON AND ON WITH THE ANECDOTES. THEY'RE THE language in which roster chemistry must necessarily be advocated—at least, for the present. Science, however, is scratching around at the edges of this weighty subject.

In *The Talent Code,* author Daniel Coyle examined the historical phenomenon by which marked achievement has periodically clustered in seemingly random locales and times: through art in Florence in the fifteenth century; poetry and fiction in the Brontë household of rural Yorkshire, England, in the nineteenth; soccer in Brazil in the twentieth. Addressing this curiosity from a physiological perspective, Coyle's narrative focuses on the wonders of myelin, an insulating element in the nervous system that quickens the transit of the electric signals that command human activity. Of more interest to the chemistry question, however, are the *social* aspects of the cluster paradigm: how the immediate presence of others engaged deeply and successfully in a certain pursuit can galvanize a fellow's fondness for it, harden his ambition along those lines, establish a model, signal a direction; how the communicable properties of proximity can, by what would seem to be osmosis, make him *better.*

On this point, Coyle quotes Geoff Cohen, a psychologist at the University of Colorado. "We're the most social creatures on the planet,"

Cohen said. "Everything depends on collective effort and cooperation. When we get a cue that we ought to connect our identity with a group, it's like a hair trigger, like turning on a light switch. The ability to achieve is already there, but the energy put into that ability goes through the roof."[17]

And so it happens that Indiana boys develop an unusual proficiency for shooting a basketball; that female golfers suddenly pour out of South Korea; that the Dominican Republic comes to account for more than ten percent of Major-League ballplayers; that Mozart, Beethoven, Schubert, Strauss, Liszt, Brahms, Mahler, and Haydn all had ties to Vienna; that as soon as he was traded from Houston to Cincinnati before the 1972 season, Morgan bought himself a Big Red Machine T-shirt to wear every day under his uniform, just for the feeling of belonging there.[18]

The connection of all this to myelin comes through the cycle by which the insulation grows and strengthens when the nerve circuits are firing—that is, when mind and body are conspiring in what is commonly recognized as muscle memory. Myelin, consequently, is built up by repetition, by *practice*. "To sum up: It's time to rewrite the maxim that practice makes perfect," wrote Coyle. "The truth is, practice makes myelin, and myelin makes perfect."

And when practice itself approaches perfection, remarkable things ensue. That's where the local environment comes in. The quality of practice, Coyle found out, is directly related to the level at which one identifies with the particular activity.

The critical association between achievement and identity was brought to light in a 1997 study by an Australian music psychologist, Gary McPherson, who set out to determine why it was that, in the matter of music lessons, some kids made better progress than others. He tracked a group of children from the time they chose their instruments (typically at age seven or eight) through graduation from high school. Ultimately, as McPherson studied the results, he saw that the disparities were largely unrelated to intelligence or motor skills or sense of rhythm. The key was in the answer to a question he posed to every boy and girl at the very outset: How long do you think you'll play your new instrument?[19]

> When McPherson saw the graph, he was stunned. "I couldn't believe my eyes," he said. Progress was determined not by any measurable aptitude or trait, but by a tiny, powerful idea the child had before even starting lessons. The differences were staggering. With the same amount of practice, the long-term-commitment group outperformed the short-term-commitment group by 400 percent.[20] When long-term commitment combined with high levels of practice, skills skyrocketed. . . . "It's all about their perception of self," [McPherson said.]
>
> —Daniel Coyle, *The Talent Code*

So, if commitment is fundamental to success, self-perception (i.e., identity) is fundamental to commitment, and identity is a product of relationships . . . that is to say, if certain relationships supercharge ability and trigger achievement . . . would not the right set of teammates—guys who contribute to a compelling, enriched environment—elevate the outlook, dedication, and bottom line of a baseball player? Wouldn't it empower his talent?

And isn't that *chemistry*?

When the matchups are favorable, chemistry can be a salve for an athlete's self-assurance, a conditioner for his states of mind and readiness, bread crumbs for his path, open arms to his sense of identity. Pride in a franchise or allegiance to a colleague—better yet, both—can occasion a substantial investment in the common cause, widening chemistry's circle well beyond the general helping out that occurs among good teammates. Caught up in a self-sustaining subculture, a ballplayer gets a glimpse of what it's like to be a marathoner from Kenya, a seven-footer in a Duke shirt, a shortstop from San Pedro de Macoris, the youngest in a family of valedictorians, a San Francisco Giant in the postseason. And he is better for it.

FIVE

CHIEF BIG FIST

AS A BASEBALL WRITER FOR ESPN.COM, JAYSON STARK MAKES THE ROUNDS OF SPRING training every year, team to team, on the lookout for whatever might be different or indicative. In the midsection of March 2009, fresh off his journalistic coverage and literary examination of the Philadelphia Phillies' first world championship in twenty-eight years, Stark stopped over in Sarasota, Florida, to check out the reinvented Cincinnati Reds, who happened to remind him very much of the club to which he'd recently devoted so many of his thoughts and words.

"There's something happening here in Reds Land," he noted. "Something building. Something growing. There's as much spring buzz about the Reds as there is about any team in Florida. And frankly, Junior Griffey and Adam Dunn needed to get out of the way for that buzz—and this team—to prosper. . . . Scouts who have followed the Reds this spring have talked nonstop about the energy that seems to jump off the field at you when you watch them."[1]

In the absence of Griffey and Dunn, the Reds were leaning heavily on twentysomethings Jay Bruce, Joey Votto, and Brandon Phillips. The three had accomplished substantially less than the trio of Phillies (Ryan Howard, Jimmy Rollins, and Chase Utley) who stepped up in rank when Bobby Abreu was traded, and were assuming prominence on a team with less recent success. Consequently, Stark was not predicting an imminent pennant for the Reds. He was, however, like the scouts he consulted, recognizing that the intangibles he had observed so vividly in Philadelphia were indicators to be taken seriously.

Of course, team sports involve myriad moving parts, and the upshot of roster evolution is a complex and sensitive proposition. If, for example, the exchange of years for youth prompts a boost in energy, it can also leave a void in leadership. That appeared to be the case in Cincinnati.

For Dusty Baker, it was a ranking issue. As a champion of the human dynamic in baseball, the Reds' skipper was particularly attuned to the presence of leadership on his teams, and insistent upon it. Baker, in fact, sought his leaders out, actively searching for them, even as a rookie manager in San Francisco in 1993. While standing by the batting cage during spring training that year in Arizona, he noticed that players tended to gravitate around Robby Thompson at second base and Willie McGee in right field. He invited Thompson and McGee to a tennis tournament taking place in Scottsdale, suggesting that the two of them drive together and he would follow. He wanted to see how much talking they did in the car ahead. The players chatted all along the way and, when they arrived at the tournament, told Baker that there were some things they wanted to discuss with him. He had his leaders.

"A lot of times the leaders are not necessarily the best ballplayers on your team," said the grape-growing, jazz-loving Californian, who began his nineteen-year playing career with the Atlanta Braves. "Your team leader has to be somebody the guys can go to with their problems, and who can accept listening to them even though he has problems of his own. You need a leader among your starting pitchers, a leader in the bullpen, a leader in the infield, a leader among the extra guys to get them to continue to work. But the epitome of leadership is when your best player is also your best citizen."

That was what the Braves had when Hank Aaron would counsel Baker and Ralph Garr, among others, on such basics as when to get up (in time for breakfast), what to have for lunch (a big meal around one o'clock), and how to stay in shape in the off-season (basketball alone is not sufficient). A rebuke from Aaron was enough to end a teammate's bad habit. "I used to throw my helmet," recalled Baker, "and one day Hank told me, 'If you throw that helmet one more time, we've got a problem. It's not your helmet's fault. You take that helmet and set it over by that bat rack and act like a professional.'"

There was no Hank Aaron on the Cincinnati roster, and no amount of creative recruiting on Baker's part could make one materialize. Even so, the Reds were hoping that Votto and Phillips would show the way. As the 2009 season got rolling, however, that plan began to look a bit improbable.

In August 2008, Votto's impressive rookie year had been darkened by the unexpected death of his father, Joseph, back in Toronto. Joey's dad, a chef and avid baseball fan, had been his first and enduring connection to the game. Votto is an uncommonly intense player, and after his father's passing, that intensity urged him through the rest of the season. But once the games ended, grief and despair pushed into the void. It was a difficult off-season for the reflective first baseman, and he welcomed the return of full-time baseball. For the first month of the '09 season, Votto played every inning, his rugged plate approach and explosive left-handed swing marking him as one of the most dynamic, well-rounded hitters in the National League.

In a bad loss to the Milwaukee Brewers on May 6, he left the game early with a respiratory infection that was making him dizzy. He didn't start any of the next four, and the inactivity treated him cruelly. His mind wandered and reeled. On May 10, Votto entered against the Cardinals as a defensive replacement and homered in his first at-bat, suggesting that he was ready to resume his regular duties. He wasn't. In all, Cincinnati's top offensive threat missed a dozen starts and was excused early from three other games before, with the Reds' record at 26–20, he left one against the Brewers for stress-related reasons. The next day, batting .357, Votto was placed on the disabled list. Cincinnati went 8–14 without him.[2] But nothing, it seemed, stated the impact of Votto's absence like his *presence.* On his third day back, playing in his hometown against the Blue Jays, he lashed a go-ahead home run and three other hits, two of them driving in runs, as the Reds halted a four-game losing streak.

While Votto's commitment was never seriously called into question, the downtime he needed was a deterrent to leadership. Nor was guidance being lavished upon the young Reds by the everyday veterans—shortstop Alex Gonzalez, who had missed all of the previous season with a knee injury; center fielder Willy Taveras, whose influence was undercut by his prodigious struggles in the leadoff slot; and catcher Ramon Hernandez, acquired in a winter trade with Baltimore, and splitting time with the less experienced Ryan Hanigan. Role models were lacking for the likes of Bruce; third baseman Edwin Encarnacion, a low-energy power hitter; Chris Dickerson, an athletic but unpolished outfielder; Paul Janish, a strong-armed, weak-bat shortstop; and developing pitchers Edinson Volquez, Johnny Cueto, and Homer Bailey. Jonny Gomes, signed as a free agent, had brought over some of the toughness and one-for-allness that had distinguished his tour with Tampa Bay, but his influence was restricted by part-time duty.

Meanwhile, Phillips, coming off his first Gold Glove, could be an inspiration through his bursts of joy and dazzling improvisation, but he had not yet embraced the unrelenting attentiveness to the task that the renovated Reds were looking for in a leader. In the way of intangibles, the versatile second baseman flashed a stirring good side and, now and then, a nagging bad one.

Case in point, Phillips thinking on the fly: In an early May game against Arizona, Votto advanced Jerry Hairston from second base to third on a long fly ball (no mainstream stat for that) and Hairston scored on a soft single from Phillips. On a subsequent base hit by Bruce, Phillips slowed as he approached second, causing center fielder Chris Young to relax his attitude toward the throw, then dashed safely to third.[3] He scored on a sacrifice fly by Hernandez, chalking up an unrecorded, second-level stat point, the RBI accruing to Hernandez but facilitated by Phillips. (The night before, Phillips had executed a similar play, expanding a single into a double when Diamondbacks left fielder Eric Brynes made a casual throw to the cutoff man. For that piece of heads-up running, however, he was statistically rewarded in total bases, isolated power, and slugging percentage.)

Case in point, Phillips defying the manager: In a loss at Kansas City in mid-June, Phillips ignored a take sign on a 3-0 count. Dusty Baker said it was the first time in his sixteen years of managing that one of his players had done that. Phillips apologized and a fine was assessed.

Case in point, Phillips encouraging less established players: Talking to beat writer John Fay of the *Cincinnati Enquirer*, Phillips volunteered praise for Cueto and platooning left fielder Laynce Nix. (At the same time, he took a jab at Adam Dunn's legacy, saying of Nix, "He's a great teammate. . . . It's good to have a guy in left field who can hit and catch the ball.")

Case in point, Phillips not running hard: Playing in Los Angeles shortly after the All-Star break, the Reds had a chance to knock out starting pitcher Jason Schmidt and put the Dodgers away in the first inning when Phillips, batting cleanup, came to the plate with two runs already in and Votto at third base. Disappointed when his fly ball floated inauspiciously into right-center field, he lowered his head and jogged out of the batter's box, speeding up belatedly when the ball unexpectedly dropped in a spot where doubles often land. Votto scored easily but Phillips, doomed by his slow start, was thrown out at second by right fielder Andre Ethier. Schmidt lasted five innings without giving up another run and the Reds eventually lost, 7-5. Baker was publicly peeved, letting it be known that he and his star second baseman had often discussed such indiscretions.

To Baker, equally troubling was the virus of bad ballplaying that was spreading throughout his club. During a particularly unsightly stretch of July baseball, rookie pitcher Josh Roenicke failed to cover first base; Nix made baserunning mistakes on consecutive plays; Taveras attempted to throw out a runner at home plate when he had no reasonable chance to do so, allowing the batter to reach second and eventually score; and the Reds, together, dropped irreversibly below .500, out of the division race.

Finally, after his team went down on a one-hitter by Mat Latos and a couple of San Diego relievers, the manager vented. He went so far as to question the club's effort and enthusiasm, the very qualities that had so impressed Jayson Stark in spring training. "This is totally unacceptable," Baker told Mark Sheldon of the MLBlogs Network. "It's embarrassing. . . . We're not getting after it. This is pitiful."[4]

Two days later, at the trade deadline, Walt Jocketty made a seemingly peculiar move for a young team out of contention, swapping Encarnacion, Roenicke, and touted pitching prospect Zach Stewart to the Toronto Blue Jays for Scott Rolen, a thirty-four-year-old third baseman with a damaged shoulder and chronically aching back.

CONCERNING THE FIRST DECADE OF THE TWENTY-FIRST CENTURY, THERE ARE THOSE WHO maintain that the connected fates of the Reds and St. Louis Cardinals were set in motion by a trade that occurred, and another that didn't, on July 29, 2002. That was when Jocketty, who, at the time, occupied the general manager's office in St. Louis, acquired Rolen from the Philadelphia Phillies in a five-player swap that sent infielder Placido Polanco the other way. Jocketty's counterpart in Cincinnati at the time, Jim Bowden, had also been trying to land Rolen, who, at the age of twenty-seven, had just played in his first All-Star game. The two midwestern river cities are the same distance from Rolen's hometown of Jasper, Indiana, a pertinent consideration for a player whose parents attended as many games as they could. Bowden, angling for a right-handed power hitter to place between Griffey and Dunn, had a deal lined up for the Gold Glover that allegedly involved his own popular third baseman, Aaron Boone, whose father, Bob, was the Cincinnati manager, but Reds owner Carl Lindner nixed it. He was unwilling to bump his payroll during the season.

On the day that Rolen changed into a Cardinals jersey, the Reds, at 54–50, trailed St. Louis by four games in the National League Central. They finished 78–84, straggling in nineteen lengths behind Rolen and, in his second big-league season, Albert Pujols. Two years later, the Cardinals won 100 games and made it to the World Series. The year after *that*, they won 105. The year after *that*, they won the World Series. From the moment of the 2002 trade until Rolen, courtesy of Jocketty, finally turned up in Cincinnati seven years later, the Reds, never reaching .500 for a season, won 120 fewer games than their division rival to the west.

Yet the 2009 trade was met, both locally and nationally, with the utmost skepticism. Over the previous four and a half years, Rolen had managed just 54 home runs. He was aging, hurting, and dropping off. He'd also feuded with his managers in both Philadelphia (Larry Bowa) and St. Louis (Tony La Russa). Jocketty looked beyond all that. He saw the kind of leadership—the kind of player and pro—that he sorely needed in Cincinnati.

"Scott Rolen isn't your prototypical leader where he's out there yelling stuff," Jocketty remarked not long thereafter, "but he talks to players individually or in a group about trying to play the game the right way. You watch the way he practices and goes about his business, and the young guys see that."

In his effort to rebuild the culture of the Reds, Jocketty, along with scouting director Chris Buckley, had made a priority of drafting players in part for their love of the game and inclination to play it properly; but those qualities, much like hitting and pitching skills, had to be not only acquired but developed. The organization had an educational responsibility. "We're trying to teach guys how important it is to do the little things to win," Jocketty said. A player like Rolen was a major asset in that area. A 245-pound example, anchoring the infield.

Jocketty, of course, had observed firsthand what Rolen's intangibles meant to the Cardinals. Going back a little further, an even more compelling precedent involved another former third baseman and Cardinal.

Terry Pendleton's seventh season in St. Louis had been a very bad one. An unacceptable OPS of .601. That year, 1990, was the ninth in which John Schuerholz served as general manager of the Kansas City Royals, and upon its conclusion he accepted a similar position with the Atlanta Braves, which a lot of baseball people didn't understand at all. With a record of 65–97, its best year of the past three, Atlanta had just completed its seventh consecutive losing season. So, Schuerholz's first move in the new job? Acquiring Pendleton, a thirty-year-old former Gold Glover who only twice had batted over .264 and had never managed more than thirteen home runs.

"When I signed Terry Pendleton as our first free agent," recalled Schuerholz, "it was referred to by Furman Bisher [noted sports columnist for the *Atlanta Constitution*] as the dumbest move he'd ever seen." There wasn't much disagreement.

Pendleton was the sort of player whom Schuerholz's father and grandfather, both sporting legends back in Baltimore, had always spoken so highly of at the dinner table, the sort the Orioles had collected when they were winning pennants with Brooks Robinson holding down third base, the sort Schuerholz had come to admire even more through his association with George Brett in Kansas City.

"I knew Terry had playability," said Schuerholz, "but also knew he had leadership. I had watched Terry play a lot, saw him in the World Series [1985 and 1987], watched how he handled himself, read a lot of things he said about attitude. There was a leader there. It doesn't have to be a guy who's an overt communicator, an effervescent, emotional, passionate guy. The best combination I've seen is someone who has ability and does it with a joyful, high-spirited, high-positive manner."

In addition to those characteristics, there were two specific others that pointed Schuerholz toward the five-foot-nine switch-hitter. He looked at the numbers, sure enough, but he *studied* the player.

"When I was hired by the Braves," he explained, "it was clear that this was a team that had a lot of good qualities to it. But two of the essential qualities missing were capable infield defenders to support the outstanding young pitchers that [previous general manager] Bobby Cox had assembled, and winners, experienced winners. Terry Pendleton was the quintessential example of that type of player."

At the time, however, Pendleton was *not* a quintessential or any other type of batting champion. Inexplicably, that's what he became in 1991, his first season wearing a tomahawk on his chest. The unexpected title contributed materially to his even more unexpected Most Valuable Player award. And yet, from Schuerholz's perspective, it was not what Pendleton contributed most to the Braves.

"His effort at practice, preparation, excellence, whether fielding a ground ball, making a tough play, advancing a runner . . . his entire professional demeanor was something that was a model for people to just watch and see."

The team Schuerholz had inherited, like the one Jocketty took over in Cincinnati, conspicuously needed a model. Such Atlanta regulars as David Justice, Ron Gant, and Mark Lemke—even pitchers Tom Glavine, John Smoltz, Steve Avery, and Kent Mercker—were approaching or hitting their prime on a club that chronically hadn't won. "There's a very honest and real expectation that young players like [those]—guys like Carl Crawford and Evan Longoria—are going to grow into excellence because of who they are. But when they have someone to watch," said Schuerholz, "someone who can demonstrate that manner, that professional character, that preparation commitment, that winning-spirit commitment, it's easier for them to see what that model looks like. They were not sure what exactly that looks like in a human being. Here was the guy who really set the tone."

What Pendleton set the tone *for* was, almost inconceivably—going into the season, Atlanta's culture of losing was right up there with that of the Cubs—a division title and trip to the World Series. The next season was much the same. In 1995, the Braves *won* the Series. Ten years later, they pulled off their unprecedented fourteenth division title in a row (ex-cepting the 1994 season, which was not completed). From Schuerholz's arrival in Atlanta—and Pendleton's—to this day, the Braves have won more games than any other franchise in Major League Baseball.

Pendleton, however, wasn't around for Atlanta's world champion-ship in '95, supplanted that year by Chipper Jones, a former first-round draft choice of whom much was anticipated and by whom much was ultimately delivered. When Jones first reported to the Braves' clubhouse in 1993, Bobby Cox, who had returned to managing when Schuerholz became the GM, placed him at the locker next to Pendleton's.

"After games, I used to have to take his shoes off for him because his back hurt so bad he couldn't bend over to take them off himself," re-membered Chipper, his admiration undiminished by the years. "TP was the rock. Everybody knew that if you screwed up, you were going to have to answer to TP."

IN HIS SECOND GAME AS A RED, SCOTT ROLEN WAS HIT IN THE HEAD BY A PITCH FROM Jason Marquis of the Colorado Rockies, his old teammate and friend in St. Louis. He missed a couple of games after that, Cincinnati's seventh and eighth losses in a row, then returned to the lineup and hit a home run against Rich Harden of the Cubs in the victory that broke the losing streak. Rolen played one more game before being placed belatedly on the disabled list with a concussion. When he returned two weeks later, the club had lost seven of eight and, at 51–71, slipped into last place.

With their new leader back in business, the Reds immediately won five straight games. In the second of those, Rolen was on second base when Laynce Nix shot a line drive to right field. It was catchable but not positively so, and most runners would have routinely trotted halfway to third and waited to see what would happen. But Rolen, who had occa-sionally been called the best baserunner in the game (and was named by espn.com as the best at breaking up double plays), knew. He remained on second until Frank Catalanotto, backing up, had snagged the ball; then he tagged and sped to third. From there, he scored on a ground single by Corky Miller.

The five-game streak was followed shortly by runs of seven, four, and six victories in a row. Although the Reds won at a dramatically higher rate when Rolen was in the lineup, he appeared to do nothing heroic or unusually grand; he was just *there*, practicing properly,[5] running alertly, setting an undeclared, unmistakable, physically imposing example. His young teammates called him Chief Big Fist.

The fact was that Rolen's influence actually took root not when he assumed his spot in the lineup but when he was disabled and took his seat in the dugout, usually next to Jay Bruce, who was shelved at the time by a broken wrist, and who had a healthy appetite for a veteran's mentoring. The subject often turned to baserunning, which, on the recent, power-heavy Cincinnati teams, had been practiced with more gumption than purpose. Rolen preached to his protégé about the importance of getting from first to third, particularly on a single to right field, with fewer than two outs. From those conversations, the Reds developed a battle cry for the base paths: "Need ya on third, Brucie!" It didn't matter if the runner on first was Bruce or Phillips or Ramon Hernandez; for that moment, he was Brucie.[6]

The 2009 Reds would end up leading the National League in going from first to third. Jonny Gomes, who did it fourteen times, credited Chief Big Fist, explaining it this way to Tyler Kepner of the *New York Times*:

[Rolen] really challenged the players . . . to take their base running to the next level. . . . You know W.W.J.D., what would Jesus do? Here, it's what would Scott do? He doesn't argue with the umpires, he runs every single ball out, he makes great plays, he makes routine plays, he gets the runner in when he needs to get him in, he gets the runner over when he needs to get him over. He just plays the game exactly how it should be played.[7]

By September, the second-guessing of the Rolen trade was waning significantly in Cincinnati. The Cardinals were uncatchable, but the Reds roared past the Pirates and Astros. Fundamentals were looking better. Opportunism was catching on. Professionalism was taking hold.

"Everybody was talking about the numbers on the trade, but they don't see the effects that a player has on other guys," said Baker. He, however, was seeing a fourteen-year veteran with a bad back showing sprier teammates how to make a dash for every attainable base. Baker had certain expectations for the players under his charge, and he was seeing them exemplified by a five-time All-Star who had the ballclub's attention. "Guys these days are all hollering, 'I get no respect,' but Rolen just commands it through his presence. It's how he runs the bases, how he goes about his business, how he doesn't complain, just being himself."

On a seemingly insignificant play early in the month, Rolen, on first base, tagged up and advanced to second on a fly ball to right field. In a more significant situation a few games later—a tight one with the Astros—Phillips, having noticed, did the same thing. That night, with the score tied in the bottom of the seventh, the Reds' showy second baseman singled to right, sending Votto from first to third, then took *two* bases as Votto scored the winning run on a wild pitch from Houston's Jeff Fulchino. It was the kind of aggressive, improvisational baserunning that Phillips was beginning to flash on a regular basis and that Baker praised as "Jackie Robinson stuff," a description that activated the Georgian's neon smile.

Of course, that sort of thing doesn't always work out for the best. Aggression on the base path is a form of risk taking that results inherently in checkered returns. The attending spirit of opportunism has its rightful place in a winning, make-it-happen attitude, but it can also be counterproductive in the wrong heads. In other words, cues taken from teammates—that is, the effect of a player's intangibles—can cut both ways.

That pesky point, understandably, is the sort that leaves the intangibles argument exposed to the jaws of saber-toothed metricians.[8] It's logical and undeniable that leaders, no matter how worthy and well-meaning, often guide their teams in unfortunate directions, which is to say that the intangibles economy is not a linear, predictable affair. One cautionary example would bundle Scott Rolen, Brandon Phillips, and baserunning.

Statistical analysis shows that, as a runner, Phillips indeed became more aggressive around the time Rolen was acquired by the Reds. Over a five-season period from 2007 to 2011, he posted a 4.4 percent jump in his attempts, successful or otherwise, to take extra bases. But in the two seasons prior to Rolen's arrival, he was far less inclined to run into outs than in the two seasons after. It might be concluded that Phillips was actually a more effective runner in the earlier stretch. Additionally, data showed that, as baserunners, the Blue Jays—including Rolen himself—conducted themselves in quite a safe and certain manner when Rolen was among them, suggesting that perhaps, in Cincinnati, Rolen was not only influencing but, in fact, *being influenced* by reckless tendencies that the Reds had already picked up. Upon further examination, Rolen's running record appears to consistently reflect, more than anything, the message of his manager. Over seven seasons, his worst baserunning—judging, that is, by the percentage of outs made while attempting extra bases—occurred during his first two in Cincinnati.

Nevertheless, it was evident in September 2009 that in the fresh company of Chief Big Fist, Brandon Phillips, in step with his club, was on a roll, playing some of the best baseball of his colorful career. And he wasn't shy about stating why.

"I don't really know exactly what Scott Rolen brought to the clubhouse," he said, "but I know what he did for me. He showed me what type of player I'd love to try to be like." Rolen recognized in Phillips a deep-seated desire to be a teammate around whom others rallied, and supported that ambition by word and example. He also suggested, specifically, that the second baseman not stand and watch his home runs leave the playing field but commence trotting without ostentation. "I thought I was doing okay," reflected Phillips, "but when I saw the way he approached the game it really woke me up a little bit. I've been a team player my whole career, but now, watching him, I'm learning to be a *real* team player. He's teaching me how to be a leader."

Over their final forty games—a period starting when Rolen came off the disabled list—the Reds clicked off an unforeseen record of 27–13, the best in either league. Of course, September performances are infamously misleading, most notably when the clubs in question are far removed from a pennant race. Cincinnati's 2009 team qualified in that respect. Meanwhile, the sharp turnaround might be ascribed to any number of things, including luck, sample size, relative health, maturation, dramatically improved pitching, and various personnel considerations, the Rolen effect among them. To the extent that Rolen *did* make a difference, was it chiefly his example or merely his ballplaying? (He was, after all, a more productive third baseman than his predecessor, Edwin Encarnacion.)

We'll never have that breakdown in precise percentages. When the book is complete on a team's season—or a player's, for that matter—intangibles haven't told the entire tale, and neither have the numbers.[9] There's an intriguing hookup between the two, and a tinge of mystery in every chapter and passage.

THE TURNAROUND OF THE CINCINNATI PITCHING STAFF WAS IN CONCERT WITH HOMER Bailey's.[10]

Although he'd spent parts of the previous two years in Cincinnati and taken a lengthy turn as the organization's top-ranked pitching prospect, Bailey, a twenty-three-year-old Texan with a tattoo of an arrow running the length of his forearm, had begun the season with the Reds' Triple-A affiliate in Louisville. His work there was somewhat disappointing until, late in May, before a game in Scranton, Pennsylvania, he conferred on the outfield grass with teammate Justin Lehr, a thirty-one-year-old knockabout who had pitched in South Korea the previous season and been freshly acquired from the Phillies organization.

Bailey had charted Lehr's most recent start and was impressed by the way in which the unspectacular veteran consistently got hitters out with a dipping, off-speed, split-finger fastball. He asked about it, and Lehr advised Bailey to take his usual fastball grip but move his index finger to the other side of the seam. With the talent of a first-round draft choice, which he'd been five years before, the lanky right-hander picked it up immediately. Bailey inserted the split-finger in place of a changeup that he'd never been enamored of, and without delay began to dominate the International League.[11] In late June, he left Louisville for the last time.

Success in Cincinnati did not come immediately. After a typically rough start in mid-August, his earned run average stood at a ghastly 7.53. Thereafter, it was 1.70, the best number in all the Major Leagues. Coincidentally or not, Bailey's dramatic improvement kicked in shortly after Lehr, who by that time had wrapped up the International League's Most Valuable Pitcher award, was promoted to the Reds.[12] (For his part, Lehr, pitching in the big leagues for the first time in three years, struggled with a groin injury after arriving in Cincinnati and throwing a shutout. His final numbers were pedestrian; his value was concealed in the *second-level statistics* he contributed to the calculus of Bailey's columns.)

Rick Sweet, the Louisville manager, had lobbied for the in-season acquisitions of both Lehr and Corky Miller, a mediocre-hitting, thirty-three-year-old, fiercely mustachioed, freakishly popular catcher who, by 2009, was in his twelfth minor-league season with six organizations. Sweet knew the pair to be players who could model the baseball ethics he was trying to instill in Cincinnati's next generation of big-leaguers. "We talk to them about situations; but a guy like Justin Lehr, a guy like Corky Miller, they go out and *do* it," Sweet said. "They *show* them how to play the right way. It is probably the most important aspect of putting a winning team together."

Like Lehr, Miller was rewarded with a late-season call to the Reds. And, like Lehr's, his biggest contributions were of the indirect variety. In Miller's eighteen starts behind the plate, Cincinnati's pitching staff went 13–5 with a 3.02 ERA, a run better than the club's other catchers combined.

Given that the Reds were not contending for a pennant in late summer, they could afford to devote a few roster spots to the nurturing of young players and the continued crafting of team culture. And, sure enough, the concerted effort showed signs of working for them. At the same time, it ought to be noted that the Yankees won the World Series that year (beating the Phillies in six games), and while they were captained by Mr. Intangible himself and he was in league with such professional paragons as Andy Pettitte, Jorge Posada, and Mariano Rivera—they even added the acclaimed teammate Eric Hinske for the second half of the season—it would be plain foolish to credit their success to any sort of subtle underpinning, inasmuch as they trotted out a monstrous daily lineup in which every starter but one (center fielder Melky Cabrera at a very respectable .752) piled up an OPS of more than .850.

In Cincinnati's case, however, the operative elements remained more elusive and indistinct. Grayer. More provocative. The very vagueness, the impossibility of boiling it all down, magnified the intrinsic inscrutability of the game, which so many fans find so addictively compelling.

Was the late rally real enough to be sustainable? Were the Reds onto something? Would their chemistry carry over to 2010?

To some of us, baseball's mystery is not unrelated to its allure; not at all.

SIX

JETERSHIP

FOR DEREK JETER, THE LATTER STAGES OF THE 2009 SEASON WERE, IF NOT UNCHARACTER-istic, eventful. In August, on his way to batting .334 at the age of thirty-five, he broke Luis Aparicio's career record for base hits by a shortstop. In September, having exceeded 200 for the seventh time, he broke Lou Gehrig's career record for base hits by a Yankee. In October, his team completed its regular season with more than 100 victories for the fifth time, wrapped up its eleventh division championship, beat the Minnesota Twins in the first round of the playoffs, beat the Los Angeles Angels for its seventh American League pennant, and beat the Philadelphia Phillies for its fifth World Series title, which is one more than Babe Ruth racked up in a New York uniform.

It was the seventh World Series in which Jeter, starting pitcher Andy Pettitte, and relief ace Mariano Rivera had banded together, and the sixth for those three and catcher Jorge Posada, the most for a Yankee quartet since Mickey Mantle, Whitey Ford, Elston Howard, and Bobby Richardson in the fifties and sixties. Posada, Rivera, Pettitte, and Jeter, referred to as the "core four" of the contemporary Yankees, first shared a clubhouse in Columbus, Ohio, the organization's Triple-A affiliate, when Jeter was promoted to that level in 1994, and between them—along with the likes of Bernie Williams, Paul O'Neill, Scott Brosius, David Cone, and company, not to mention such epic predecessors as Mantle, Ford, Gehrig, Ruth, and Joe DiMaggio—there has emerged a brand of player identified by the somewhat grandiose term *True Yankee.* Jeter has become the face of that breed. True Yankeeism is a contrived conglomeration of class, professionalism, eminence, and intangibles, which are loosely defined as whatever Jeter does. "To describe the overzealous praise of Jeter's intangibles," Joe Posnanski made up a word: *Jeterate.*

Overzealousness aside, Jeter does nicely as a prototype for the intangibles superstar. "When it comes to intangibles," said former Atlanta manager Bobby Cox, "the number one guy today is Derek Jeter." Cox was using the word as a catchall for makeup, fundamentals, instincts, approach, and whatever becomes a ballplayer. He was using Jeter as an example of the type of player he would like twenty-five of. "Now, I'm sure he's made mistakes like any other player in the game, but not many. And he carries himself well in the public eye and with the fans. The ultimate professional sports guy? Derek Jeter."

Bear in mind, Cox managed Chipper Jones and Greg Maddux, on whom the words *ultimate professional* could properly be pinned. They apply, as well, to such solid baseball citizens as Albert Pujols, Chase Utley, Jim Thome—once rated by a Tribune Company survey as the Best Teammate in Baseball—and Scott Rolen. And yet, it is Jeter who, by playing the game so conspicuously and triumphantly right, has brought intangibles to the big stage and come back for curtain calls.

That's not to say he has acquitted himself impeccably. The captain has been known for intolerance toward those of whom he disapproves. His distaste for teammate Alex Rodriguez has occasionally gone public; there was, for instance, the punishing look Jeter directed at Rodriguez in 2006 when the third baseman bumped into him and made him drop an easy pop fly. Privately, Yankee general manager Brian Cashman once appealed to Jeter, for the team's sake, to please fake it with A-Rod.[1]

Some Yankee watchers also whisper that Jeter doesn't always run his hardest to first base. Others were disappointed that he didn't volunteer to move off shortstop when A-Rod was acquired. Under the magnifying glass, those are but impurities in a dazzling diamond. In relative mortality, baseball division, Jeter's feet touch only the top of the grass.

Torre, whose history with Jeter covers a dozen seasons as Yankee manager, has never forgotten when the future Hall of Famer was a twenty-two-year-old Rookie of the Year in 1996 and, by late summer, older teammates were looking his way when a play needed to be made or a hit delivered. From the beginning, the kid shortstop was a player who would assume responsibility and answer for the outcome. "His mom and dad made him sign a contract when he was a teenager, about what are his responsibilities, what he had to do," observed Torre. "All that stuff, to me, is what you call intangibles." Jeter's had the visibility of pinstripes and New York City, and were sharply accented by his talent, from which they couldn't be separated.

"Even though he was gifted as an athlete, he didn't think there was anything free that went with that," Torre said. "He was always earning his way. He had the sense of responsibility ingrained in him. That's what I got from him. He's not someone who's going to talk a lot in the clubhouse. He's not going to open his mouth just for the sake of opening his mouth. He's a guy who's competitive, competent, yet doesn't need to talk about it. A guy you can look in the eye. I have a deep appreciation of Derek."

And yet, with respect for all the Jeteration, what are the elemental traits that make up a do-right, good-to-the-bone, holistic player such as the truest Yankee? If the question referred to physical attributes, the familiar five tools—ability to run, field, throw, hit, and hit with power— would fill out the checklist. What, though, are the more abstract assets that complete the profile? What are the performance-enhancing qualities (PEQs) that represent a full set of intangibles?

Given that we've classified intangibles into two basic types, some of the PEQs would be situational in nature—the little things that improve the circumstances on the field—and the majority would fall into the category of environmental subtleties, the steady showering of character that raises all the boats in the clubhouse.

Together, the accumulated qualities would constitute a communicable competitiveness that I call teamship. If a word, deed, or example somehow aids the collective cause, it's an act of teamship. If it makes somebody better, it's teamship. If it's what you'd want your teammate to do, it's teamship. Teamship is what intangibles amount to.[2]

Honestly, there are dozens of PEQs that contribute to the total package of teamship, but in the effort to isolate the ones that best complement each other and as a group account for all the necessities, and since acronyms seem to be pretty popular for this sort of thing, I've broken it down as follows:

Toughness
Execution
Accountability
Moxie
Supportiveness
History
Intensity
Passion

TOUGHNESS

Watching Pete Rose bat, with either hand, I always had the general impression that he was simply too tough, willfully and physically, to get the best of when it counted most. It had to do with the intensity of his crouch and concentration, the thickness of his legs and forearms, the clench of his jaw, the challenge in his eye, the combative, bring-it-on attitude, the

whole defiant package. Subjectively, if not statistically, he was the ultimate "tough out."

However, the issue here is making teammates better. How does
toughness do that? How does it empower those in its company?

It demonstrates the fighting spirit. Toughness animates the refusal
to lose or even be hurt. It rouses purpose and tightens determination. It
girds a ballclub for the wilting weeks of July and August. It stays the surrender when a losing streak reaches five games and a deficit stretches to
seven. As a six-month grind, a baseball season is best suited for grinders,
for tough guys.

Observed in a teammate, toughness rallies resolve. Was there any
chance the Dodgers would let the 1988 World Series get away from them
after Kirk Gibson limped to the plate and ended game one? Could the
Cardinals have been found wanting in 1967 after Bob Gibson pitched
to three batters on a broken leg? Could the Red Sox have succumbed to
the Yankees in game seven of the 2004 ALCS after Curt Schilling won
game six with his sock soaked in blood from a ruptured ankle tendon?
Could the St. Louis club have quit on the 2011 season after Albert Pujols
returned from a fractured wrist on the seventeenth day?

Then there was the unflinching courage of first baseman Jim Bottomley, who played for the Cardinals in the early 1920s, when they were
managed by Branch Rickey. On this day, Rickey had given his team a
typical pep talk about paying the price for success. Bottomley had a nasty
infection on his right hip, which caused the Cardinal captain, Burt Shot-
ton, to report to Rickey that Bottomley most likely wouldn't be able to
play that afternoon against the Pirates. Bottomley, however, insisted that
he would, with Rickey insisting in turn that if he was forced to slide, he
was to stay off his right side. The game unfolded as a tight one, and it
happened that, with the score tied and two outs in the ninth, Bottomley
reached base with a walk. The next batter was the estimable Rogers
Hornsby, who, in those days, was averaging in the general vicinity of
.400. So, Bottomley proceeded to do what he knew to be the proper

thing in that situation. He lit out for second. The catcher's throw to Rabbit Maranville, the Pittsburgh shortstop, came in on the third-base side of the bag, and to beat it Bottomley flung himself into a right-leg slide that brought him in safely, with his St. Louis teammates holding their breath in the dugout. As Bottomley took his leadoff and pulled his trousers away from the sticky wound, Cardinal pitcher John Stuart called out in a bugle voice, "He paid the price! He paid the price!" Naturally, Hornsby drove in Sunny Jim with a game-winning single. Afterward, Rickey asked Bottomley why in tarnation he hadn't slid on his *left* side. "Mr. Rickey," he replied, "didn't you see where Maranville was standing?"[3]

And on the Jeter meter: Since he became a Yankee regular in 1996, Jeter has played in more games than anyone else and has played them with a recklessness exemplified by the catch he made in 2004 in the twelfth inning of a tie game against the Red Sox, snatching the pop fly from Trot Nixon on the run, crashing into an empty seat, and cutting up his photogenic face. The thing was, the ball would otherwise have landed fair and scored a run or two. The captain was, of course, back in the lineup the next night. As a standard practice, when he is, say, hit on the hand with a fastball and the trainer recommends an X-ray, Jeter firmly declines. He would rather play than know the extent of his wound.

Of course, playing through injury is not always the best thing for a ballclub. And yet, as that spirit ripples through a roster, it well serves any member confronted with adversity, whatever the stripe. When the going gets tough, as you might have heard . . .

EXECUTION

Execution is a situational, game-time intangible: attention to detail, taking care of the dirty work, the fulfillment of duty that constitutes playing the game right. Skillful, scrupulous execution is what makes a ballplayer a *ballplayer's* ballplayer, and very much a manager's. It's the salute to little things.

To execute properly on the baseball field, a player requires, first, an understanding of the game, accompanied by the willingness to do whatever, for the team's sake, ought to be done. And, of course, the technical mastery to *get* it done. Implicit in that paradigm are a dedication to both the craft and the ballclub and a spirit of sacrifice if it happens to be in order. Execution is no accident.

To wit, if little David Eckstein were to come to bat with no outs and a teammate on second base, he would know that, short of producing a base hit himself, he must at least direct the ball to the right side of the field to advance the runner to third. Because he has embraced his complementary role on the roster, he would be eager to do that. And, because he would never have made it to the Major Leagues on speed, grace, or power, he would bring to the plate a practiced, purposeful knack for putting the bat on the ball. Neither his batting average nor his on-base percentage would prosper from a productive groundout, but his team invariably would.

"Those guys are the hardest to evaluate," said Tim Naehring, a Major-League scout for the Yankees. "It makes it a lot tougher having the Ecksteins of the world in the equation. You look at his tools and talent level and say, This guy may not be a shortstop. But he's a guy who continually made plays and brought a level of winning environment to the club. He had a great career because of those intangibles."

Eckstein, of course, would not hesitate to let a strike go by in the interest of allowing a teammate to steal a base. As a runner at first base, he would not neglect to take his secondary lead in order to perhaps break up a double play or make it to third on a single. As a shortstop, he would not forget to position himself for a relay throw or back up the teammate who had that assignment, much as Marco Scutaro, playing second base, did for the Giants in the second game of the 2012 World Series.

Scutaro's handsome piece of execution occurred with no outs for the Detroit Tigers in the top of the second inning, when Delmon Young shot a double to left field and Gregor Blanco mishandled it long enough for hefty Prince Fielder to attempt to score all the way from first. It appeared that Fielder would do so when Blanco's throw badly missed its relay target, shortstop Brandon Crawford. Scutaro, accounting for just such a scenario, hastened over to back up Crawford and met up with the ball on the third-base line, whirling and pegging it to the plate just in time for catcher Buster Posey to slap a quick tag on Fielder. The game remained scoreless until the seventh inning, and the Giants pulled it out 2-0 on their way to a sweep.[4]

Not coincidentally, the most celebrated play of that sort happens to be another reading on the Jeter Meter. It was 2001, game three of the AL Division Series, seventh inning, two outs, Oakland leading the series two games to none but the Yankees leading the game 1-0. This time the runner on first was Jeremy Giambi of the A's, the double was struck down the right-field line by Terrence Long, and the wild throw came from right fielder Shane Spencer. The relay target was second baseman Alfonso Soriano and the backup was first baseman Tino Martinez. Spencer overshot both of them. The ball came down in the vicinity of the first-base line, where, to the astonishment of most, Jeter, sprinting madly, caught it on the bounce. With his momentum carrying him toward the New York dugout, he had no option but to flip the ball backhanded, across his body, on the run, twenty feet or so, to catcher Jorge Posada, who swiped at Giambi's right foot and executed the tag. Mariano Rivera went two innings for the save and the Yanks took care of the next couple of games to move along on their way to another World Series. "I don't have a clue as to how or why he was even involved in that play," said Oakland manager Art Howe. Except he did: "Shows what kind of player he is."[5]

Of course, Jeter's dazzling execution underscored Giambi's breach of it. It happens a lot, perhaps most often on the base paths: runners misjudging the ball off the bat, runners misreading the outfielders (or neglecting to read them at all), runners taking timid or lazy leadoffs, runners sliding inefficiently, runners averting their eyes, runners squandering opportunities, runners picking the wrong time to steal or stay put, runners neglecting to consider *other* runners, runners failing to understand the possibilities involved in a play. An alert and fundamentally sound baserunner, on the other hand, will draw pickoff throws just to let his teammates see the pitcher's move. He'll get himself in a rundown when it's advantageous to somebody else. He'll slide hard enough, or avoid a tag long enough, to preclude a double play. He'll rarely, if ever, miss a sign. (Pete Rose claims that he never missed one his entire career.)

In the field, the subtleties of execution extend even to efforts that can only be heard. History has charged Johnny Pesky, the Boston shortstop, for blundering away the seventh game of the 1946 World Series when he held the relay throw too long and allowed Enos Slaughter to score from first base on what was ruled a double by Harry Walker but, by most accounts, was actually a single to left center. Slaughter, however, placed the blame not on Pesky but on second baseman Bobby Doerr and third baseman Pinky Higgins for not shouting instructions to Pesky when his back was turned to catch the throw from the outfield.[6]

Failure to communicate, while inexcusable, might be considered a passive transgression, but it can have a willful, sinister side. When the great Edd Roush arrived in Cincinnati in 1916, his manager, Christy Mathewson, installed him in center field, scooting Greasy Neale over to right. Even back then, the custom was for the center fielder to take charge of any fly ball he could handle, but Roush soon learned to keep a wary eye on Neale. Finally, after some awkward weeks of outfielding, Neale sought out the future Hall of Famer in the dugout, sat down, and said, "I want this to end, Roush. I guess you know I've been trying to run you down ever since you got here. I wanted that center field job for myself, and I didn't like it when Matty put you there. But you can go get a ball better than I ever could. I want to shake hands and call it off. From now on, I'll holler."[7]

ACCOUNTABILITY

A player's accountability for *himself* is evident, to a large extent, in the statistical judgment of his performance. His work ethic, professionalism, preparation, practice habits, and so on, redound materially to his own credit. Accountability for his *team,* however, while slipping covertly under the numbers, can mean even more to the collective mission.

It's a question of ownership within the ranks. Of personal responsibility for final scores and standings, a stake in the fortune of not only one guy, but twenty-five.[8] But it starts, of course—necessarily—with number one.

Accountability is dotting all the i's, and Carl Yastrzemski, without saying a word, articulated it when, at the age of forty-three, in his twenty-third season with the Red Sox, he took early batting practice on the road. It's crossing all the t's, as Roberto Clemente demonstrated when he was entertaining a guest on a summer afternoon and a hard rain started up, prompting him to rush off to the ballpark and grind through a set of drills on the wet grass in right field, which he knew he'd have to deal with that evening. It's Dale Murphy winning the National League MVP award in 1982, then assigning himself to the Florida Instructional League to clean up a few things.

Accountability is staying on task, and Gaylord Perry demanded it when he would tell younger players who wandered down to his end of the bench and made the mistake of striking up a random conversation, "We're talkin' baseball down here. These are working hours. You wanna talk about something else, go the hell down to the other end."[9] It's helping out, which George Brett made a habit of when he would arrive early at the ballpark to throw batting practice left-handed (yes, he threw right-handed from third base) to Kansas City's bench players, then, after shagging fly balls and taking his regular and extra infield practice, fill in at first base to accommodate the reserves.[10]

Accountability is self-discipline, which Tom Seaver took to the extreme when, returning to New York from a road trip at about ten o'clock one night, he grabbed a cab to Shea Stadium, slipped into his uniform, and fired baseballs into the bullpen screen because, well, it was his day to throw and he hadn't had the chance. It's preparation, which for Joey Votto involves poring over video of that night's pitcher from both the windup and stretch positions, and doing the same for every reliever who might make an appearance. And, on the road, being in the exercise room at six-thirty in the morning.[11]

Accountability is a conscientious, thorough approach to the game, and Jim Palmer personified it so completely that when young players asked Earl Weaver what they should do in spring training, the skipper simply said, "Follow Palmer."[12] It's doing all you can do, and doing it so fervently that the consummate devotion will make the sort of impression Pete Rose made on Mike Schmidt. "Rose," stated Schmidt, a teammate during the Hit King's advancing years in Philadelphia, "was probably the ultimate gamer. That's probably the best thing that can be said about a player. He plays hard; he'll do what he needs to do to help win that game that day—take out a runner, break up a double play, slide hard into home, knock a guy over, play hurt, play the whole game even if it goes seventeen innings, do whatever it takes. And then show up the next day ready to play again, even if Nolan Ryan is pitching."[13] The effect, Schmidt said, is that "Pete Rose makes me look in the mirror. If what he's giving is a hundred percent, then my hundred percent must be coming up short."[14]

Accountability happens also to be the message on a sign that hangs in the Yankees' spring training complex, the facility which long ago occasioned Jeter, not yet a Major Leaguer, to move to Tampa in order to be near it in the off-season.

MOXIE

The dictionaries favor moxie with multiple definitions,[15] including backbone, courage, verve, nerve, know-how, skill, and aggressiveness. It seems a bit remiss, however, considering that the term owes its legs to plucky players who've got a lot of it, that none of them alludes to a situational intangible pertaining particularly to baseball.

While some might loosely characterize moxie as the ability to operate out of the box—to take the game to another level—it issues from a firm grip on fundamentals.[16] When a player has the basics covered, improvisation is only a circumstance away. Jeter provided a conspicuous demonstration of this when he lateraled to Posada to startle Giambi.

More clinically, that sort of spontaneous comprehension has been linked to the psychological term *chunking*, which refers to the ability to mentally store patterns and scenarios as ready reference material, to grasp the big picture at a glance and respond to it reflexively. A *New Yorker* article touching on the subject explained the genius of Wayne Gretzky by describing him as "hockey's greatest chunker."[17]

Jeter showed more of his chunking prowess in Boston in 2009, when Dustin Pedroia smacked a ball off the Green Monster and on the hard carom it sailed over the head of left fielder Eric Hinske. The Yankee captain, characteristically, anticipated that possibility, and dashed into the outfield, where he scooped up the baseball, whirled, and zinged it to third, nailing Pedroia for the final out of the inning—an implausible short-to-third assist on an attempted triple. Then there was the moxie that he sported, ethically or otherwise (baseball hardliners took no issue), when, representing the tying run in the seventh inning of an important game against the Rays late in 2010, he clutched his elbow and hopped away from the batter's box after a pitch from Chad Qualls bonked the knob of his bat and bounced into fair territory. Jeter was awarded first base by umpire Lance Barksdale, and, once there, he persisted with his persuasive pantomime before scoring on Curtis Granderson's home run.

Moxie takes over when the business at hand can't be game-planned or signaled in from the bench. It's value added, a bonus point for audacity, ingenuity, or derring-do. In 1986, while on first base with Mike Schmidt at third, Glenn Wilson of the Phillies actually faked tripping over his own feet to draw a throw from the Mets' pitcher, allowing Schmidt to score— a play, needless to say, not reflected in Wilson's Win Shares rating.[18]

Baseball tends to tolerate a certain degree of deviousness if it can be passed off as moxie. Sign stealing might fall into that category. It is, at any rate, an art to which some illustrious players have been devoted.[19] In the first game of the 1922 World Series, Heinie Groh, the New York Giants' third baseman, figured out the signs that Yankee manager Miller Huggins was flashing to his hitters and was able to anticipate every bunt and swing-away in the Giants' four-game sweep.

In these endeavors, Groh may have had some conspiratorial assistance from the Hall of Fame shortstop next to him, Dave Bancroft. When he was traded to the Giants from the Phillies in 1920 and pulled aside to go over his new team's signs, Bancroft asked, "Why, have they changed?"[20]

SUPPORTIVENESS

In May 1947, Jackie Robinson, having broken baseball's color line, was in his first tour of the National League. He'd already been to Philadelphia, where the Phillies, on orders from manager Ben Chapman, welcomed him with a storm of racial insults. Cincinnati was more southern by both geography and nature. As Robinson assumed his position at first base, the Crosley Field organist greeted him with the strains of "Bye Bye Blackbird." The fans and the Reds themselves joined in, creating an atmosphere so harsh that the Dodger shortstop, Pee Wee Reese—a native Kentuckian whose family had expressed concern that Reese might be contaminated by his association with a so-called colored player—was moved to walk across the diamond and place a supportive arm around Robinson's broad shoulder. The response in the ballpark was astonishment. For his part, Branch Rickey, the Dodger executive who had chosen Robinson as the right man to integrate the game, was so impressed that he promptly appointed Reese the team captain. When the captain began to take his meals with Robinson, theirs became the popular table among the players. The Dodgers, ennobled and unified—and with four Hall of Famers (Robinson, Reese, Duke Snider, and Roy Campanella) in the lineup for most of the period—went on to win six pennants over the next ten seasons.

Supportiveness is the essence of teamship. It's the proactive concern for the well-being of all the guys in the room. It's having the other fellow's back. In the interest of the collective effort, a supportive player puts all he can offer at the disposal of his teammates, be it counsel, humor, insight, experience, time, sympathy, or a foot in the hindquarter.[21]

For Joe Morgan, coming up with the Houston Astros, the Reese role was played by aging Nellie Fox, whose second-base job Morgan was in the process of taking away. Knowing that precocious rookies can often meet resentment from veterans who have each other's backs, Fox approached Morgan in training camp, put his hand on the rookie's shoulder, and walked him out to the field. "Listen," he told his more familiar teammates, "this guy is special. I'm gonna do the best I can to help him and I want you to do the same."[22] The show of support was invaluable, and Fox was true to his word, patiently schooling his replacement on the game's demands and finer points. "I can't imagine what kind of career I would have had without the presence of someone like Nellie Fox," Morgan wrote in his autobiography.[23]

While his Hall of Fame credentials were ultimately carved out with the Reds, it was in Houston that Morgan came to understand what one teammate can mean to another. As a rookie, in a duel that saw Don Nottebart match Sandy Koufax for eight scoreless innings, he failed his pitcher in the ninth by allowing a ground ball to roll through his legs and bring in a run. When he stepped up to bat in the ninth inning, there were tears in his eyes. After the defeat had become official, Morgan was so obviously disconsolate that Fox walked over to tell him about a game the year before in which Fox had committed a two-out, ninth-inning error that lost the game for Ken Johnson, in spite of a no-hitter. Walt Bond, a hulking first baseman, urged Morgan—forced him—to come out for a drink. Mostly, it was a talk. After a couple of hours, Bond's calming intervention had restored the spirits and confidence of the budding Hall of Famer. "I believe, absolutely, that a single game can make or break a player because of what he carries away from it," Morgan reflected. "I might have been derailed by that Koufax game. My moods ran that deep. But Walt Bond instinctively knew that and saved me from myself."[24]

In Cincinnati, Morgan was enduringly grateful for Pete Rose's lectures about turning back the temptations of temper, resentment, and nagging pain. He was impressed, also, by Rose's willingness to suffer on the ballclub's behalf. When Charlie Hustle sensed that a team meeting was in order, he'd invite Sparky Anderson to go ahead and chew him out in front of everybody if that would help.

For all his personal ambition—no great player has ever lacked it—Rose was a staunch supporter of teammates, and Morgan especially. The way it worked in the Cincinnati clubhouse was that Morgan lockered next to Rose, Perez buddied up with Bench in the opposite corner, and every day was another lively game of psychological two-on-two, with the other Reds swept up in the current. It was a classically jocular support system, the four stars needling each other into heightened readiness, all the while making sure to fold in useful observations from which the rest of the room could benefit as well.[25]

Jeter's style is more statesmanlike, but he sees to it, just as furiously, that the bar is set and the spirits lifted on the club he captains. "He'll go to the mound in the World Series, and he's smiling, and when they all walk away, they're all smiling," said Mark Newman, a Yankees vice president. "He's able to lighten the mood, ease the burden, and help people around him relax and be confident."[26]

It would seem intuitive that collegiality encourages productivity and thereby avails a ballclub's bottom line, as it would any company's. A study by Rutgers University confirmed as much, according to a report in the *Philadelphia Inquirer*.[27] The study focused on the dynamic of subgroups within a baseball roster, and determined that teams with strong ones reflect a cohesiveness that corresponds with success. Chester Spell, an associate business professor who conducted the research, attributed the outcome to the players' support of each other. "They provide kind of a comfort zone," he said.

Though he didn't use the word, because it really isn't one, Spell was speaking of teamship.

HISTORY

In a game as chronicled as big-league baseball, a player never leaves home without his reputation. It figures into how he's paid, pitched, approached, and generally regarded. Among teammates, a lofty reputation is the currency of credibility.

Reputation is largely a matter of personal history—numbers put up, dollars earned, rings collected, headlines made, and the like. A player's history alone doesn't make the next guy better, but it can get his attention. It can make him look and listen. The tidier the history, the mightier the clout. And if a player with plenty of cachet puts it to proper use . . .

"It's a wonderful advantage when your best players set the best examples," said Tony La Russa. "Albert Pujols is the perfect teammate. He'll take you to spring training and tell you to show up at seven-thirty with me; watch me work; I'll tell you what I'm doing; I'll help you during the season. He pulls for his teammates. He helps whoever is willing to work, but you've got to *work*."

When, after eleven historic seasons in St. Louis, he signed with the Los Angeles Angels of Anaheim in 2012, Pujols was well aware of his reputation, and well aware that the Angels were well aware of it. In spring training that year, he took more bus trips than any other veteran on the team. He arrived at the complex early and left late. "He showed us he was not bigger than the game," teammate Torii Hunter told *USA Today*. "Here's a guy who has three MVPs, two World Series rings and did some real damage in the National League. But now that he's with a new team and a new league, he wants to do even more damage." When Pujols was taking batting practice, two younger Angels, Howard Kendrick and Peter Bourjos, wouldn't look anywhere else.[28]

As manager of the Braves, Bobby Cox observed the assiduous game preparation of Greg Maddux trickling down to the rest of Atlanta's superlative pitching staff. By the time Cox's successor, Fredi Gonzalez, took over, the organizational culture was firmly established, and he reached out to Chipper Jones and All-Star catcher Brian McCann to perpetuate it. "Those guys handle stuff in the locker room that the manager then doesn't have to handle," noted Gonzalez. "I think that has more of an impact than the manager or one of the coaches doing it. They can come in and say, 'Hey, we don't do that here.'"

The game has been generously graced by illustrious players who have applied their personal stories to the highest purposes of the ballclub, and virtually every manager and general manager can provide a classic example or two. Wayne Krivsky, a former Reds GM, points to Craig Biggio and Jeff Bagwell, longtime teammates with the Houston Astros. John Schuerholz is a George Brett man. Charlie Manuel speaks of Chase Utley in the same sort of terms that La Russa reserves for Pujols. Dusty Baker can never say enough about Hank Aaron. Bob Gebhard, an Arizona Diamondbacks executive and original general manager of the Colorado Rockies, sings the praises of Kirby Puckett in that context.

And yet, no other player so categorically personifies the breed as Derek Jeter.[29] "Jeter," said Gebhard, "is the one guy you would use to build a mold for a player. He's got that combination of players respecting him for what he can do on the field plus having a perfect character of being no-nonsense when he puts on the uniform."

The on-field part—the body of work—is fundamental to the effect. For Jeter, that entails practically perennial All-Star appearances, frequent passes at the MVP award, five Gold Gloves (controversial or not) at a critical defensive position, well over 3,000 hits (the most ever by a Yankee or a shortstop), five World Series titles (one short of Lou Gehrig, two of Mickey Mantle, four of Joe DiMaggio, five of Yogi Berra), a celebrated gift for making plays, and a long history of delivering dramatically.

"I'm a little prejudiced," remarked Torre, "because I had him from a baby, and it was really hard to fathom what we would have done without him. It's tough to imagine anybody being a better teammate than Jeter."

So resonant is Jeter's reputation that even a bitter rival can admire it.[30] "He plays the game right, the way it's supposed to be, and he never gets caught up in all the crap like some of us," said David Ortiz of the Red Sox. "The thing that gets me is I hear people talking about his game and people don't appreciate all that he does. This guy has been doing it for years. His game is at a high level at all times. Same effort, same results, and you've got to have a super pair of nuts to say bad things about a guy like that. I play in Boston and if somebody says something bad about Jeter, I say, 'Dude, you better check your book.'"

INTENSITY

For baseball, the notion of intensity takes on a different timbre, one adjusted, necessarily, to the lingering, slow-twitch season. Unlike the sudden intensity—the game-time explosion of pent-up competitiveness—suited for football, hockey, soccer, even basketball, baseball's variant is an unrelenting, more demanding, equally ferocious pursuance of the sport. It's the abiding edginess that characterizes the pitcher Roy Halladay made himself into, and Joey Votto the hitter, and Bob Gibson the dreaded opponent. It's the quality that Pat Gillick credited with making champions of both the Blue Jays and the Phillies.

By natural order, baseball lacks the luxury of football's weeklong buildup to a feverish state of "let me at 'em." Transported to baseball, the raging pregame pep talks of Ray Lewis, the maniacal former Baltimore Ravens linebacker, would take on a droning tone by the second week of April. Teammates would avert their eyes from his daily introductions dance. On the field, his primal screams would be answered with fastballs to various regions of the body.

And yet, if an intensity as concentrated as the extraordinary Raven's would prove impractical for baseball's pace and sensibility, its underlying *spirit* impacts every pennant race. Intensity, after all, is a quickened form of conscientious. It's energy incarnate. It's the motor that commentators go on about, the hustle that fans go wild for, the focus that seizes the moment. If it was unproductive for Mike Piazza to scream obscenities and slam the wall of the dugout with his fist when he struck out, that same fury of ambition also drove him—a courtesy draft pick in the sixty-second round—to become the greatest-hitting catcher of all time.

During the course of the workweek, when he had no running back to tear into, Lewis exercised his intensity through a driving dedication to his task, studying film so thoroughly and intelligently that, come the eve of the game, he would hand his defensive coordinator a sheet of recommended looks and formations for various situations. His routine, on a seven-day cycle, was a close match for Maddux and his five-day schedule, only the pitcher's came around about twice as many times a year. A fully engaged hitter—Votto, Tony Gwynn, Ted Williams—does the drill daily. The effect on teammates is bound to be comparable, and that's before anybody hits the playing field.

"You know what happens when Ray Lewis is in the locker room, and on the field?" asked his former teammate, offensive tackle Tony Pashos. "Guess what, you just maximized your entire salary cap, because everyone around him is playing at the highest level he can play."[31]

Intensity is an unequivocal devotion to the endeavor at hand. It's unsparing attention and effort, an animated message that this game, this play, calls for all you can give; that it urgently, desperately *matters*. It's compelling, hell-bent vigor.

In the simplest form, the dynamic works something like this, according to Jonny Gomes: "You see a guy beat out an infield hit and you see the crowd go crazy, you applaud with them, and then you think, 'I want to do that. I want that for *me*.' Then you play the game *that* way."

A ballplayer's intensity has been known to impel his teammates toward a redoubled commitment. Concerning Gibson, Tim McCarver said, "I was driven to win, but not like Bob Gibson, not with his intensity. His desire to win and succeed influenced me and all of our teammates. We revered him as a teammate."[32]

A player's intensity can *shame* other players into equaling it, or at least attempting to. Regarding Jackie Robinson, Carl Erskine said:

"Jackie played so hard, with such intensity, that he made you try that much harder. You simply couldn't let up if you were on the same ball club as Jackie Robinson."[33]

There's nothing in those last three quotes about banging heads against lockers. Nothing about Knute Rockne speeches. There's quite a bit, though, about effort, competitiveness, and example.

"Baseball's a little different deal than football, basketball, and other professional sports," said Mike Radcliff, a veteran executive for the Minnesota Twins. "There's a lot of downtime between pitches, between innings." It's the downtime and baseball's halting, summer-long pace that present a special challenge to an athlete's focus, engagement, and summoning of energy. Intensity has to balance with patience, suddenness with steadiness, explosion with calm. "Therefore, one of our hallmarks, our foundational beliefs, is that intangibles do separate out. Michael Cuddyer, when he goes on the field, is able to channel his natural aggressiveness, to focus in each and every at-bat. He tackles the preparation part of the game with similar intensity. He [was] one of our shining examples."

Of course, *baseball's* shining example captains the Yankees, and he, too, had one of those as a younger player. Actually, he had a few, but in terms of day-to-day intensity, his guy was Tino Martinez.

Jeter's intensity takes him into box seats chasing pop flies, into left field in pursuit of balls off the wall. It puts him, occasionally, in teammates' faces. It makes him the hitter a pitcher doesn't want to face in the ninth inning, with the winning run in scoring position. Jeter's intensity is always turned on, though seldom too loudly.

"Derek Jeter," wrote Joe Posnanski, "almost the second they begin to say his name (before they get the 'urr' in DEH-rick JEET-urr) holds out his glove toward the fans. He does this without looking, while staring in at the batter." While maintaining his intensity, in other words, sticking doggedly to the task, even as he acknowledges the commotion outside the lines on his specific behalf. "It feels to me like the perfect Derek Jeter gesture."[34]

PASSION

Branch Rickey was general manager of the Pittsburgh Pirates when, in the winter following the 1953 season, he journeyed to Puerto Rico and, one afternoon, took notice of the nineteen-year-old left fielder playing next to Willie Mays for the Santurce Crabbers. After the game, he called the kid over for a chat, during which one particular thing that the youngster mentioned made a deeper impression on Rickey than even his excellent range or extraordinary throwing arm. Roberto Clemente, who had been signed by the Dodgers but hadn't yet played in their farm system, said that he loved baseball more than eating. A year later, Rickey, remembering, selected Clemente in the Rule 5 draft.

Rickey, of course, knew talent to a famous degree, and understood what brings it to full flower. He knew, for instance, that in a pursuit such as baseball, loving the game and eating aren't all that different to begin with: The lack of either leaves a player undernourished. He knew that Clemente's passion, paired with his very special physical tools, would make him spectacular.

He also knew what his future fan, Joe Maddon, had learned when he said, "If you've got a kid with talent who loves the game and a kid with even more talent that doesn't love the game, I'm gonna say the one who loves the game becomes a star. I think the other guy will wane at some point."

In his renowned wisdom, Rickey would have appreciated, as well, what the great Japanese slugger, Sadaharu Oh, was talking about when he said, "My baseball career was a long, long initiation into a single secret: At the heart of all things is love."[35]

To Rickey, passion and enthusiasm were inseparable. Concerning the latter, he felt as Ralph Waldo Emerson did when he said, "Nothing great was ever achieved without enthusiasm."[36] Enthusiasm, meanwhile, was never achieved without passion. Rickey knew that, whatever the undertaking, passion points the way. Passion lights the fire. Passion lifts the burden. It speaks for the heart, urges the body, charges the room, spreads the virus. Passion tramples the excuse.

When passion is brought to a sport, playing it hard becomes innate. Sprinting to first base on a walk didn't make Pete Rose great, but it *revealed* what made him great. Passion is why uncommon players keep playing until they sense it missing.

As a cardinal enabler, passion is more than a love for the game itself; it's a love for being good at it, for *winning*. Genuine passion can't be summoned in the seventh inning; it's a constant companion. It's the hand that sets the alarm clock and the first foot that hits the floor in the morning. It's what gets Votto into the hotel exercise room in the wee hours of the A.M. It's what put Piazza in the batting cage every midnight on New Year's Eve. It's what kept Tony Gwynn in front of the video player. It's what all sports-minded parents can only wish their sports-minded children had, *really* had.

When he managed the Red Sox, Terry Francona liked to hang around the back fields on spring-training mornings, just to see which players approached their jobs with passion. One of his guys was Kevin Millar, who said, "I love this game more than anybody out there, but I can't run, can't hit, can't throw, can't do any of the five tools. But I'm going to dig in for you and give you everything I have every night." Millar lasted twelve years in the big leagues. Teammates swore by him.

Passion might be a lot to ask for at a holding company or machine-tool plant, but a good baseball team seeks it out. "Look," said J. P. Ricciardi, a New York Mets executive and former GM of the Blue Jays, "everybody makes money in this game. So, what makes a guy who's making a lot of money push himself and drive himself? That's got to be his inner being. That's got to be the way you were raised, the foundation that you had, the self-pride, and you *want* to be good." Ricciardi's experience has convinced him that passion—the overwhelming desire to be the best player possible—is the most important quality in the making of a Major-Leaguer. He hasn't seen as much of it as he thinks he should've, but has come across enough to know what it looks like in a uniform. "Dustin

Pedroia's that kind of guy. Kevin Youkilis is that type of guy. Aaron Hill is that type of guy. Scotty Rolen is that type of guy. Derek Jeter is that kind of guy."

Of course, Jeter.[37] For all his refined professionalism, Jeter, remarked baseball columnist Jerry Crasnick, "plays the game with an exuberance typically reserved for Williamsport."[38]

Posnanski recognizes the same thing in the unimpeachable shortstop: "He clearly loves his job. His game has been joyous."[39]

It has been, in the broader view—the passion, the moxie, the toughness, and all the intangibles that make Jeter their grand exemplar—the stuff of teamship. To the letter.

SEVEN

THE TRUMP CARD

IF THERE REMAINED SKEPTICS CONCERNING SCOTT ROLEN'S SIGNIFICANCE TO THE REDS, Walt Jocketty was not among them. A week before Christmas of 2009, as a practical acknowledgment of Rolen's part in the provocative finish to the season just completed and, more to the point, in the culture change to which Cincinnati's general manager had pledged himself, Jocketty signed his workmanlike third baseman to a two-year contract extension that would keep him in town through 2012.

While adding $12 million to Rolen's negotiated earnings,[1] the deal offered the Reds some short-term benefits. Rolen had been on schedule to earn $11 million in 2010. In exchange for the two additional years, he agreed to play the upcoming season for $6 million instead, leaving available $5 million that Jocketty used to acquire veteran shortstop Orlando Cabrera on February 1 and bring back Jonny Gomes—who had become a free agent—three weeks later, with $2 million left over. Those bucks were put to good advantage in the signing of Aroldis Chapman, a lanky, heat-seeking lefthander by way of Cuba.

The Reds had been whispering bidders in the Chapman market and, to some, their winning of his services—for $30 million over six years—signaled a new level of seriousness. But if the purposeful pursuit of Chapman spoke convincingly to the club's commitment, the Cabrera signing said a significant amount about the ideology guiding it.

At age thirty-five, Cabrera was coming off a decent hitting season (.284 average, .705 OPS for Oakland and Minnesota) in which most of his fielding metrics were among the worst in the game at his important position. Bear in mind, this was a player with two Gold Gloves to his name—one in each league—whose midseason acquisition by the Red Sox in 2004 was credited by *Sports Illustrated* with marking (along with other Boston moves) a defensive renaissance.[2] The man was clearly on the downside of his career. But Cabrera, even in decline, was *one of those guys*, one of those who happen, year after year, coincidentally or not, to show up on teams that kick quite a bit of backside.

It started as soon as he left Montreal in his eighth season there. At the time, the Red Sox were eight and a half games behind the Yankees and trailing in the American League wildcard race. Their cult-figure shortstop, Nomar Garciaparra, had been out of sorts and spreading the mood. And so, just under the trading deadline, Boston joined in a four-team swap that, among other things, sent Garciaparra to the Cubs and brought Cabrera to Fenway Park along with first baseman Doug Mientkiewicz from the Twins. On the same day, the Red Sox, stressing defense and teamship (by whatever name), also traded for outfielder Dave Roberts of the Dodgers. Cabrera started at shortstop the following afternoon and homered in his first at-bat. After the trades, Boston went 42–19, rallying to the wildcard berth in the playoffs. Cabrera had never participated in a postseason game and, along the way, was so intent on doing so that he berated Manny Ramirez one day for complaining of a headache and wanting out of the lineup. Ramirez played. The new team-friendly shortstop batted .379 in the epic AL Championship Series comeback that toppled the Yankees, and the Red Sox went on to whip the Cardinals for their first World Series title since Babe Ruth pitched for them.

In Anaheim, where Cabrera spent the next three years and shared in two division championships, Angels manager Mike Scioscia made a point of moving the locker of Howie Kendrick, his young second baseman, next to the sociable Colombian's. In 2008, Cabrera won a division title with the White Sox. In 2009, he was traded to the Twins at the deadline, when they stood third in the AL Central, joined in another division championship, and played in his fifth postseason in six years, with four different teams.

In Cincinnati, he would be stationed across the bag from Brandon Phillips, who had started in the Montreal organization when Cabrera was a mainstay there. With the Expos, Cabrera somehow became acquainted with Phillips's mother and father, who were aware that the older player had taken their son under his wing. "Get him straight," said Brandon's dad. Cabrera promised that he would.[3] Upon his arrival at the Reds' new spring training facility in Goodyear, Arizona, he also took an interest in Joey Votto, goading him, challenging him, pushing his buttons. During one game, Cabrera ribbed Votto so ruthlessly—distracting him, actually, to make him relax—that the quiet first baseman screamed back across the diamond.[4]

"It's important to recognize the good ones," Cabrera said. "Because you really don't want to waste your time." With a practiced eye for the intangible, the veteran infielder was keen to pick out players with the kind of will he could work with. "I look for the one I want to push. I can see those guys. I believe one of my legacies when I leave the game is knowing that I influenced some people in a good way, how to play the game and how to beat other teams. That's what I love: Take guys and show them weaknesses of the other team and how we can just attack."

When the season began, however, the Reds were hard-pressed to reprise the momentum of late 2009. In the last week of April, they fell four games below .500 in a loss to the Padres, during which they forfeited baserunners in three consecutive innings, two of them (Phillips and Gomes) on pickoffs. The inning after those, center fielder Drew Stubbs caught the second out and tossed the ball into the stands, thinking it was the third. After the game, Dusty Baker, an accommodating man by nature, was so agitated that he refused to talk to the press. A few days later, cued by heady baserunning from Stubbs and Votto's two-run homer, Baker's reprimanded fellows showed some signs of bearing down, beating Houston ace Roy Oswalt for only the second time in twenty-five decisions.

They were, in fact, straining to get back to .500 on the final day of the month and were leading the Cardinals 3-2 in the sixth inning, when hard rain hit St. Louis. The game was delayed two and a half hours, during which time, according to Jay Bruce, Cabrera made certain the club stayed focused. Then, in the seventh, with no outs and David Freese representing the tying run for the Cardinals at second base, the shrewd shortstop broke behind the runner, blocked the base with his knee, snatched the pickoff throw from catcher Ramon Hernandez, and slap-tagged Freese for an out that proved critical in the 3-2 victory. It was Cincinnati's fifth straight.

The Reds eventually lost that series, two games to one, but might have swept the next one, against the Mets, were it not for an untimely outbreak of Bad Brandon. With one out in the third inning of the middle game, Phillips launched a high fly off the wall in left-center field. He thought he had hit it well enough to reach the seats and jogged out of the batter's box, warming up for his home run trot. He was about halfway to first base when the ball struck the fence, caromed oddly back, and eluded center fielder Angel Pagan. Phillips ended up with a double that, in all likelihood, should have been a triple. He was, of course, unable to score when Votto followed with a long out to left. New York ultimately claimed the game, 5-4, with a run in the ninth.

Afterward, Baker repreached the now familiar fiery sermon to his occasionally unholy second baseman. Phillips was once more repentant and, for at least the next few weeks, full of base-path brimstone. Superficial or not, it was noted. Around town and the ballpark, conversation, even excitement, made the rounds in response to the vigor and sense of purpose that had suddenly consumed the Reds.[5]

As Phillips was finding his hardball religion, the club at large was drawing closer with postgame outings at Cabrera's house, winning picked up—nine out of ten in the middle of May—and the auspicious karma manifested itself in comeback victories and last-bat triumphs that led the Major Leagues in number. Jonny Gomes, whose vitality never flagged but whose bat had a tendency to, was on a hot streak, pushing himself frequently into the thick of the drama. On one of the telecasts in the middle of the month, Reds broadcaster Thom Brennaman quoted the Cardinals' redoubtable manager, Tony La Russa, to the effect that Gomes was "the kind of player who scares you to death, because he plays every game like it's his last one."[6] The Reds player who most frightened *pitchers*, however, was Votto, who, unencumbered by the complications that had sidetracked him in 2009, was hitting at the highest level in the game. Meanwhile, the pitching side picked up notably, owing in large part to the crafty work of Arroyo,[7] the arrival of rookie Mike Leake, and the sharp improvement of young starter Johnny Cueto, who credited the strategic examples of the other two.

The subject of credit had become a popular one in Cincinnati. A significant portion of it was heaped on the broad, cranky back of Rolen. In spite of his continuing physical misfortunes—after three surgeries on his shoulder, he had compromised, and reinvented his swing, conceding much of his power—Rolen was producing handsomely, holding down the cleanup spot, fielding splendidly, influencing teammates, and humbling his many critics. In May, a leader of that band, *Cincinnati Enquirer* columnist Paul Daugherty, confessed, "Some of us might have questioned the trade for Scott Rolen. A portion of us might have suggested that the Reds were, you know, nuts. . . . It can now be said that Walt Jocketty and Bob Castellini acquiring Scott Rolen was pretty much a masterstroke."[8]

C. Trent Rosecrans was jogging around the same track, as he explained at CNATI.com: "There's a confidence in the clubhouse I don't think I've seen in my seven years here, and it has a ton to do with Scott Rolen and Orlando Cabrera. . . . I wasn't for either move when it was made, but they were made to contend in 2010, and now, in May, they're working out just that way."[9]

By all accounts, Jocketty's vision was beginning to play out nicely in the real time of the pennant race. After five straight series wins (Mets, Cubs, Pirates, Cardinals, Brewers), things were looking particularly good on May 20 in Atlanta, as the Reds headed into the ninth inning with a 9-2 lead and a solid bullpen to protect it. The eighth batter of the inning, an unheralded pinch-hitter named Brooks Conrad, arrived at the plate with the bases loaded, one out, and the score now 9-6. Francisco Cordero, the Reds' closer, was summoned to face him. On a 2-2 pitch, Conrad, a switch-hitter batting left-handed, lofted a deep fly down the left-field line. The ball glanced off the glove of left fielder Laynce Nix and dropped over the fence. The Braves had won, 10-9. The Reds, it was presumed, were devastated.

It soon became apparent, though, that their special talent was the capacity *not* to be devastated. They bucked up to take their next two games, seven of their next nine. They jockeyed with the Cardinals for the division lead. Goosed by the bump of Phillips into the leadoff spot late in June—Stubbs and Cabrera had proven inappropriate for the role—the Reds carried the resiliency thing so far as to finish the month in first place by winning two of three from the Phillies.

The game they lost in that series was the one that Rolen didn't start, which wasn't unusual. What *was* unusual was the reason he didn't start it. It was a night game, to be followed by a series-ending day game that, typically, Rolen would sit out in deference to his shoulder and back. Miguel Cairo would ordinarily start in his place. Cairo, an upbeat, conscientious veteran and former teammate of Rolen's in St. Louis, had won a roster spot at the end of spring training when Rolen had approached Baker and convinced him of his old friend's underlying value. Cairo, indeed, had proven to be a reliable substitute, and Rolen, among others, appreciated his presence. He also noted that if Cairo were to be in the lineup the next afternoon, the itinerant Venezuelan would inherit the thankless task of taking on Roy Halladay. Just two starts prior, Cairo's spot assignment had been Kansas City ace Zack Greinke. Rolen didn't think that was fair to his backup, so he asked Baker if he could switch his day off. Such is teamship.

The Reds weathered that defeat and won five of their next six games, the last of those in New York, a week before the All-Star break. In spite of his status, as voiced by various writers and critics, as the best player in the National League, Votto had not been elected by the public as an All-Star starter at first base (that honor went, not undeservedly, to Albert Pujols) nor appointed as a reserve by Phillies manager Charlie Manuel. He was, however, on the ballot for the popular vote to send one more player to the game. Cincinnatians mounted a spirited campaign on behalf of their handsome hero, and the Reds themselves printed T-shirts bearing the oversize message: "Vote Votto." When a reporter asked in the clubhouse whether the players might wear them for batting practice, Jonny Gomes piped up and declared it mandatory. Even the coaches joined in. Votto was elected overwhelmingly and his team won two out of three at Citi Field.

Thus it was that the Reds held a three-game lead over the Cardinals when they landed in Philadelphia for a hefty four-game series. In the opener, they tied the score with a run in the ninth and lost on a home run by Brian Schneider in the bottom of the twelfth. In the second game, the Reds led 7-1 in the bottom of the ninth and—Atlanta redux—lost 9-7 in the tenth. The third night, the Reds' rookie left-hander, Travis Wood, took a perfect game into the bottom of the ninth, but against Halladay, Wood's team hadn't scored, either. Philadelphia won in the eleventh, 1-0, on a two-out single by Jimmy Rollins. In Sunday's finale, the Reds got another great start from a rookie pitcher, this time Matt Maloney, and the Phillies completed the sweep, 1-0, behind Cole Hamels. At the break, Cincinnati's division lead was down to a single game.

And yet, even at the All-Star event in Anaheim, there was an indication that the club's will had not weakened. The moment was inspired, tellingly, by a little thing. With the National League trailing 1-0 in the seventh, Rolen singled to center field. When Matt Holliday did the same, Rolen wheeled safely into third base. In the dugout, Phillips, proud and energized, clapped his hands, found the camera, and shouted, "Yeah! That's how we do it in Cincinnati!"

The record shows that Phillips was quite right. Inspired by Rolen, urged by Cabrera, and paced by Bruce (66 percent) and Stubbs (60 percent), the risk-taking Reds (46 percent) led the Major Leagues that year in attaining extra bases on batted balls. It should also be noted that they led the Major Leagues in running into outs.

True to form, they came out full speed ahead when the season's second half got under way, winning their first two games, four of their first five, fifteen of their first twenty-two. And the Cardinals stayed with them. The separation was only two games when Tony La Russa's team stopped in Cincinnati on August 9.

The rivalry between the Reds and Cardinals had become a brisk one, if westward leaning and only recently relevant. The plot included a spirited subrivalry between Baker and La Russa, in their fourteenth year of managing against each other. They went nose-to-nose in the 2002 playoffs, when Baker skippered the Giants. They pointed and shouted at each other in 2003, when Baker was with the Cubs. As recently as 2009, Baker's second season in Cincinnati, they'd been at odds when La Russa, pitching coach Dave Duncan, and Cardinal pitchers John Smoltz and Chris Carpenter lodged various complaints about pine tar in Arroyo's cap and the baseballs at Great American Ball Park not being properly rubbed up.

The latter incidents prompted Brandon Phillips to offer a few statesmanlike words on the subject of the St. Louis club. "Let me make this clear," he said before the opening game of the series. "I hate the Cardinals."[10] By way of elaboration, he called them "whiny little bitches," which of course caught on quickly as a Cincinnati catchphrase.

Apparently, it wasn't until after the Cardinals and Carpenter had won game one, 7-3, that the visitors were apprised of Phillips's remarks. They weren't the first team he had offended in 2010. At Washington in

June, he incurred the wrath of the Nationals when, advancing from first base on a wild pitch, he rounded second in such a way that he drew an obstruction ruling on shortstop Ian Desmond. Washington manager Jim Riggleman argued the call to the point of ejection. Then, from third, Phillips broke for home on Rolen's ground ball to Desmond, who threw to catcher Wil Nieves, who dropped the ball as Phillips crashed into him. On his way to the dugout, Phillips thumped his chest and indulged in some celebratory styling that, next time up, got him hit by a pitch from Miguel Batista.

Rolen had succeeded somewhat in tempering Phillips's body language, but his *actual* language, in reference to the Cardinals, had violated etiquette. And so it was that, when the Reds' chatty second baseman stepped into the batter's box the next night to lead off the bottom of the first inning and in his customary greeting tapped the catcher's shinguards with his bat, the catcher in question, Yadier Molina, stood up and got in his face. Phillips removed his helmet, Molina removed his mask, and suddenly Rolen was on the scene, holding back his former St. Louis teammate. Occupants of both benches reconvened on the playing field. Things were settling down, however, until Carpenter shouted something at Baker, who was discussing the situation with La Russa. By this time, Rolen had switched his bouncer duties from Molina to Carpenter, a long-time friend, and to distance him from Baker he physically urged the big pitcher in the direction of the backstop. That sent the whole scrum moving in the same direction, and backed Johnny Cueto, the evening's starting pitcher for the Reds, against the screen. Crowded in with nowhere to go, Cueto hopped onto the rail, facing the action, and, as another Cardinal catcher, Jason Larue—a former Red—advanced toward him, Cueto lashed out with his feet, landing at least one of them on Larue's head and causing a concussion that ended the veteran's season, which was the last of his career. Baker and La Russa were ejected. Cueto was fined and suspended for seven games. Phillips paid the pitcher's fine.

The Cardinals won that one, as well, 8-4, the biggest swing being a two-run homer by Molina, at the expense of Cueto. Then they won the

Wednesday matinee, 6-1, knocking around Arroyo in a four-run fifth. The ringing sweep put St. Louis back in first place, and the Reds, so it seemed, in *their* place.

Faced with yet another opportunity to reel, Cincinnati instead swept the Florida Marlins. In the final game, won 2-0 on a strong start from Homer Bailey, Cabrera, on the disabled list, took over the batboy duties. He retrieved foul balls sent back to the screen. He delivered water to the home-plate umpire. He put away the helmets and placed the batting donuts in the on-deck circle. He kept the club on the uptick while the Cardinals were digging into a five-game losing streak.

On the West Coast, the Reds' winning string expanded to seven games. As August wound down, they returned home and closed out the month against the Milwaukee Brewers on a Tuesday night that marked the debut of Aroldis Chapman, who was on record as having thrown the fastest pitch—102 miles per hour—in the history of Cuban baseball. In his last minor-league game before the promotion, the Cuban Missile, as he quickly became known, had been clocked at a ludicrous 105. Against his first Major-League batter, catcher Jonathan Lucroy, he hit 103.9. It was a strikeout. When Chapman relieved again on Wednesday, in the seventh inning, the Reds, throttled by Brewers lefthander Chris Narveson, trailed 1-0 in front of an understandably quiet crowd.

Sometimes, a player's intangible value is found simply in his extraordinary talent. With a fastball the likes of which they had seldom if ever seen, Chapman electrified the 16,000 folks on hand. As Baker put it, "[Chapman] changed the energy in the ballpark."[11] He struck out a couple of Brewers in his perfect, flaming, wildly cheered inning, and in the bottom of the seventh the Reds erupted for six runs, three of them on an unlikely home run by catcher Ryan Hanigan. The 6-1 victory completed the sweep.

Next came a trip to St. Louis, and by the time the Reds took the field there, it was September 3 and their lead had ballooned to an astonishing eight games. Jay Bruce was unavailable for the Cardinal series (and the next two), suffering from pain in his side, and the defending division champs won two of three. When the Cards pulled within five games, however, Votto swatted them away. His cranked-up hitting down the stretch closed out personal National League titles in on-base percentage, slugging percentage, and, of course, OPS. He was the league's MVP. Cabrera still wouldn't get off his back. Votto was grateful.

Meanwhile, his sidekick, Bruce, returned to the lineup on September 13 and ripped two home runs against the Diamondbacks, then went one for ten over the final three games of the series. After that, the Reds traveled to Houston, where Bruce lives. So does Kevin Millar, a friend of Rolen's. Rolen stayed at Millar's house, and one morning they picked up Bruce and took him to a local batting cage to tinker with his swing. For his subsequent work over the final two series of the season, the young Texan was named National League Player of the Week. He belted four home runs over that stretch. One of them, against left-handed reliever Tim Byrdak, was a walkoff blow on September 28 to beat the Astros at Great American Ball Park. It clinched Cincinnati's first division title, and first trip to the playoffs, in fifteen years. The winning pitcher, in relief, was Aroldis Chapman.

IT WAS ON THE BASIS PRIMARILY OF THEIR BATTING—THEY HAD LED THE NATIONAL LEAGUE in runs, hits, batting average, home runs, slugging percentage, total bases, OPS, and OPS-plus (adjusted for ballpark effect)—that the Reds were given a sporting chance in the National League Division Series against the Philadelphia Phillies, the NL's two-time defending champions, the winningest and, by most accounts, preeminent team in the loop. The Phillies' chief advantage, in addition to their considerable postseason experience, was a pitching staff built around superlative starters Roy Halladay, Roy Oswalt, and Cole Hamels.

While Oswalt, a two-time twenty-game winner with the Astros who had been acquired by trade in late July, was a notorious dominator of the Reds, and Hamels, who also wielded a fearsome history against Cincinnati, had been the MVP of both the League Championship Series and the

World Series two years before, the assignment for game one went unsurprisingly to Halladay, even though he had never in his twelve prior seasons thrown a playoff pitch. Halladay's jump from Toronto to Philly had seen him pace the National League in wins, complete games, shutouts, innings, and, ironically, hits—in spite of the fact that he had pitched a no-hitter against the Florida Marlins in May—all of it adding up to his second Cy Young Award. More than by his numbers, though, Halladay was defined by his precise professionalism and consuming intensity. In contrast, none of that description applied to his opposite number, Edinson Volquez, who had returned to the Reds' rotation in July after more than a year off for elbow surgery.

Against Volquez, the Phillies put up four runs in the first two innings. Lefty Travis Wood replaced Cincinnati's starter, and, batting in the top of the third, put the barrel on a pitch from Halladay, driving it to right field, where Jayson Werth made a diving catch. It was the hardest ball the Reds would hit. Brandishing an exceptional curveball, Halladay was working in near-perfect concert with his catcher, Carlos Ruiz, and the home-plate umpire, John Hirschbeck. He would throw more than three strikes for every ball. Of his 104 pitches, the Reds chose not to swing at forty-eight, of which twenty-five were balls and the other twenty-three were called strikes by Hirschbeck. Of the twenty-eight hitters Cincinnati sent to the plate, twenty-five fell behind on the first pitch. The only Red to reach base was Bruce, who walked on a 3-2 delivery in the top of the fifth. The final was 4-0. Halladay's no-hitter was the first the Reds had suffered in thirty-one years. It was the first in the postseason since Don Larsen's perfect game in the 1956 World Series.

By the midpoint of game two, however, Cincinnati was showing signs of the resiliency that had characterized its season. Roused by a leadoff home run from Phillips against Oswalt, the Reds placed a 4-0 lead into the hands of Bronson Arroyo and a decorated defense that featured three past or present Gold Glovers[12]—Rolen, Phillips, and Arroyo—and had tied for the league lead in both fielding percentage and fewest errors. What followed was therefore inexplicable.

In the bottom of the fifth, Rolen and Phillips made back-to-back errors, which enabled Chase Utley to drive in two runs with a single. With one out in the bottom of the sixth, relievers Arthur Rhodes and Logan Ondrusek hit back-to-back batters with pitches, then Ondrusek walked in a run. With the Cincinnati lead down to 4-3, Baker summoned his secret warhead to pitch the seventh. The first batter was Utley. Chapman hit him in the hand with a 102-mile-an-hour fastball. Or did he? Replays said no, Utley said he wasn't sure, and umpire Bruce Dreckman awarded him first base; or, rather, didn't prevent him from taking it. With one out, Rolen fielded a ground ball from Werth and threw to second, Utley appeared to be out on a force play, and umpire Ed Rapuono determined him safe. Then Rollins lifted a routine fly ball to Bruce, which the Reds' right fielder couldn't locate in the lights. Utley scored easily, and when Bruce finally picked up the ball on the track and relayed it to Phillips for a play at home on Werth, Phillips fumbled the throw for the Reds' fourth error in three innings. Rollins scored Philadelphia's fifth unearned run on a groundout. The Phillies won 7-4 in the only postseason game ever to include four errors and three hit batsmen by the same team. The Reds hadn't done that, in any type of game, since 1939.

When the series switched to Cincinnati for game three, Hamels happened. The bright-lights lefty shut down the home team and Johnny Cueto, 2-0.

The Reds had been outclassed. Their humbling performance brought back the stoical remark that Oakland general manager Billy Beane made in *Moneyball,* after his 2002 Athletics had lost in the American League Division Series for the third consecutive year: "My shit," said Beane, "doesn't work in the playoffs."[13] While both the Reds and A's had succeeded during the regular season in optimizing the resources available to small-market franchises—in effect, attaining the positive arbitrage that the Tampa Bay Rays so diligently pursued—Cincinnati's shit, in baseball terms, was thoroughly different from Beane's.[14] For starters, the team that Walt Jocketty had put together, and Dusty Baker managed with more autonomy than Beane afforded his field bosses, swung more freely than Oakland, ran the bases more aggressively, placed more trust in intangibles, and didn't pitch nearly as well. Yet when the last sweaty uniform was tossed into the laundry cart, the two clubs had merely taken separate routes to the same destination. Bottom line: The Reds' developing game, while sufficient to run away with the NL Central, had failed ingloriously in the face of the more poised, pitch-perfect Phillies.

With nearly a week to rest up for the League Championship Series, the Phillies, in fact, were looking very Fall Classical. Next on the docket were the San Francisco Giants, another team loaded with nobody who had been around for the organization's last postseason appearance.

FOR THE LENGTH OF THE 2010 SEASON, THE GIANTS WERE A GRADUALLY EVOLVING CLUB. Their starting pitching—notably Tim Lincecum (with two Cy Young awards to his credit), Matt Cain, Jonathan Sanchez, and twenty-one-year-old Madison Bumgarner—was young and brilliant, and the seasoned general manager, Brian Sabean, had cobbled the rest of the roster around it.

Sabean has been often described as old school, which essentially means that he trusts his scouts, having been one. Of course, scouting is but a method of gathering information and doesn't preclude *other* methods, of which the Giants, like all teams, availed themselves. For example, their director of minor-league operations/quantitative analysis, Yeshayah Goldfarb, had been instrumental in the drafting of Lincecum and Buster Posey, a fast-rising, total-package catcher. On July 1, 2010, Sabean traded away veteran catcher Benjie Molina to formalize the transition to Posey, whose May promotion from Fresno had preceded Bumgarner's by about a month.

Goldfarb also had input on several of the experienced retreads whom Sabean thoughtfully acquired. Those included, before the season, shortstop Juan Uribe and first baseman Aubrey Huff,[15] and *during* the season, reliever Javier Lopez, infielder Mike Fontenot, and outfielders Jose Guillen, Pat Burrell, and Cody Ross, the last pair by waiver claims. If there was a theme to Sabean's wholesale purchasing, it seemed to be stocking up on gamers. Tough guys, mentally and physically.

That was just fine with Sabean's manager, Bruce Bochy, a former big-league catcher. They say that a ballclub, to some degree, assumes the personality of its manager, in which case it stands to reason that Bochy's team would be stuffed with tough customers. Brian Wilson, the closer, messed up a side muscle in the first inning of his 2006 debut, recorded his three outs, then returned to the mound and did it again. In April 2010, center fielder Aaron Rowand was hit by a fastball that broke three bones in his face, then shagged flies the next afternoon, spent his fifteen days on the disabled list, used the time off to adjust his swing, and resumed his season with a seven-game hitting streak.[16] Remarked Huff, a bounce-around player on his fifth team in as many years, "He'll play if he's ten percent. That's how tough he is."

It was also not uncommon for Bochy's clubs to pitch exceptionally, and, in that tradition, his 2010 Giants led the National League in (park-adjusted) ERA-plus. In the first round of the playoffs, capitalizing on game plans informed by reports from multiple scouts[17] and executed by pitchers with the skill and willingness to make them work, San Francisco held the Braves to a .175 batting average.

In the NLCS, the Giants held the Phillies to .216. Game one, Lincecum beat Halladay, 4-3. Game two, Cain shut out Hamels, 3-0. Game six, it was Sanchez, Jeremy Affeldt, Bumgarner, Lopez, Lincecum, Wilson, and a nervy 3-2 victory that sent San Francisco to the World Series. The MVP, unforeseeably, was Cody Ross, whose three home runs matched Philadelphia's.

At twenty-nine, Ross, like Huff, was on his fifth Major-League team. But, in a way with which he closely identified, this one was not like the others. Ross looked around the Giants and saw a roomful of nonstars like himself. "Our team," he said, "is made up of guys who play with a lot of heart. Not so much the tools side of it, with the five-tool guys, and this and that. It's more of being good at playing baseball. This team figures out ways to win. Our common goal in the clubhouse is just to win the game that day.

"Tell you what, I've never been on a team like this where it's all about playing baseball and caring about winning a game and getting better, where the organization and the coaches just let you go out and play and not worry about all the other little stuff that organizations and owners worry about." In his itinerant career, Ross had known teams that, to him, seemed preoccupied with irrelevant rules: what players could or couldn't wear for batting practice, what they could or couldn't drink in the clubhouse, what they could or couldn't listen to their music on, how long or where they could grow their hair. Those were clubs lacking the personality of the champion Red Sox or the old A's or Orioles, or Bochy's Giants. "I've played on teams where I don't remember half the guys on the team," reflected Ross. "But I'll never forget each and every player I played with on this team."

The memory was burned in deeper by the World Series, when the Giants held the Texas Rangers to a .190 team average. Cain, Lopez, and Guillermo Mota shut out the American Leaguers in game two. Bumgarner and Wilson shut them out in game four. Lincecum and Wilson whipped them in game five to wrap it up. The MVP was thirty-four-year-old shortstop Edgar Renteria, who, during the regular season, had started 100 games on the San Francisco bench.

EIGHT

THE BOTTOM HALF OF THE PIE CHART

INEVITABLY, IN HIS QUARTER CENTURY WITH THE SCOUTING DEPARTMENT OF THE ATLANTA Braves, Hep Cronin had suffered the disappointments of prospects he loved but, for whatever reasons, couldn't land. Just four years into his summer job, Cronin took a shine to a six-foot-five-inch, left-handed-hitting catcher named Dave Parker, who, as a scholastic athlete, was more renowned as a 225-pound running back for a Cincinnati vocational school called Courter Tech. Parker, however, hadn't made it through the first quarter of the first football game of his senior year when he wrecked his knee, which not only caused him to miss the rest of the season but gave him another reason, in addition to some difficulties he had with the Courter Tech coach, to forgo his senior baseball season as well.

"I was just starting out scouting," recalled Cronin, "and I told the guy in charge of our area about Dave because I'd seen him play in the summer." Cincinnati had a proud tradition of summer-league baseball, and Parker, who grew up a block from Crosley Field idolizing Reds outfielders Frank Robinson and Vada Pinson, made a substantial mark on it. Accordingly, Cronin arranged a workout for Parker in front of Atlanta scouts, but the area man, wanting no part of a youngster who hadn't finished high school ball, canceled it. In spite of massive talent that would produce two Major-League batting titles, an RBI crown, three Gold Gloves, and an MVP award, Parker slid down to the fourteenth round of the draft, where the Pittsburgh Pirates were ready and fortunate.

Fifteen years later, with a little more sway and a healthier player to tout, Cronin was able to surmount another high-school irregularity. His prospect, David Justice, had attended an elite private institution that didn't offer baseball and graduated its students at age sixteen. Justice moved on to play ball at Thomas More College, an inauspicious Division III school in northern Kentucky. When his junior season began at Thomas More, he was eighteen. Although he played the outfield and pitched a little, Justice was classified as a first baseman in light of both his arm and speed grading poorly. Cronin, however, knew that the young player was holding back on his throws from the outfield in order to save his arm for pitching, and that his running was temporarily compromised by a basketball injury. The scout couldn't help but notice, also, that Justice had a certain spark to him, a substance of spirit and personality. "The kid was intelligent," Cronin said. "He had instincts. He didn't have any bad baseball habits." When Paul Snyder, the Braves' scouting director, came to watch Justice run, throw, and swing the bat, he wondered out loud why the kid wasn't a first-round pick. The answer was that he didn't conform to convention. The Braves grabbed Justice in the fourth, and four years later he got started on his 305 Major-League home runs.

It was in 1988 that Cronin thought he was going to ring the bell. The Braves had the third pick in the draft. And Cronin had the guy, a nearby infielder, Mark Lewis. Snyder was sold. Bobby Cox, the general manager, was on board. The trouble was, the Cleveland Indians were thinking along the same lines, and they had the *second* pick.

And so, two springs later, in his twenty-fifth year of beating the bushes, with his franchise in possession of the very first selection in the June draft, Cronin was craving to feast his eyes upon a young man worthy of that calling. He would find satisfaction in Jacksonville, Florida, in the person of switch-hitting Chipper Jones of Bolles High School.

"We were shorthanded down there," Cronin recollected. "We'd just hired a first-year guy in Alabama, and he was having trouble getting away from home. Paul sent me down. I saw Chipper on a Friday night and called Paul on Saturday morning. I said, 'Paul, I know we pick first but you'd better get down here. He's better than Mark Lewis. That's all I can tell you.' So he and Bobby Cox came the next day. That was the end of that."

What they saw was a player without a physical or mental imperfection. He hit with bat skills and power from either side. He'd been taught the game by a father who'd played and coached at the college level. And his instincts were way ahead of the curve. Cronin always made a point of watching a player run the bases, gauging not only his speed but the prospect's grasp of the game, and Jones negotiated them like a big-leaguer.

But there was a catch. Actually, two. The first was Todd Van Poppel, an acclaimed prep pitcher whom the Braves had scouted feverishly, but who expressed an acute disinterest in playing for them. Eventually Cox, fed up, informed his scouting personnel that if they drafted Van Poppel it would be at the expense of their jobs. That left Jones at the top of the list, with one caveat, one vital area in which Cox still had to be convinced. As Cronin explained to author Bill Shanks in *Scout's Honor:*

> Bobby loved the ability but was worried about his makeup, his toughness. He wore a different T-shirt than the rest of the kids. He wore orange and they wore black. He was kind of aloof. The thing that won Bobby over was when some kid on another team yelled at Chipper's pitcher. Chipper decked him. Bobby said, "He's my guy."[1]

Jones actually broke his hand when his blow connected, but, in a close vote, the scouting department stuck with him. By Atlanta's way of thinking, a hand injury was temporary but makeup lasted a career. As it happened, the career in question would encompass 468 home runs,

1,623 RBIs, a .930 OPS, an MVP award, and a dozen postseasons in a nineteen-year tour of duty, all with the team that drafted him instead of Todd Van Poppel (eleven years, six organizations, 40 wins, 52 losses, 5.58 ERA), whose stubbornness, incidentally, dropped him to the fourteenth selection.

By investing in Jones, the Braves got started on the teamship paradigm that would underpin the organization for the next generation. It became institutional when, in October of the same year, John Schuerholz took over as Atlanta's general manager, returning Cox to field managing.

For Schuerholz, makeup was not a tiebreaker in assessing ballplayers; it was a prerequisite. It was, in fact, the sporting ethic he had grown up with. Back in Baltimore, his father and grandfather and most of his uncles had been distinguished athletes, and some of them coaches. The family conversation tended to revolve around teammates and what the best of them were made of. That was the prism through which Schuerholz followed the hometown Orioles and Colts and the standard by which he measured the high school and college teams he played for. Soon thereafter, when he took a starter job in the Orioles' front office, it was also the professional culture he fell into step with. By accidents of family and geography, Schuerholz had become a student of character—more specifically, of athletes who had a lot of it. "I learned," he said, "that the more of those guys there are on your team—if they can play, if they have the ability—the better your chances of winning."

As general manager in Kansas City—even before then, as first farm and then scouting director—Schuerholz put his theory into practice and maintained his faith in it, affirmation coming with the World Series title the Royals won in 1985. His commitment to character was what led him, seemingly moments after taking over in Atlanta, to the inspired acquisition of Terry Pendleton. (It also precipitated his prompt hiring of Bill Lajoie, the former scouting director and GM of the Detroit Tigers— a veteran baseball man well-known for his emphasis on the human side of the game—as a special assistant.) Over the years, Schuerholz's sense of teamship would guide a good many of the roster changes he made on a regular basis. He found, for example, that players with super egos, as he called them, often have a difficult time folding them into the best interest of the ballclub. That was why he traded Deion Sanders to the Reds in 1994. ("Good player. Good riddance," Schuerholz wrote in his book, *Built to Win*.)[2]

Schuerholz and Cox were in perfect harmony on that score,[3] and Lajoie and Paul Snyder with them. To a man, they were people people. There are, however, subtle distinctions between the intangibles that are vital to a team—the disposition of its members to make each other better—and those pertinent to a prospect and, by extension, to the scouting of undeveloped players. In an up-and-comer, a discerning talent evaluator is looking for characteristics that will propel the player toward the flowering of his natural ability. For that artful challenge, the scout requires an eye that sees beyond video, stat sheet, and stopwatch.

Verily, there's a healthy crossover between the tools of teamship and the affirmative traits that avail a rising athlete. The wise scout, a term that *Moneyball* threatened to make oxymoronic,[4] understands that a young man's sense of accountability will professionalize his preparation; his toughness will fortify him as he scraps through the minor leagues; his passion will push him. But while a general manager puts together his roster with players who, ostensibly, produce the maximum value, a scouting director stocks the farm system with those who, individually, offer the maximum *potential*:[5] Players whose compounded personal qualities, matched with their physical wherewithal, give achievement a sporting chance.

An Atlanta scout was wasting his time if he spent it on a player who conspicuously or otherwise lacked the requisite makeup. The bird-dog might not have been able to fully describe the particular polymer of character that the organization was in the business of rounding up, or spell it out on the scouting report, but he was duty bound to recognize it, and typically did.

"We had a box to check," said Cronin. "But in forty years I never figured out what it meant. I just checked it every time. It was a box for 'Braves type player.' I knew what they were looking for; hell, I wouldn't be reporting on him if I didn't think he was that kind of player. They didn't want bums. I can remember a predraft meeting when one of the young scouts was talking about how good this player was, going on for about ten minutes. Then he said, 'He's just got one problem. If he beats the conviction . . .' Schuerholz looks up. Paul Snyder looks up.

" 'What conviction?'

" 'Well, he's presently charged with rape. But if he gets off, we could have a hell of a ballplayer.'

"The next sentence was Schuerholz saying, 'Let's move on to the next guy.' "

And yet, while integrity and rectitude, as social traits, translate fluently between life and vocation, it was a *baseball* integrity, a *baseball* rectitude, that Schuerholz and Snyder demanded foremost of their uniformed employees. If a high-school prospect was so scrupulously honest as to have never let his eyes stray to the test on the next kid's desk, that was very nice, but if he was so scrupulously *competitive* as to never take his eyes off the opposing *pitcher*, that was draftable. That was conducive to winning, which, according to the school of Schuerholz, ensues organically "if you have the physical tools and high character. And I'm not talking about moral character necessarily, but about athletic, competitive character."

As for what constitutes competitive character—in the vernacular, *makeup*—well, the elements are numerous and nuanced, but the Braves were especially partial to moxie and passion, and, in turn, intolerant of the lack of either. When All-Star, Gold Glove center fielder Andruw Jones once loafed after a fly ball, Bobby Cox pulled him off the field before the inning could continue. On the other hand, while they would have welcomed a little more sock from a little guy like Mark Lemke, they held his gritty style in high esteem. "We had a guy in Mark Lemke who did a little bit of everything you look for in the 'intangibles' player," noted Cox. "He couldn't run, couldn't throw, wasn't a good hitter, had no power, but you won with him. He was MVP of one of the playoff series [1992 NLCS]. He did everything right."

When speaking of passion, which he does passionately, Schuerholz sounds very much like Branch Rickey, Pat Gillick, and Joe Maddon. "Have you ever seen anybody really, truly successful," he asked, "who hasn't had a measure of passion or enthusiasm? I've not."

His scouts got the message. It was passion, right along with bat speed, hand-eye coordination, and base-path cunning, that Cronin searched for on the amateur circuit. A fundamental tool of teamship, passion is also basic to a young person's sense of purpose, store of energy, and willingness to work; to his chances, that is, of actually reaching the big leagues.[6] In its pursuit, Cronin solicited clues from coaches, teachers, teammates, and fans in the stands. He looked for it on the field, naturally, but also in the living room. He consulted his ears, his eyes, and the *kid's* eyes.

"Sometimes," he said, "you get into the house and come out thinking this guy doesn't want to play. Paul Snyder always said that if you go into their homes and listen more than you talk, sooner or later they'll tell you what they're about." Cronin could sense when a prospect, perhaps at the behest of his parents, was in the conversation for the money more than the baseball. That was a red flag. Another was when the kid looked at the floor and fidgeted. "If you really don't want to be there, you're not going to do very well."

Occasionally, though, an Atlanta scout would meet the steady gaze of a prospect like Jeff Francoeur, a hometown kid and renowned all-around athlete who, coming out of high school in 2002, was offered a football scholarship to Clemson University. It was generally believed that, if he were to announce his intentions to pursue a baseball career, Francoeur would be chosen high in the first round of the June draft. However, uncertainty along those lines left the powerful outfielder on the board through twenty-two selections, during which time the drafted players included Prince Fielder, Zack Greinke, Nick Swisher, B. J. Upton, and Cole Hamels. The Braves had the twenty-third pick, and they also had a ringing recollection of Francoeur from the home visit paid him by Snyder, player development director Dayton Moore, and area scout Al Goetz, which occurred a week before the draft. When Schuerholz's men arrived, Francoeur asked his parents to please leave the room. He had something to say to the three gentlemen from the team he grew up watching: He wanted to be a Brave, and he was willing to give up football to chase that desire. On draft day, the organization was only too happy to accommodate him.[7]

Make no mistake—Francoeur's athletic ability was the flashing neon sign that got the attention of Atlanta's scouts and every other team's. But, for the Braves, the deal was sealed by the young man's self-assurance and strength of conviction, by the monumental decision he insisted on making alone and declaring under the glare of influential adults. He had shown them what some old-timey scouts might have called *the good face*. He had character.[8]

In his blueprint of Atlanta's scouting philosophy for *Scout's Honor*, Bill Shanks outlined fifteen defining themes. At the top of the list was the term the Braves, like other teams, commonly use for character. The buzzword is makeup.[9]

> This is the most important word used in Braves Nation. Whether it's the scouting of an amateur player, of a minor leaguer that might be promoted, or of a potential addition from another team, it's all about makeup. To the powers that be in the Braves' organization, makeup is just as important as on-base percentage.[10]

The club's approach to personnel was unchanged when Roy Clark succeeded Snyder as scouting director in 1999. Rather, Clark wrestled with the actual makeup of makeup. It remained an indistinct proposition, but he knew, at least, that it had to do with the way a player handled various situations, and to gauge that, it was necessary to observe him in as many as possible. Said Clark:

I like to see a guy at his best and I like to see a guy at his worst. I want to see how he handles adversity. I like to see him play other sports. I like to see him in crucial situations, game on the line, title on the line, state championship on the line. I want to see how they react. The ones that have a strong makeup, the ones that we're looking for, are the ones that thrive in that situation.[11]

Chipper Jones, as you might suspect, was among those, high among them. But there was something more. Jones separated himself not only in talent and instinct, but in aspect. He was a presence among players, and Cronin wasn't the only Atlanta scout who picked up on it.

"[Jones] was General Lee up there sitting in a gray uniform on a horse leading the troops," said Dean Jongewaard, a Braves cross-checker. "He was a leader. You really get happy when you see that. There's not even one in every draft."[12]

In time, Jones's leadership came to involve such items as switching from third base, where he had been an All-Star for five of the previous six seasons, to left field to accommodate free agent Vinny Castilla; switching back two years later; working alongside the Braves' batting coaches; tinkering in the off-season with the swings (steady your head, unwrap your bat) of teammates like Francoeur; meeting others in the video room for instructional viewing and consultation; showing up for extra spring-training batting practice at seven in the morning; forgoing potential windfalls by reupping repeatedly; playing hard and hurt; and, by word and example, urging younger teammates (Jason Heyward, for one) to do the same.

When, in 2011, Heyward told reporters that he didn't think he ought to come off the disabled list until his injured shoulder was completely healthy, Jones, who at age thirty-nine was playing with a torn meniscus, told reporters that the gifted outfielder was about to rub the other Braves the wrong way and that Heyward, in the tradition of the colors he wore, should be eager to return to duty at 80 percent. Had those remarks come from any other player, Heyward might have been offended. But since they came from Jones, a figure the precocious twenty-one-year-old had admired while growing as a Braves fan and now admired even more as a teammate, he got the message.

In Atlanta, though, the imperative to battle through injuries—to suffer a little pain on the ballclub's behalf, if need be—was advanced from many more corners than just the hot one. The clubhouse was stocked with guys who embraced the ethic that the front office promoted. "The Braves won 14 consecutive division titles," wrote Jim Bowden, the former Reds and Washington Nationals general manager, "and they did so with rosters of players who always played hurt. I remember as a young general manager when then–Braves GM (now team president) John Schuerholz, one of the greatest GMs of our era, took me aside at one of the Winter Meetings and shared with me his philosophy that games played and games started were an integral component on how he evaluated players."[13]

Here, "games started" referred, of course, to Atlanta's clockwork pitching rotation. As the Braves dominated the National League for a decade and a half, it was the triumvirate of Cy Young Award winners— among them, John Smoltz, Tom Glavine (a two-timer), and Maddux (four in a row) were so honored for six straight seasons and seven of eight[14]—that set the franchise apart. And yet, even then, Chipper Jones was the organization's essence, the leading edge of the Tomahawk Chop. He gave the Braves more RBIs than any other third baseman has produced in the game's history; a .300-plus lifetime average from both sides of the plate;[15] a stunning career on-base percentage of .401; and a complete set of the right stuff: toughness, execution, accountability, moxie, supportiveness, history, intensity, and passion. As a paragon of teamship—the Derek Jeter of the National League—he was the ultimate Brave.

The case can be made that since the baseball draft was initiated in 1965, Jones has, in fact, been the finest first selection of all.[16] When Cronin, Snyder, and the Atlanta brain trust identified in him a synthesis of talent and makeup that exceeded every other available player's, and chose accordingly, they hit the jackpot. In addition to the titles that soon thereafter piled up so prodigiously, there was, symbolically, this: From Opening Day of 1995, when he replaced Terry Pendleton as the Braves' starting third baseman, until his retirement at the conclusion of the 2012 season, Larry Wayne Jones participated in 1,449 Atlanta victories and 1,049 Atlanta defeats. At the time he called it quits, only one other active player had taken part in as many as 400 more wins than losses.

That was Jeter.

IN HIS FIRST BASEBALL JOB, WITH THE HOMETOWN BALTIMORE ORIOLES IN 1966, JOHN Schuerholz worked for and learned from the club's newly named player development director, Lou Gorman, who worked for and learned from the Orioles' newly named general manager, Harry Dalton, who in the mid-fifties had worked for and learned from a Shakespearean scholar and ferociously thoughtful scouting and farm director, Jim McLaughlin.

Because of his refusal to sanction the folksy, intuitive styles of the good-old-boy scouts in the Baltimore system, and because he had better ideas, McLaughlin became roundly known for "making scouting a more scientific process."[17] He, in fact, might have been the first to publicly ridicule the time-honored scouting standard of "the good face" as talked up by the likes of former Dodger executive Al Campanis[18] and the fall guys in *Moneyball*. "I used to hear scouts talk about 'the good face,' as if they could tell about a kid's makeup just by looking at him, instead of taking the trouble to get to know him, or studying the results of a psychological test," McLaughlin said. "I used to hear those 'good face' stories and they'd drive me up the wall." In his view, scouting was fraught with assumption, myth, and brainless prejudice. It was unevolved and grossly unenlightened. "I wanted rationality. I wanted science."[19]

McLaughlin's more sophisticated techniques involved early-edition psychological testing;[20] visits from FBI agents to educate scouts on conducting background checks; the introduction of cross-checkers; health and fitness evaluations; and, for the minor-league managers charged with molding the prospects into professionals, seminars designed by Dale

Carnegie, the guru of friend winning and people influencing. If scouts were reluctant to modernize, McLaughlin weeded them out. "Basically," wrote Ben Lindbergh, "he's the patron saint of scouting for anyone who believes in an objective approach to baseball."[21]

And yet, McLaughlin was not too objective, or too scholarly, or too clinical, to embrace the notion that personal, interpersonal, nonphysical, nonmechanical, inherently subjective *qualities* were germane to the potential and value of a ballplayer. In fact, his quaint old pie chart, "The Whole Ball Player," helped define the Oriole heritage and endures as one of his most abiding contributions to the game at large.

The chart is a circular affair divided in halves. The top portion is labeled "Can Be Seen with Eye," and includes visible standards for pitchers (arm strength, fastball, curveball, slider, other pitch, control), infielders and outfielders (arm strength, use of arm, speed, hands, fielding, range, hitting, power), catchers (arm strength, use of arm, hands, hitting, power, speed), and all players (stamina, durability, anticipation, hustle, reflexes, size, coordination, agility, poise, instinct, baserunning, eyesight, and "record if in pro ball").

The bottom half, "Can Not Be Seen with Eye," is where McLaughlin, completing the composite of "the whole ball player," revealed his appreciation for the abstract virtues. It's grouped into five categories.

Attitude: desire, drive, willingness, hunger, ambition, aggressiveness.

Mental: intelligence, baseball sense, teachability, knowledge of game.

Personality: improvement, consistency, maturity, adjustment, stability, temperament, disposition.

Winner: stomach, heart, competitiveness, pride, confidence.

Background: family, habits.

It was in the purposeful pursuit of the whole ballplayer that the Orioles, under McLaughlin's and subsequently Dalton's watch at the head of the scouting department,[22] signed and developed Jim Palmer, Dave McNally, Boog Powell, Davey Johnson, and Brooks Robinson, the core— along with Frank Robinson, who was acquired from the Reds by Dalton shortly after he took over as GM in late 1965—of two World Series champions. In the case of Brooks Robinson, in particular, the bottom half of McLaughlin's circle was, in effect, a treasure map, the course to a trove of fifteen straight All-Star games and sixteen consecutive Gold Glove awards.[23]

Nearly two decades after the Orioles spirited Robinson out of Little Rock, Arkansas, in 1955, they identified less conventional qualities in a switch-hitting catcher (at the time) from Los Angeles. Eddie Murray was a calm, expressionless prospect whose muted manner was interpreted by many scouts as an absence of energy and passion. But he happened to graduate from high school in 1973, the same year in which general manager Frank Cashen appointed a former military officer and bank executive, Dave Ritterpusch, as the Orioles' scouting director. Another protégé of McLaughlin, Ritterpusch was an ardent advocate of psychological testing, and he read Murray's profile the way a grizzled scout might watch him blast batting-practice pitches onto intersecting streets. Where others suspected laziness, Ritterpusch recognized in Murray an extraordinary level of self-control that concealed a healthy strain of ambition.[24] Murray went to Baltimore in the third round, and to Cooperstown thirty years later.

Like McLaughlin, Ritterpusch—who left the Orioles for various other careers, including one in military intelligence, then returned as the organization's director of baseball information systems—was a practitioner of both the objective and the subjective, a science-minded administrator who applied empirical standards to his study of what, in a player's composition, might be relevant to his possibilities in baseball. Murray's emotional control, for instance, was pertinent not only with the bases loaded, but with the crowd in a frenzy, with personal distractions pressing down, with the tedium of the season wearing on him, and with claims being staked by highs and lows and streaks and slumps. In many ways, baseball is a sport for the even-keeled. Ritterpusch happened to believe that starting pitchers, in particular—an emphatic and longstanding point of strength for Baltimore—could be picked out, to some extent, by that element of their psychological profiles.

In the modern lexicon of the Tampa Bay Rays, the Orioles' long-term, dedicated emphasis on character traits was the organization's positive arbitrage. In the language of *Moneyball*, it would represent the club's exploitation of a market inefficiency. As Ritterpusch put it, there is a "tendency by people in baseball to not want to go beyond the physical." That camp would build its cases on the testimony of measuring devices, with willful disregard of anything those devices couldn't rank. "The same people believe the earth is flat."[25]

For at least a quarter of a century, Baltimore's front office was a laboratory for thinkers out of the box, a haven for appreciators of the not so obvious. It was surely not a coincidence that the Orioles' baseball staff in that period produced seven general managers—Dalton, Gorman, Schuerholz, Cashen, Hank Peters, Jim Frey, and, toward the tail end, John Hart (another future GM, Pat Gillick, pitched in the Baltimore farm system for five years, and yet another, Bill Lajoie, entered the game working under McLaughlin with the Cincinnati Reds)—and developed a Hall of Fame field manager, as well. McLaughlin happened to know Earl Weaver's father from St. Louis, in the Orioles' previous life as the St. Louis Browns, and hired the feisty former minor-league infielder to manage in the Baltimore farm system. It was in this capacity that Weaver became the chief on-field executor of "the Oriole way," a complete guide to training and fundamentals, based on an original manual written by general manager Paul Richards and amplified by McLaughlin.[26]

And it was in the same deep-seated culture that Schuerholz, for an annual salary of $6,500, was introduced to professional baseball. "When I began my career with the Baltimore Orioles," he reflected, "I quickly learned how important to that organization were not only the access [to] and accumulation of talent, which they did superbly, but the measurement of character, the measurement of intrinsic things, the measurement of qualities, through which the organization found it easier to rely on this particular person in the effort to win. It was a combination of (a) people who had ability, and (b) character. That 1966 team, my first year, when we won the World Series in four games, at every position there was someone who was a reliable professional. That was at the plate, in the front office, on the management staff, the field staff, everywhere. The organization was filled with those kinds of people. Never was an analysis of a player done that didn't include—and this was the mid-sixties—looking at the statistics we measured in those days, for production assessment, but also talking about who the person was, what's he like."

Schuerholz had been with the Orioles for only two years when Lou Gorman was hired away as the first farm director of the new Kansas City Royals franchise and took his assistant with him. The Royals' owner, Ewing Kauffman, was a forward-thinking billionaire with an appreciation for both the empirical and the abstract. It was Kaufman who, pairing science and scouting, conceived the Royals Baseball Academy in Sarasota, Florida, with the mission of making big-league prospects out of unsung, undeveloped athletes with speed, strong arms, and promising psychological profiles. In the Kansas City system, Gorman and Schuerholz were free to do their thing. They were in the whole-player business.

"Lou was principally responsible for the construction and growth of the player development program," Schuerholz said. "So, that was a big aspect for us. We started there to look for players who obviously had the physical skills but whose character even more assured us. We didn't always get it right, because we're dealing with human beings, doing both the playing and the assessing."

But with the glitches and growing pains, there was George Brett. And when the Royals routed the Cardinals in game seven, 1985, there was validation.

AS MUCH AS HE EMBRACED STATISTICS, AND AS PROGRESSIVE AS HE WAS IN THE ACQUISI-
tion of talent, modern sabermetrics would have been of little use to Branch Rickey when he set out to integrate professional baseball. The numbers would not have led him to Jackie Robinson.

Robinson had been an outstanding baseball player at Pasadena Junior College and UCLA—and a celebrated football player, basketball player, and track sprinter—but there wasn't much data to show for it; and although he batted .414 in his partial season with the Kansas City Monarchs of the Negro American League, the sampling was only sixty-three plate appearances. There was but one home run involved, a single triple, a measly pair of stolen bases.[27] Of necessity, Robinson was judged by his conspicuous athletic talent and, perhaps more important, the matching heart—with a premium on courage, forbearance, and resolve—that Rickey knew would be mandatory for the man who would break baseball's color line.

Robinson thus became a case study in subjective scouting, and an epic triumph for investment in a player's conquering spirit. "Of course, there are fundamental qualifications for all positions," Rickey said. ". . . But over and above these basic qualities, there is a great common denominator for all positions: a driving spiritual force that puts a man over." Force of character was the magnetic field that pointed Rickey's compass to not only pioneers, but all preferred prospects. "If you haven't got a heart at eighteen, you'll never get one later on."[28]

For all the illumination that objective analysis has brought to the predictive side of player evaluation, baseball scouting remains, inherently, an exercise in people reading. It's a skill at which Rickey still ranks as champion.

That's not to suggest that his supersensitive eye, for example, was what most accounted for his accumulation of talent and pennants in St. Louis and Brooklyn. Rickey improved the odds by investing in vast farm systems—in effect, hoarding prospects. He leveraged the ultimate market inefficiency when he dipped into the rosters of the Negro Leagues. He was a master of positive arbitrage. But through it all, he was also, with a religious devotion, a sucker for the driving characteristic held in common by Dick Groat, Roberto Clemente, Jackie Robinson, and inevitably, as his system institutionalized, by countless kids he had signed without ever seeing. He wanted a player who wanted to play, and he trusted the scouts who knew it.[29]

Rickey's talent seekers were scrutinizing their subjects for much the same stuff that the Jim McLaughlins and Lou Gormans would be seeking out in Baltimore and the Paul Snyders and John Schuerholzes were later looking for on Atlanta's behalf. From the stands and in the kitchens, they were tuned in with all three of their applicable e's: eyes, ears, and experience.

"We're in the personnel business," said Pat Gillick, the old Oriole minor leaguer. "You should have some kind of instinct of what kind of individual you're looking for. Statistically, I can't do that. I don't know how it is statistically possible to evaluate somebody's makeup. The only way to do it is with visual observation, then talking to a lot of people about the individual and meeting the individual."

"Our first question," said Jack Pastore, a former Phillies scouting director who also got his start in Baltimore, hired by Gorman and arriving there a year after Schuerholz, "is, 'how bad does this kid want to play professional ball?' And our scouts get paid to have an informed answer to that question. As for physical tests, I just don't believe they give enough of the picture. There are too many intangibles . . . you're dealing with the human individual and you're looking so far in the future."[30]

"Scouts," said Gorman, "don't see themselves as scientists; they see themselves as artists. Of course, a lot are neither one, but the best really do have a gift."[31]

In that perception—scouts as artists—Gorman of course was neglecting the disposition of McLaughlin, and deviating, as well, from the perspective of Ritterpusch, who said, "In a line of work where there's so much emotion and hearsay and folklore, the scientific opportunities are tremendous. Even simple objectivity is rare and valuable."[32]

In spite of their professed differences, however, the self-styled artists and scientists in question were of one accord on the importance of scouting for character. Both undertook to build organizations on players with passion for the game, a professional's makeup, and a relevant array of intangibles. To oversimplify: One camp sensed those characteristics; the other tested for them. As Kevin Kerrane put it in *Dollar Sign on the Muscle*, "McLaughlin and Ritterpusch were left-hemisphere critics, believers in rigorous quantitative analysis. Pastore and Gorman were right-hemisphere poets, attracted more to the exception than the rule, more to qualities (personality, intuition) than numbers. Both sides meant to study 'the whole ballplayer.' " [33]

That prized creature, the "whole ballplayer," is the guy with the tantalizing, rainmaking talent you see right away and the vaporous, whispering stuff that you don't, the guy with *two* sets of tools. Arms get tender, legs get tired, and bats get fooled, but a proper, competitive makeup comes to play every day, every year. When a scout sees a prospect with a work ethic, a measure of confidence, a feel for the game, and a driving desire to succeed in it, he sees, if not a high floor, necessarily, at least a head start. He sees a kid who can be counted on and coached, if not into stardom, at least into usefulness. He sees an asset to the organization.

That was, for instance, what a Detroit Tigers scout, Ed Katalinas, observed so clearly back at midcentury when he caught an accidental look at Al Kaline as a wiry Baltimore teenager. "He was about 5'10" and weighed maybe 140, but he hit line drives, ran beautiful, and threw the shit out of the ball," recalled Katalinas. "Fourteen years old. I watched him all through high school, saw him get stronger and fill out to about 180, and the amazing thing was that he had all the intangibles. Didn't lose his temper, had time for people, and just wanted to be a ballplayer. He was *oozing* with it." [34]

Let's break down that profile just a bit, to see what in it, theoretically, might have portended a player who would become a batting champion at age twenty and a first-ballot Hall of Famer at forty-five. The arm, legs, and bat were of course foremost. Without them, there would be no career. But even *with* them, unaccompanied, there would be no relative certainty. The aspect of Kaline that Katalinas found "amazing" was not the prospect's athletic wherewithal, but the attending qualities that would nurture it:

"Didn't lose his temper . . ." Even as a teenager, Kaline showed conspicuous control of his emotions, the same characteristic that impressed Dave Ritterpusch so much when he identified it in Eddie Murray. Baseball folks speak often of the need to avoid temperamental highs and lows in a six-month season. The same, for that matter, applies to a nine-inning game. Kaline's even disposition would be an ally for the length of his twenty-two-year career.

"Had time for people . . ." Teammates are people. Consideration for a teammate is the first step in helping one, in the collective effort the game expressly requires.

"Wanted to be a ballplayer . . ." The kid who wants to play is the one who stays on the field for as long as it takes to get where he's desperate to go, the one who accepts instruction and rejects excuses, and the one who will push his team in the spirited process of pushing himself.

"Was *oozing* with it . . ." This was not a young man to whom liking the game was the simple enjoyment of fresh air and sporting recreation. This was a kid whose soul was stitched with four seams, a kid who lived not just to play, but to *practice*, the rare prospect to whom baseball was self-expression.

"Makeup, as far I'm concerned, is half the equation," said Bill Lajoie, the subject/coauthor of a scouting tome, *Character Is Not a Statistic.* "Ability will get you to the big leagues and makeup will keep you there." [35]

Contemporary scouts may be scattered along the qualities-quantities spectrum, but few, regardless of how conversant they might be with sabermetric acronyms, would entirely dismiss the value of intangible virtues. They follow the game, after all.

"We go through our checklists all the time and we see that two of the top ten players in the American League [this was in 2009] are [Dustin] Pedroia and [Kevin] Youkilis, and they have no skills," said J. P. Ricciardi. "You have to look for *baseball players.* A scout actually has to live with the guy to find out, be so tight with a player that he knows what makes him tick. But for somebody to say one side is more important than the other, that's a mistake. There's a lot of value to having a statistical guy onboard and there's a ton of value to having scouts. This isn't the Arabs and the Jews trying to live together."

And yet, in the ideological skirmishes that have raged in the fervid scouts-versus-stats conflict, relations have sometimes been strained.

Needlessly so. The two, in truth, round each other out, like the halves of Jim McLaughlin's circle. As that reality becomes increasingly and sometimes dramatically evident, détente proceeds, club by club.[36]

"If you hire the best scouts," said Theo Epstein, who turned around history as Boston's GM, then repaired to Chicago to see about the Cubs, "put them in a position to see the player at the right time and get good solid accurate scouting reports, you see the player through a strong traditional scouting lens. If you hire the best analysts, get the most accurate data, make the best adjustments, do the most thorough analysis, and you come out with the best available statistical information, that's another lens [through] which to view the player. The way to see the player most accurately, to get the truest picture of the player, is to put both those lenses together and look through them simultaneously."[37]

THE SCOUTING OF PITCHERS, OWING TO INJURIES, NUANCES, AND THE MYRIAD WAYS IN which success can avoid them, is a capricious discipline. Hence the arcane acronym TINSTAAPP: There Is No Such Thing as a Pitching Prospect.[38]

In the requisite attempt to identify one anyway, it's intuitive to gravitate first toward the very popular live-arm individual, the effortless young thrower of, say, ninety-four- to ninety-nine-mile-an-hour four-seamers. And many scouts, of course, do, although few are unaware of the high incidence of flameouts even among the most generously armed, not only pitchers who break down physically but those, also, who fail on any of innumerable other accounts: flatness of the fastball, lack of secondary pitches, absence of finesse, self-defeating wildness, subtler trouble with command, an easy-to-read delivery, insufficiency of concentration, weakness in strategizing, neglect in conditioning, reluctance to learn hitters, shortage of confidence, poor poise, lukewarm competitiveness, counterproductive temperament. . . .

The fact is, more than that of any other player on the field—with the possible exception of the catcher's—a pitcher's performance turns on subtleties and fine points. Innately, it's tethered fast to the individual's mental, emotional, and competitive architecture. When the ball is in the pitcher's hands, so is the game. Preparation is paramount. Focus cannot be breached. Situations, like fastballs, must be commanded. Pressure must be mastered. Gamesmanship must be relished, responsibility embraced, results accounted for.

"You have to have a gut feel and instinct when you're scouting pitchers," said Cronin. "Anybody can hold a radar gun. I'll ask a guy, how'd he *pitch*? He'll say, 'He was ninety to ninety-three.' Well, I could send a monkey to get that. I know we're not considering the guy if he's throwing eighty."

"Let me hear about fastball velocity, fastball command, and fastball movement," added Terry Ryan, longtime general manager of the Minnesota Twins, speaking at the 2012 national SABR convention. Under Ryan's effective stewardship, the Twins' pitching has been known to feature control to a distinguishing degree. "Mechanics, athleticism, makeup, delivery, arm action. Those are the types of things you want to hear when you're in the room." [39]

The organizational emphasis on command requires that Minnesota's pitchers know how to use that particular skill. There being no advantage to spotting a fastball in the *wrong* spot, it's essential that they absorb scouting reports and exert the conviction—sometimes the courage—to carry them out. They have to understand hitters and scenarios. They have to parlay their control into craftsmanship. As a rule, *all* good pitchers have to do that. The Twins, angling for value in the marketplace, have simply edged a bit further than most teams toward the intangibles of the game's most important position.

Through the early stages of a season's scouting process, when prospects are being winnowed, it's typical and understandable that floor-level talent is diagnosed according to physical facility, which consequently predominates in the written reports. The abstract considerations are the stuff of judgment calls, tiebreakers, and draft-room editorials.

"In the draft meetings," wrote Kerrane, referring specifically to those of the Phillies, the team he closely tracked, "as the scouts rated players with comparable physical tools, makeup became more significant. For a catcher this was brute toughness and a willingness to 'sacrifice his body.' For a pitcher it was grace under pressure and readiness to 'dump hitters on their asses.'" A mean streak, in Philadelphia's template, was nearly as vital to a pitcher as velocity. Other organizations might place their premiums on confidence, poise, ambition, or *pitchability*, the feel for the art. ". . . Most scouts would say that with pitchers you have to forget about distinguishing sharply between tools and makeup, the physical and psychical—if you really ever separate them in the first place."[40]

Tim Naehring, who was player development director for the Reds before joining the Yankees, has never divided the two while appraising pitchers. When he scouts a guy on a mound, he notes not just the repertoire and results but also such character clues as facial expressions and interactions with teammates. In the absence of absolute answers—there's no such thing when it comes to projecting pitchers—clues have to suffice, and scouting is an exercise in collecting them. "The biggest problem in dealing with an amateur is that the young man may not know yet who he's gonna be," Naehring said. "You obviously keep your ears open and listen to a lot of things being said. You can sit in the stands and mix right in the trenches with the students, the fans, the parents.[41] I like to read the paper for what kind of comments are being made by the player. The biggest thing is what I can gather about how this guy competes, how he makes adjustments, what kind of work ethic I see, how he deals with staff members I talk to."

All of that might sound distinctly traditional and tobacco stained. Is it not, though, scientific in its own devices? Isn't it data gathered from multiple sources and senses—from watching, listening, reading, all of it supplementing the psychological tests and complementing the analytics? And, yes, even sabermetrics can be applied to the examination of a player's constitution. And even scouts appreciate that.

They have, in fact, appreciated it for decades. When Jack Morris pitched for Brigham Young University, he put up pedestrian numbers that, taken alone, made him a marginal prospect.[42] But when, in the spring of 1976, a Detroit Tigers scout named Dick Wiencek showed up at a California tournament to watch a coveted lefthander named Floyd Bannister pitch for Arizona State, he couldn't help but notice the losing pitcher, a tall, athletic, highly competitive right-hander who actually threw harder than Bannister. Following up on Wiencek's observations, Bill Lajoie, Detroit's scouting director at the time, looked deeper into Morris's college performances and noticed that the Minnesota native had pitched extremely well against the best competition. With little previous pitching experience, Morris showed an uncommon capacity for raising his game when the situation demanded it, a trait that later showed up in his 254 Major-League victories with a less impressive 3.90 earned run average. By matching impressions with ad hoc numbers, the Tigers were able to snatch a five-time All-Star in the fifth round.

"Now, with the use of statistical type things," said Naehring, "everything is weighed with different leverage situations. We look at that and see the guys who perform better in the clutch. When you try to evaluate the back end of your bullpen, you immediately look at how the guy handles high leverage. Does that tell you something about his makeup, his intestinal fortitude? Yes, no question."

And does makeup, in turn, tell you something about the player's potential?

"Talent is number one, no doubt," stated Ryan. "[It goes] talent, makeup, talent, in that order."

NINE

EXPECTATION AND PUJOLS

THE REDS OPENED THEIR 2011 SCHEDULE AGAINST THE FASHIONABLE FAVORITES IN THE NL Central, Milwaukee's Brewers, whose status resulted from a loaded lineup (Ryan Braun, Prince Fielder, etc.) and a pitching rotation reconfigured by trades for a premier starter (Zack Greinke) and a very good one (Shaun Marcum). The defending division champions were not so bold in their off-season activity but considered themselves upgraded by the return of right-hander Edinson Volquez, which they celebrated by naming him the Opening Day starter.

The Brewers celebrated the very same thing with long home runs by their very first batter, Rickie Weeks, and second, Carlos Gomez. While Volquez ultimately lasted for six innings, Milwaukee got six better ones from Yovani Gallardo, and the Brewers took a 6-3 lead into the bottom of the ninth. It was 6-4, with two outs and Votto and Rolen on base, when Ramon Hernandez, the Reds' veteran and generally unspectacular catcher, shot a line drive down the right-field line that cleared the fence and, after the smoke from the fireworks had abated, the premises. Cincinnati also won the next two against the Brewers, and the following two against Houston. Just like that, the Reds' magic number was down to 156.

Time-sharing his position with Ryan Hanigan, Hernandez brought along an evident advantage in power and a less conspicuous one in veteranness. The latter quality, though, was caught on camera one mid-April afternoon in San Diego. Aroldis Chapman, summoned in the eighth inning to protect a 2-1 lead, was throwing less blurry fastballs than usual, and when he walked the first batter, it prompted a visit from Hernandez, who turned to the dugout and called for the trainer. Chapman assured everyone that he was fine, threw wildly to first base, faced one more batter, and was replaced in a double switch by Nick Masset. Hanigan entered, as well, with Hernandez joining Chapman in the dugout, where he turned to the Cuban Missile and verbally cut loose, the veins popping out visibly in his thick neck. The catcher's message had to do with more honesty, less machismo, and the foolishness of pitching hurt in the first weeks of a long season.

Masset took the loss in the ninth inning, and with the squandered lead went the inertia that had carried the club two and a half games ahead of the rest of the division. In an extra-inning victory just the night before, game-saving plays had been made in the eighth inning by Phillips, who ranged far to his right, barehanded a ground ball hit by the swift Will Venable, and, throwing across his body as his momentum carried him toward left field, nipped his man at first by half a step;[1] in the ninth by Jay Bruce, who with the bases loaded and two outs had picked off a line drive on the run; and, in the tenth, by Gomes, who leaped to snare a screaming bullet. While it was far too early to reach conclusions about a club's character, which assumes its shape over the crucible of spring and summer, the Reds had been taking on that refuse-to-lose look, the one that Walt Jocketty, by recasting the roster with the likes of Rolen, Gomes, Hernandez, and Orlando Cabrera, had been so intent upon crafting. (Jocketty had not re-signed Cabrera for 2011, but replaced him with the closest thing, thirty-four-year-old shortstop Edgar Renteria, a two-time World Series champ and a hero on both occasions; he was, in fact, fresh off his Series MVP award with the Giants.)

The daytime defeat in San Diego was an aura changer, the first of six losses in a seven-game swatch that saw the Reds squander their division lead at home, caught by the Cardinals. Then they moved along to St. Louis, where rain clouds were approaching. The pain in Rolen's left shoulder had already arrived.

For the series opener on Friday night, Rolen was not in the lineup—he was about to go on the disabled list—and neither, controversially, was the Cardinals' previously announced starting pitcher, Kyle McClellan. It was another of the little dustups between the quarreling clubs, without the dust. The weather report distributed to the Reds and umpires indicated that the rain would reach Busch Stadium around forty-five minutes after McClellan's first pitch, except that, as it turned out, reliever Miguel Batiste would be throwing it instead. Tony La Russa insisted that he was operating under the same official forecast as the other principals and that he'd already made the decision to hold back McClellan by the time, around fifteen minutes before the scheduled start, the Cardinals received a call from somebody on I-270 who said that the rain was already in the vicinity. As it happened, Batiste delivered six pitches before the downpour hit, necessitating a two-hour, ten-minute delay. When the game resumed, Volquez, who had already warmed up earlier, would not take the mound. McClellan, who had *not* warmed up earlier, replaced Batista, threw six strong innings, and got the win in a 4-2 decision. At the end of the long night, Dusty Baker was perturbed and the Cardinals were in first place.[2]

They were still there when the Reds left, and also when the rivalry resumed in Cincinnati three weeks later without La Russa, who stayed home to get treatment for his bout with shingles. (The testiness between the two teams and their managers didn't preclude Baker from leaving a supportive voice mail.) But the St. Louis lead was only a game and a half, and sitting uneasily.

"The Cardinals are barely a month into the season, and it's already a nerve-racking adventure," noted Bernie Miklasz in the *St. Louis Post-Dispatch*. "There have been cruel injuries, including the loss of rotation ace Adam Wainwright and the broken hand suffered by hard-luck third baseman David Freese. . . . There's been an emergency appendectomy (Matt Holliday) and a lingering eye infection that's caused La Russa to look like a battered fighter in an MMA event. There have been inspiring comebacks, holes in the defense, old-school scrappiness from [newcomer infielders] Nick Punto and Daniel Descalso. . . . And there are a lot of games that have us reaching for the Tums. But overall, I admire this team for a simple reason: It's tough and resilient."

There was poignant irony in the columnist's remarks. As much as Cincinnatians deplored the Cardinals, that was the way they wished to admire their *own* team. And that was the very kind of ballclub Jocketty was trying to give them.

"No team can win without sufficient talent," Miklasz continued, "but La Russa's best St. Louis teams have possessed a grind-it-out mentality. That's the kind of compliment that makes the sabermetric scholars wince, but it's true. Most of this game comes down to performance, but you can't take the human element out of the equation. Some teams compete harder than others."[3]

The series opened on the night Rolen returned to the Cincinnati lineup, with three hits. It was a ninth-inning single by Phillips, however, that kept the game going and gave the Reds a chance to win one admirably. That happened after Hernandez led off the bottom of the tenth with a double. He was thrown out on a ground ball by Chris Heisey, but not before the catcher engaged the Cardinals in a rundown—no statistical reward for creating distractions—that allowed Heisey to reach second base. From there, Heisey scored the winner on a two-strike single from Votto.

Hernandez cracked a couple of homers the next day off McClellan, Phillips added another, and Cueto pitched the Reds to a breezy victory. They were positioned to send the Cardinals away in second place by taking Sunday's rubber game, but Chris Carpenter would have to be dealt with. Cincinnati hadn't beaten him in five years, during which time the strapping right-hander had become an enemy of the people of southern Ohio.

There were several factors contributing to this. Carpenter was a petulant pitcher whose carping and various complaints put a face to Phillips's description of the Cardinals as "whiny little bitches." He was also competitive to the point of being flagrantly combative on occasion. To wit, he once struck out Gomes to end an inning and then proceeded to yap at him, afterward telling Miklasz that he didn't remember doing that. Miklasz described Carpenter as "a figure of controlled rage. It's fascinating," he wrote, "to watch him go into psycho mode out there; Carpenter's starts become extended sessions of primal-scream therapy. . . . With La Russa, Carpenter, Pujols and catcher Yadier Molina, there's no backing off with this psycho bunch."[4]

Carpenter's ornery side might not have seemed quite so onerous to Reds fans if he hadn't been so very *good*. On that point, the Queen City's annoyance with him derived not just from Carpenter's prowess, but from its spontaneity. Over six years in Toronto, he had put up only mediocre numbers, and yet, the moment he arrived in St. Louis, he became an ace and a major player in pennant race after pennant race. In that respect, Carpenter personified a phenomenon that made the Cardinals a seemingly irrepressible organization—a marvel to its admirers and a bane to its adversaries. On a regular basis, the Cardinals, notably their starting pitchers, succeeded to degrees that they simply weren't *supposed* to. A long litany of them—the likes of Carpenter, Woody Williams, Jeff Suppan, Braden Looper, and Kyle Lohse, among others—became significant winners for St. Louis after pedestrian work elsewhere.[5]

The standard explanation for this pattern was Dave Duncan, the Cardinals' longtime, magic-making pitching coach. "The Cardinals seem to have a reclamation project for Dave Duncan every year," observed John Perrotto in *Baseball Prospectus*. "In fact, if the Hall of Fame ever begins allowing coaches to be considered for induction, then Duncan should be right at the top of the list. The number of careers he has revived is amazing."[6]

Writing for *SB Nation*, Rob Neyer took a good look at what he called the "Dave Duncan Effect," examining the dynamic from the other end—the success that St. Louis pitchers experienced after moving on. His sample was the twenty-first century. "I believe in the *Dave Duncan Effect* when it comes to pitchers who *joined* the St. Louis Cardinals," Neyer submitted, wondering at the same time whether the effect wore off when the Cardinal uniform was removed and Duncan was left behind. "A few of these guys did *okay* after leaving St. Louis, but all of them fell off some. As a group, they allowed 4.6 runs per nine innings in the two seasons before leaving St. Louis, and 5.1 runs per nine innings in the two seasons after (or in Looper's case, one season after)."[7]

Duncan was an American League catcher who worked with Catfish Hunter, Vida Blue, Ken Holtzman, and Rollie Fingers in Oakland and finished his career in Baltimore, where his best friend on the ballclub was Jim Palmer. Along the way he became a champion of the ground ball, and he effectively pounded that philosophy into his Cardinal pitchers, all the while cultivating a subculture that flourished in spite of personnel that regularly turned over.

In at least one evident respect, Duncan tapped into the gestalt of players making each other better. Perhaps uniquely, he developed the custom of sending his entire rotation to the bullpen when one of its members was due to throw between starts. The others simply observed, learned a little, and shared any observations that might be useful. John Smoltz, the erstwhile running mate of pitching maestros Greg Maddux and Tom Glavine, had won 212 games and saved 154 by the time he caught on with St. Louis late in 2009. He was taken aback when Carpenter, Adam Wainwright, and others accompanied him to his first side session as a Cardinal. He was flabbergasted when they commenced to call his pitches as they were being delivered. He'd been tipping them. "When 'Carp' and the other guys were down there and they knew every pitch I'm throwing, I didn't have to look at any film of what I was doing wrong," Smoltz told the *Post-Dispatch*. "I knew if they figured it out that easily out there, then I had to be doing the same thing in a game."[8]

Because of that nourishing cycle, virtually every St. Louis starter was, in fact, more productive than his numbers represented; each was supplying second-level statistics to the ledgers of his rotation mates. And so, when the Reds attempted on that Sunday to sweep the Cardinals by beating Carpenter for the first time since 2006, they were getting a little piece of Wainwright, as well, and perhaps a dab of Lohse.

On this occasion, however, any ancillary help that Carpenter might have received from his fellow pitchers was negated by the misplays of his defense. In the fourth inning, with the score 2-2 and the Cardinal infield playing close in deference to the presence of Rolen on third base, second baseman Tyler Greene momentarily booted a ground ball, and while he was able to retire the batter at first, avoiding an error, the glitch enabled Rolen to give Cincinnati the lead. Carpenter was already perturbed by the smoke that had lingered in the air from the fireworks the Reds set off after Hernandez homered in the third, and he became increasingly piqued as his afternoon worsened. His infielders did what they could to calm him down, but in the sixth, Rolen ripped his seventh hit of the series, an apparent double down the right-field line that Lance Berkman allowed to roll past him and along the wall. Rolen ended up at third base, Phillips—who had reached first on an error by Pujols—scored, and Carpenter briefly snapped at the well-respected outfielder. He was finally knocked out in the seventh, when the Reds' sixth run scored on a double by Phillips.

It was 9-2 going into the ninth inning, when Chapman entered and walked four Cardinals. Masset relieved him and gave up a double to Ryan Theriot. Francisco Cordero relieved Masset and gave up a double to Nick Punto. Then, on an 0-2 count, he hit Pujols on the hand. Pujols acknowledged after the game that Cordero would not intentionally hit him in that situation; but Gerald Laird, the Cardinals' backup catcher, nevertheless saw fit to holler at Cordero from the dugout. Finally, with the tying runs on base, after Pujols had broken up a potential game-ending double play by sliding late and hard into Phillips, Cordero struck out Berkman for the twenty-seventh out, at which point he jabbed a finger toward the St. Louis bench and jerked his arms in a what-the-hell-is-your-problem twitch. Hernandez ran out to restrain Cordero. Johnny Cueto was suddenly there, chirping at the Cardinals. Carpenter and Duncan strained at the edge of the dugout, giving Cordero what for. Duncan, filling in for La Russa, screamed at the Reds' reliever to get off the field.[9]

"Is the Cardinals' psychological advantage over the Reds now a thing of the past?" asked Miklasz in the next day's column. "We'll have to wait and see. But certainly this was a big deal to the Reds, to finally win a series from STL and do so with authority."

It was a bigger deal, however, to Reds *fans,* gratified to watch not only the color change of the rivalry, but the full blooming of the game itself. For a vibrant weekend—and Cardinals fans could appreciate this part, as well—the manifold splendor of the sport was unfolded in plain sight, the myriad skills, intangibles, and emotions spilling out before them as two compelling teams did all they could to settle a score by a score. "If you try to be objective about this," Miklasz went on, "you'll conclude that (A) the bad blood is genuine; (B) both teams can be incredibly annoying to the other side; (C) and the fans get into it with the kind of pure vitriol that we don't see in the Cubs-Cardinals rivalry. . . . Say this for the Cardinals, the Reds and their fans: this stuff is rough. It's old-school baseball."[10]

THE REDS' DIVISION LEAD WAS NOT TERRIBLY DIFFICULT TO SUSTAIN ON A TWO-DAY VISIT from the Cubs, who, among other offenses, made four errors in a game, committed a TOOTBLAN (Thrown Out On The Bases Like A Nincompoop) or two, and gave up a couple of runs on a sacrifice bunt.

Runs, however, were not doled out so generously by the Pirates, Indians, or Phillies, the effect on the Reds being a six-game losing streak and a dogged descent from the top of the standings. Baker's guys fell out of first place in Pittsburgh, shorted by as many as four runs through base-path gaffes by Phillips and Heisey. In Philadelphia, Phillips was at second base with one out in the eleventh inning when he took his lead-off, chatting amiably as he did with Phillies shortstop Jimmy Rollins. Meanwhile, second baseman Wilson Valdez darted to the bag, fielded the throw from pitcher J. C. Romero, and picked Phillips off. Philadelphia won in the bottom of the nineteenth. Said Phillips, "I fell for the banana in the tailpipe."[11]

As his custom had become, Phillips responded to his breach of base-ball by playing it very right for a while. Less than two weeks later, in fact, looking to square his moxie ledger, he actually did unto another as Rollins had done unto him, more or less. It occurred, not surprisingly, in Chicago. With two outs and two Cubs on base, Carlos Pena singled to right field. Jay Bruce made a strong peg to home plate and Pena rounded first, prepared to move along when the throw went through. But Phillips sneaked in behind him, took the bullet from catcher Ryan Hanigan, and applied the tag to end the threat.

Cincinnati's season lurched back and forth in that fashion, the little things piling up in two heaps: give and take. In San Francisco, the Reds took a fourth-inning lead owing, in part, to a subtle contribution from Votto, who, after being hit by a pitch from Jonathan Sanchez, disturbed the Giants' lefty with his supersized leadoffs. They led to a walk for Bruce, and both ended up scoring. In the subsequent inning, however, Volquez gave back, delivering a rare single but inexplicably stopping at second base when Stubbs's apparent double bounced around in the left-field corner. Votto's fly ball to the warning track would have easily scored Volquez if he'd been at third. Instead, he started for third, stopped, and got himself doubled up at second. The Giants rallied to win, 4-2.[12]

At home against Toronto, Stubbs ran out an inside-the-park home run made possible when the Blue Jays' center fielder, Corey Patterson, neglected to tell their right fielder, Jose Bautista, whether he intended to make the catch. The next night, Heisey was unable to track down a long fly in the gap, but his enormous effort persuaded the runner on first,

Adam Lind, to hold up long enough that he was unable to score. Gradually, the balance of small stuff was tipping in the Reds' favor, and the standings reflected it. By Sunday, June 19, only two games stood between them and the Cardinals—and Milwaukee, as well.

That was the day Pujols broke his left wrist when he came off first base to catch a wide throw and collided with Wilson Betemit of Kansas City. The reports said he would miss four to six weeks.

He made it back in two and a half.

In that time—in fact, for an inconceivable stretch of more than five weeks—Cincinnati, its gestalt proving spurious, was unable to chase one victory with another. Bronson Arroyo, pitching through lingering mononucleosis, was not himself, and Gomes was in a batting slump, but the troubles went deeper. In spite of a scoring differential that was the best in the division, the Reds were dropping one-run games with dispiriting regularity. Perhaps they missed Cabrera's spunk and confidence, or the solemn example of reliever Arthur Rhodes, lost to free agency.

Meanwhile, by whatever synergy they seemed to perennially summon, the Cardinals, without Pujols—they were already playing the season without Wainwright, second and third in Cy Young voting the previous two seasons—had clung to the division lead and doubled the spread over the team that visited Busch Stadium on the Fourth of July. True to form, Carpenter ruined Cincinnati's holiday with eight shutout innings in a 1-0 decision. The Reds managed to win only the final game of the series, which took thirteen innings, and there was grim foreboding even in the long, rare victory. It was the occasion of Pujols's return.

On the flip side, Rolen started the All-Star game and was on the disabled list ten days later. Same shoulder. Surgery was in store. He was finished for the season.

Four days after that, Gomes was traded for two minor leaguers.[13] His suddenly former teammates responded by committing three errors, which could have been five, in their worst effort of the year, part of a four-game sweep, in Cincinnati, by the New York Mets.

The Reds were as done as their third baseman. By the second week of August, their deficit had reached double digits. Milwaukee had taken hold of the division race.

In spite of Pujols's presence, the Cardinals, schlepping through the straightaway of summer, were also slipping hopelessly behind the Brewers. Their best bet for the postseason appeared to be the wildcard berth; but Atlanta was making a shambles of that derby. After being swept and humiliated by the Dodgers on August 24, exactly five weeks before the end of the regular season, St. Louis trailed the Braves by ten and a half games.

THE CARDINALS HELD A TEAM MEETING THE NEXT DAY AT BUSCH STADIUM. IN TALES LIKE this one, there's always a meeting. Carpenter led it. Pujols spoke. Berkman spoke.

Berkman's voice had become a leavening agent in the Cardinal clubhouse. In that respect, it didn't hurt that St. Louis had resuscitated his bat in a way that turned heads. More than that, though, the eminent switch-hitter, after twelve eventful years in Houston and part of one with the Yankees, had developed a seasoned aspect that balanced the steaming intensity of La Russa, Duncan, Pujols, Carpenter, and Molina. "Teammates, opponents, managers, fans, media members and scouts regard Berkman as an uncommonly nice person and the classic case of an athlete who has his act together," observed Jerry Crasnick of espn.com. ". . . The Cardinals also love Berkman's intangibles."[14] Spread around with perspective and humor, Berkman's niceness was not merely an endearing characteristic but a mood changer that blended well with the Cardinals' methodical mien. At the same time, his professionalism made an immediate impression on his teammates, and he had addressed the club, to winning effect, in just the season's second week, after a 2–6 start. He fully understood, however, that the notes he struck were amplified by the chorus.

"You've got to have guys that are good guys, that are true professionals that buy into a team concept," Berkman said. "If there's anything that

I've learned about a Major-League clubhouse it's that it's not one guy. You really need to have four or five veteran guys. Preferably a bullpen guy, a starting pitcher, an everyday superstar type, and a bench guy; you really need someone from every phase of the game to have a really good, effective clubhouse culture." Berkman's convictions were informed by his experience in Houston, where the Astros took their cues from Jeff Bagwell and Craig Biggio, and reinforced during his partial year with Jeter. The stars provided the teamship model for contiguous subcultures, and, together, those subcultures constituted an atmosphere. "Clubhouse culture is a commitment to winning and to playing the game hard on a daily basis. Be a part of a team on a daily basis. The best clubhouses are those that don't have a lot of individuals. They have a lot of guys who buy into a team and understand that it takes twenty-five guys, not just one or two.

"What's funny, though, is that one guy can spoil it or put you over the top. I'm sure there will be people that don't share this opinion, but if you look at the Yankees, they win four World Series with Andy Pettitte. He leaves, they don't come close to winning it. He comes back, they win another one. Andy, to me, is the biggest winner I've ever played with. There are certain guys who have an aura and have a presence and give the team confidence even when they're not pitching or playing. Andy Pettitte is the one guy that is head and shoulders above anyone else in terms of that sort of thing." In addition to their brief time together in New York, Berkman and Pettitte teamed up for three seasons in Houston, once reaching the National League Championship Series and the next year reaching the World Series. The Astros haven't been to the postseason since.

"It's really tough to come to the ballpark and be able to concentrate and be able to play hard every day," concluded Berkman. "Guys like Bagwell or Biggio or Jeter or Mark Teixeira, they come to play every day. Albert Pujols is the same way. Matt Holliday. You can go back and look at the teams that have won the World Series, had success. Sounds corny, but they play for each other. They play hard and don't want to let their teammates down. As you get older as a player, you really learn what wins or loses at the Major-League level. The disparity in talent from the worst team to the best team a lot of times is not much. But what separates teams is that attitude, that culture, that expectation of winning."

The last item, *that expectation of winning*, is what the Cardinals had so deeply developed over the years and were loath to let go of, whatever the circumstance. Losing slogged repugnantly down their throats. Their system rejected it. So did the St. Louis fans, a point that Carpenter brought to the attention of his teammates as he addressed them on August 25.

When the oratory was wrapped up that day, the Cardinals had four more games in their home stand, all with the Pirates. They won three of them, setting up the inspirational psalm of Rafael Furcal: "Happy flight! Happy flight!"

A longtime Braves and Dodgers shortstop, Furcal had been acquired at the trading deadline. He had squeezed in comfortably between the lockers of Pujols and Molina, and at the top of the St. Louis batting order. Along with Furcal, general manager John Mozeliak, reacting proactively in a way that Jocketty and the Reds had elected not to, had also brought in some relief reinforcements to stabilize a failing bullpen from which Ryan Franklin, the Opening Day closer, had been released. Octavio Dotel, a jocular right-hander picked up in a trade *before* the deadline, helped break the gloom and thwart a few rallies. He was joined by lefty specialist Marc Rzepczynski. After the deadline, graybeard left-hander Arthur Rhodes, the highly respected former Red in his twentieth big-league season, signed on as a free agent.

The Dotel deal, which also brought the Cardinals starting pitcher Edwin Jackson, was fraught with alchemic elements. Notably, it marked the departure of talented young outfielder Colby Rasmus, whose issues with La Russa had become a public distraction. Rasmus had been a player of symbolic significance since being selected in the initial round of the 2005 draft, the first taken under Jeff Luhnow's watch as St. Louis scouting director. Luhnow's sabermetric inclinations were not entirely consistent with Jocketty's more traditional views about the procurement of talent, a rift developed, and Rasmus was trapped in the middle.[15] Even after Jocketty's removal, the Rasmus drama dragged on. On July 27, after insisting that he wouldn't trade him, Mozeliak traded him.

With their holes plugged, their critical mass of character expanded, and their charge spelled out in the team meeting, the Cardinals began to string together happy flights. They went to Milwaukee and swept the team that couldn't be caught. At the end of the nine-game home stand, they also swept the Braves, suddenly closing within four and a half games of Atlanta's wildcard lead.

The Braves, meanwhile, were beginning to crack in a manner unbefitting their modern custom. Even their young relief pitching, extraordinary all season, was running out of stuff. In part because of that absurdly productive bullpen—notably, Craig Kimbrel, Jonny Venters, and Eric O'Flaherty—Atlanta, for the first time in seven years, was playing ahead of its Pythagorean projection (a win–loss predictor based on run differential), which a team might be expected to do if it was indeed enhancing its raw production with resourcefulness and winning intangibles. The Braves, in fact, had done it throughout the nineties and shortly into the new century.[16]

Although Schuerholz had stepped down as general manager after the 2007 season, he still served as Atlanta's president and, in that capacity, perpetuated the club's scrupulously carved culture. Bobby Cox still managed in that spirit. And Chipper Jones still set the example. Their enduring consortium would seem to lend an air of contradiction to the organization's declining Pythagorean trend, except that, in baseball, environment is a people thing. In baseball, people come, go, and retire.

Jones was six years removed from his eleventh straight postseason— he was thirty-four before he ever missed one—and the turnover had become a difficult dynamic for him to deal with. "I feel that so much of what we built in the nineties has been lost somewhere along the way," he said. "We used to play the game the right way. Used to hit behind runners, execute bunts, not give teams extra outs. Now, all of that has gotten kind of lost." As the faces around him changed, Jones made it his personal responsibility to bring back the ethic of teamship that the Braves had played and won with for most of his long career, to pass along to his young teammates what teammates like Terry Pendleton had passed along to him. "It's a transitional stage, but I've been spoiled. I'm used to the game being played a certain way and it's *not* being played that way now."

It was, though, in St. Louis. The Cardinals swept another series in Pittsburgh. Through the heart of September, they won twelve of fourteen games. And yet, such was the handicap they'd imposed upon themselves—it had remained formidable, at eight and a half games, with twenty-one to play—that, on September 24, after finally scoring on a bottom-of-the-ninth, two-out, bases-loaded base on balls by Cubs closer Carlos Marmol and then winning, 2-1, on a walkoff wild pitch, they still trailed the Braves by two games with only four remaining. Three days later, they were even.

On the final night of the regular season—oddly, it ended on a Wednesday—Carpenter shut out the Astros on two hits. And in Atlanta, the Phillies, the best team in the National League once again, presented the devastated Braves with their fifth straight defeat, 4-3 in thirteen excruciating, season-ending innings.

St. Louis was in the playoffs. Against the Phillies, who, unlike the Cardinals, hadn't needed to win twenty-three of their final thirty-two games to get there.

As division champs, meanwhile, the Brewers were preparing to begin their playoff series against the Arizona Diamondbacks. And as *defending* division champs, the Cincinnati Reds were inconspicuously dispersing, having restored their modern tradition of sub-five-hundred seasons.

PERHAPS NEVER BEFORE HAD A TEAM—NOT EVEN THE HISTORIC CARDINALS OF 1964, who stood six and a half games out of first place with thirteen to play, or the miracle New York Giants of 1951[17]—entered the postseason so steeped in the avoidance of elimination.

Tempting the odds, the wildCards lost their first Division Series game to the Phillies and fell behind 4-0 in the second. It was, bear in mind, a five-game set against a frightening starting rotation of Halladay, Cliff Lee, Hamels, and Roy Oswalt. But after Carpenter uncharacteristically faltered in game two, the Cardinals' reconstituted bullpen uncharacteristically saved the day. Six modestly armed infantrymen delivered as many scoreless innings, the last one, for the save, belonging to the surviving closer, Jason Motte, a former minor-league catcher.

Hamels then beat Jaime Garcia, 3-2, to put Philadelphia back in control and St. Louis back in its comfort zone, at extinction's brink. In game four, Edwin Jackson went six strong innings for the Cardinals and left with a 3-2 lead, owing in part to Pujols's moxie: Utley led off the sixth for the Phillies, drew a walk, and, as one of the game's savviest baserunners, noted with interest that when Hunter Pence followed with a ground ball to the left side, Furcal had to range far to his right to reach it. And so, rather than stopping at second, Utley rounded the bag and steamed for third as Furcal fired the ball across the infield. Engaging in the battle of spontaneity, Pujols stepped forward to meet his shortstop's long throw before it reached first base, then swiftly reversed it to third, where Utley was tagged out by David Freese. Ryan Howard then lifted a deep fly that would easily have tied the game by scoring Utley from third, had he been there. In the bottom of the inning, Freese, locally bred and frequently injured, banged a two-run homer. The Cardinals finished it off with their improvised bullpen cluster, Motte at the back end. The series went to its full length. It went to Halladay and Carpenter.

Furcal, leading off the deciding game, helloed Halladay with a triple. Second baseman Skip Schumaker followed with a double. The rest was Carpenter's wing and will. It was still 1-0 in the bottom of the ninth when the Phillies' final chance was formidably represented by Utley, Pence, and Howard. Three up, three down, three-hitter. St. Louis was off to Milwaukee for the League Championship Series.

There, Freese, who'd produced ten home runs during the regular season and fifteen in his career, provided the Cardinals with one in the first-game defeat and another in the second-game victory. Carpenter and the pen held off the Brewers in game three, Milwaukee evened the series in round four, and over the next eighteen innings the St. Louis offense clubbed the club clear into the World Series. Freese's three home runs were garnished by his .545 batting average. He was the MVP.

The Cardinals' challenge in the World Series would be the Texas Rangers, who'd been there the year before, as well, succumbing to the Giants. The Rangers were a muscular club that had blown away their division and taken care of Tampa Bay and Detroit in the American League playoffs. By objective standards, they were the Series heavyweights, outperforming St. Louis both offensively and defensively during the season and dwarfing the Cardinals' run differential by more than 100. If the Cards had advantages, they were intangible. The last few weeks had instilled in them a powerful sense of survival. They had, in Pujols, the game's foremost player. And they were guided by a manager who was destined for the Hall of Fame and set to retire after sixteen years on the Mississippi.

It was conceivable, and would turn out to be the case, that the Series would also mark the St. Louis farewell of Pujols, the faultless first baseman whom La Russa had described as the perfect teammate. In his eleventh season with the Cardinals, the three-time MVP (who also had four second-place finishes and a third) had led them on their protracted rally to the World Series, a pillar of fiery professionalism and willing doer of whatever it took; he even played a few games at third base, for the first time in nine years, when Freese was hurt. But, unlike other years, he hadn't piled them on his shoulders.

That, he postponed for a few more days. Pujols, in fact, went hitless in the Series' first two games, which pitching dominated and the teams split. Carpenter won the opener, with timely batting help from Freese and Allen Craig, who provided the same in game two, only to see Texas pull it out with small ball—a couple of singles, a steal, and sacrifice flies by Josh Hamilton and Michael Young—in the bottom of the ninth. For the Cardinals, the walkoff loss begged the question of whether karma was finally moving on to other matters.

But in game three, Pujols changed the narrative for a night. He already had a pair of singles to his credit when he stepped up in the top of the sixth inning against Alexi Ogando, with St. Louis leading 8-6. His three-run homer to deep left field made it 11-6. In the seventh, when Pujols became the first player to ever produce hits in four consecutive innings of a World Series game, his two-run homer to deep left-center made it 14-6. In the ninth, his solo homer—to deep left again—made it 16-7, the crazy final score.

Not even *that*, however, could keep the Cardinals' backs off the wall. Derek Holland shut down their offense to square the Series, and in game five the Rangers proceeded to once again put La Russa's club in the elimination posture, at the same time taking Carpenter out of the equation for games six and seven, obstensibly. The St. Louis ace had been spotted an early 2-0 lead and left after seven innings, with the game tied 2-2, but this time the relief relief, Dotel and Rzepczynski (thankfully, they called him Scrabble), had been unequal to the assignment. When the evening was over, Texas had but one more game to win. It would have to come after a day of travel to St. Louis. And a day of rain on top of that.

The extra twenty-four hours appeared to have no effect on the Rangers' momentum. They scored first, kept answering the Cardinals, and took their fourth lead of the game when Adrian Beltre homered to lead off the seventh inning. Nelson Cruz followed with another homer, and a single by Ian Kinsler widened the spread to a healthy three runs. That was pared a bit when Craig, in the game for Holliday, who was injured while running the bases, homered in the eighth off Holland, pitching out of the Texas bullpen. In the bottom of the ninth, batting against Rangers closer Neftali Feliz with the score 7-5, Pujols doubled and Berkman walked, but Craig fanned for the second out. The Cardinals were down to their last one. After three pitches to Freese, they were down, in fact, to their last *strike.* Feliz proposed one at ninety-eight miles an hour. Freese drove it deep to right for a game-tying triple.

In the top of the tenth, Hamilton smoked a two-run homer against Motte. In the bottom, some St. Louis small ball made it 9-8 with runners on first and third and two outs. Berkman was up, facing Scott Feldman. The count went to 2-2, once again putting the Cardinals a solitary strike from the end of the line. Berkman singled to center. It was the first time a team had ever overcome five deficits in a World Series game.

Leading off in the eleventh, Freese crushed a 3-2 changeup over the center-field fence. There would be a game seven.

And, of course, the Rangers would lead it early. They scored twice in the first against Carpenter, back on the mound by the good graces of the earlier downpour, but Freese tied the game with a double in the bottom of the inning. Craig, in the lineup only because Holliday's wrist was now in a soft cast, homered to put St. Louis in front in the third, a few more runs were tacked on, and without another plot twist the world championship was wrapped up by the pitcher who wasn't supposed to pitch again and most of the ragtag bullpen.

Was there, by this time, anyone remaining in America who didn't believe that there had been some force, some inspiration, some magic, some *some*thing beyond the pale of the tangible, metric, and overt, impelling the Cardinals through a ten-and-a-half-game breach; and then, in the postseason, through four games that absolutely had to be won, through two strikes that positively had to be hit?

Jayson Stark called them "the most improbable World Series champions who ever lived."[18] It barely qualified as an opinion. "In the history of baseball," he wrote, "only one other team has ever done what these Cardinals have just done. Only one other team—the '86 Mets—ever tumbled into that one-strike-away abyss in a World Series and survived to pop the champagne bottles. So think about that. In the first 106 World Series ever played, only those '86 Mets ever got down to their last strike and then won it all. Then *this* team found itself in that mess twice in two *innings.*"

There was no flashing, indisputable explanation for what happened in the fall of 2011. There was no lights-out object lesson in what the Cardinals pulled off. Stark's colleague Howard Bryant was one of many who made a run at understanding it, and his theory was as good as any.

"For what the Cardinals truly discovered," he reflected, "or redis-covered during this title run . . . was the importance of toughness and chemistry and, most importantly, of pride. In a game of millionaires, all supposedly detached, the Cardinals regrouped by rededicating them-selves to liking what they saw in the mirror." [19]

In the end, of course, that was not a problem. Their expectations had been met.

TEN

MR. MACK'S IMMORTALITY

IN CHRIS JAFFE'S IMPRESSIVE BREAKDOWN OF THE GAME'S ALL-TIME GREATEST MANAG-ers,[1] Tony La Russa ranks second, which brings us to the complicated matter of what responsibility he might have borne for the Cardinals' epic comeback in 2011. Some, it's safe to say.

Since *Moneyball,* a manager's impact has been an object of increasing skepticism.[2] It wasn't a matter I'd intended even to touch upon when I set out to explore intangibles—I was and am, after all, principally concerned with their part in a *player's* value—but logic and testimony eventually called the question. The logic is this: If it can be established that a manager, in ways that transcend the writing of lineups and changing of pitchers and the like, truly makes a difference through his influence on a ballclub, it follows that influencing a ballclub is actually an operative, contributing thing. The manager has no corner on such subjective contributions as informing, counseling, motivating, and leading, and if he can make a competitive difference through those means, it stands to reason that a player can, too.

Needless to say, any statistical boost that a manager might afford any team or player would be of the second-level variety. His strategic decisions represent his version of the situational intangibles he expects from the guys he puts on the field, but his setting of tone—from the guidance he offers to the confidence he inspires to the demands he makes to the buttons he pushes—furnishes a model for the environmental intangibles he counts on from his veterans and best men.

Considering how vociferously Dusty Baker has been ridiculed for his lineup choices and alleged ruination of certain pitchers, it's ironic that the first study to seriously examine a manager's effect on his players was undertaken with respect to Baker's influence on his hitters. That was in 2003, in *Baseball Prospectus,* and the conclusion was that the batsmen who played for Baker's San Francisco Giants, with whom he won three National League Manager of the Year awards,[3] improved by an average of 8 percent.[4] Among those who prospered conspicuously under Baker's stewardship were Jeff Kent, Ellis Burks, and J. T. Snow. "People skills," wrote Jaffe, alluding, by another name, to environmental intangibles, "were Baker's strong point."[5]

That mode of documentation was significantly amplified, albeit inadvertently, in a presentation by Canadian researcher Phil Birnbaum at a SABR convention in Toronto two years later. Birnbaum had set out, through dedicated algorithms, to compile sabermetric evidence that would quantify the impact of luck in baseball outcomes. His method was based on a study of a team's under- and overachievement over the course of a season, as it related to the production of individual hitters and pitchers in the context of their norms. Presumably, deviations in that production would capture and, to some extent, even measure the presence of luck, which, as the default explanation for statistical anomalies in such areas as pitcher wins and BABIP (batting average on balls in play), occupies much of the undeveloped territory that intangibles would like to claim. However, when Jaffe undertook to parse the considerable testimony that the Birnbaum Database encompassed on the effect of managers, "The results," he wrote, "never came out quite perfectly, but they consistently refuted the luck storyline. . . . The difference between the best and worst managers is about 50–60 runs, or five or six wins per year."[6]

In general, Jaffe's treatise was predicated on statistical analysis but characterized by appreciation toward that which eluded it:

> The purpose of this book is to use sabermetric methods to appraise the overall performance and particular tendencies of baseball's field generals—its managers. Although this is not the first sabermetric study of managers to be done, it is a bit different from much of what has come before it. Most other attempts to quantify managerial performances focused on the in-game decisions made. Individuals much smarter than myself have looked at very specific decisions managers make—such as sacrifice bunting, issuing intentional walks, attempting to steal, etc. These studies normally focus on how managers manage the game, but the people skills and basic management portions of the jobs are generally ignored. . . . There is a good reason for this focus of interest. None of those softer, people skills can be proven to exist solely by using statistical methods, thus the sabermetric research into these areas dies before it even begins. The existence of managerial impact on players is virtually impossible to prove by math alone, because numerous issues muddy the waters. It is necessary to separate the manager from the coaches, trainers, players' own motivations, random happenstance, aging, and God only knows what else.[7]

The "softer, people skills" to which Jaffe referred are, in effect, the personal touches with which a manager recognizes a player's essence and works with the parts of it that might have variable implications for the ballclub. Johnny Keane provides an example. When, in 1961, Keane took over the St. Louis job from Solly Hemus at midseason, Bob Gibson was a promising young pitcher with a raging need for trust. Under Hemus, Gibson had been belittled and jerked around, and he responded with a lack of confidence that exaggerated his inconsistency. Keane, however, immediately placed Gibson in the starting rotation and kept him there, even while the blazing, unpolished right-hander was leading the National League in walks. Instead of chiding Gibson for his wildness, as Hemus often did, Keane spoke to him about the things that were suddenly working for Sandy Koufax, the Dodger lefty whose career track roughly resembled Gibson's. "It was apparent to everyone," said Cardinal announcer Jack Buck, "that there was a major change in Gibson when Keane was appointed the Cardinal manager." [8] The relationship fed on itself. After Gibson had closed out the 1964 World Series with his third complete game, pitching on two days' rest and fighting through a pair of ninth-inning home runs, Keane, asked why he had stuck with his obviously flagging ace, replied, "I was committed to this fellow's heart." [9]

The manager who pointed Hank Aaron in the right direction was Ben Geraghty, an inconspicuous, plainspoken, wrinkly dressed, beer-friendly journeyman who presided over the Jacksonville, Florida, team on which Aaron, along with teammates Horace Garner and Felix Mantilla, integrated the Sally League in 1953. On the road in Georgia and South Carolina, the three black players remained on the bus when it stopped at the team hotel, whereupon they were carted to their accommodations in private homes on the other side of the tracks. Soon enough, Geraghty would show up to share beer and talk baseball with his accidental pioneers. On one occasion, the team was invited for dinner at Fort Benning, and as the white players proceeded into the dining area, their less welcome teammates were shown to the kitchen, where, moments later, their boss happily joined them. Geraghty was not a reformer, just a wise and caring minor-league manager.

"I guess Ben could sense that I was the type of kid who needed to be encouraged," Aaron wrote in his autobiography, *I Had a Hammer,* "because he was always telling me that I was going to make it big. He told some writers that I'd make people forget Jackie Robinson. I knew that was nonsense, but Ben's faith meant a lot to me." [10] The very next season, which Aaron spent in Milwaukee, was the last, until 1976, that he was not a big-league All-Star.

If Geraghty's support was instrumental in Aaron's coming-of-age, so was that of the more experienced Garner—whose veteranness was so roundly developed that the skipper counted on him to procure the beer for the long Sunday bus rides—and Jacksonville's burly white first baseman, Joe Andrews, who more than once that year was arrested for challenging fans who verbally abused the quiet teenager who would break Babe Ruth's career home run record. Of course, it's not unusual for the salutary contributions of a good manager and a good teammate to overlap. If they weren't made of much the same stuff, the latter would never become the former.

For that matter, a manager's effects, as Jaffe pointed out, can be difficult to distinguish from those of his coaching staff, as well. During the same SABR convention at which Birnbaum revealed his research on luck, Peter Bendix and Matt Gallagher introduced "The Leo Mazzone Effect," in which they demonstrated that the Atlanta Braves' wondrous pitching coach was more valuable to a ballclub than some of the highest-paid players in the sport. Another analyst, J. C. Bradbury, determined that pitchers, as a group, saw their earned run averages benefit by a hefty 0.64 on Mazzone's watch. Meanwhile, research from Max Marchi in *Baseball Prospectus* honed in on a manager's connection to his *catcher*, addressing his impact on the catcher's performance handling a pitching staff. Bobby Cox ranked at the top of the list, by a considerable margin over Joe Torre and Tommy Lasorda. (Of course, Cox, for the most part, had the advantage of Mazzone at his side.)

Marchi also ran an algorithm to examine the pairings of managers and pitching coaches. The result was that Cox saved fifty-three runs when Mazzone presided over his pitchers, and only two runs when others coached them.[11] When Jaffe examined the data, he surmised, "There is a word that can describe what is going on, and it is often a dirty word in sabermetrics: chemistry. It was not Cox, Mazzone, nor [GM John] Schuerholz—but how they all worked together."[12]

Generally, the input of a pitching or hitting coach is considered mechanical and strategic in nature, scarcely related to the sociology of the clubhouse. But coaches involve themselves as well in matters of a player's regimen, work ethic, confidence, preparation, and motivation. So can an encouraging peer. Help may be acquired, in fact, from a wide range of sources. Before Evan Longoria and psychologist Ken Ravizza worked together in Tampa Bay, they did the same at Long Beach State University, where Ravizza introduced both Longoria and his teammate Troy Tulowitzki to the advantages of slowing the game down through familiar, repeatable practices: things like the same unhurried walk to the batter's box, deliberate breathing, tightening of the batting gloves, or picking out a point of concentration on which to steady the gaze and gather one's thoughts. The lesson was about being in the moment; about releasing the last pitch and moving calmly, purposefully ahead to the next one. "The focus," Ravizza said, "is on things like controlling the controllable, playing one pitch at a time and how you actually do that." [13]

Ravizza's fundamental task was to equip his clients with the psychic structure to cope with the challenges of a demanding occupation. As he described it: "Giving them techniques to maintain confidence as they go through the grind of a season. Sharpening mental skills to deal with adversity. . . . More and more teams are looking at the mental aspects of player development."

Having benefited from Ravizza's concepts, Longoria found himself in a position to subsequently share them with teammates. In such a way, the baseball atmosphere—*any* atmosphere—is so full of influences that a ballclub would have to be tone-deaf to remain merely at their mercy. Whitey Herzog, understanding that, was in an uncommon position to manipulate the synergy of the St. Louis Cardinals when he served them as both manager and general manager for the 1981 and '82 seasons, and did so decisively. When Garry Templeton offended the sensibilities of both his manager and St. Louis itself, Herzog dug in and traded the twenty-five-year-old shortstop ("I hated to part with him") who, at twenty-three, had been the first player ever—not Pete Rose, not Mickey Mantle—to pile up 100 hits in a season from each side of the plate. Templeton's most notorious indiscretion had been grabbing his crotch as a gesture to the hometown fans, but Herzog was perhaps more disgusted by his young star's general lack of enthusiasm.[14]

"I don't have patience with players who don't work hard," wrote Herzog. "When I put a club together, I look for guys who aren't afraid to work, who don't bitch and moan and blame their troubles on somebody else—guys who can get along with each other and make the clubhouse a decent place. The writers call this 'chemistry,' but to me, it's just common sense."[15]

It worked out famously, of course, that Herzog was able to fetch and then sign Ozzie Smith in the Templeton deal. Needing speed, he also acquired outfielders Lonnie Smith from the Phillies and Willie McGee from the Yankees. The Cardinals beat the Milwaukee Brewers that year (1982) in the World Series.

When they regressed in 1983, it didn't take long for Herzog, who had surrendered the GM title but still lent considerable authority to the office, to again act boldly, this time trading star first baseman Keith Hernandez, a former MVP and batting champion and an annual Gold Glover. It was mid-June, and the return from the New York Mets, Neil Allen and Rick Ownbey, was inconsiderable. But they weren't the most compelling reasons for the swap.

> I've got two basic rules—be on time and hustle—and [Hernandez] was having trouble with both of them. A couple of the players came up to me and asked why Keith was loafing. I couldn't tell them. . . . His practice habits were atrocious. He'd come out for batting practice, then head back to the clubhouse to smoke cigarettes and do crossword puzzles. . . . It was getting to the point where I was fed up with him. A couple of my coaches even told me, "You'd better get rid of that guy. He's poisoning the whole ball club."[16]

While Hernandez marched on as a .300 hitter and one of the best-fielding first basemen the game has ever seen, critics took Herzog to task, calling the trade the worst he ever made. Herzog steadfastly disagreed, insisting that Hernandez would not have prospered in St. Louis as he did in New York—where he was not only an All-Star but also a teammate held in the highest esteem—and that, furthermore, he would have been the ruination of the Cardinals, who returned to the World Series in 1985 and 1987. In between, Hernandez won a Series ring with the Mets.

The case of Keith Hernandez remains especially provocative in light of the professionalism with which he is generally associated. It speaks to the complexity of the clubhouse cocktail. The fact is, a player's effect is substantially dependent upon the players in his proximity. On a highly charged, twenty-five-man roster, symbiosis is thoroughly entangled, fundamentally personal, and profoundly *subjective*. Whitey Herzog's reality, in the context of Hernandez, was nothing like that of Mets pitcher David Cone, in whose opinion "Keith was a leader on the Mets in the late 1980s in the same way Don Mattingly was on the Yankees. He didn't have to say anything, but everyone saw how he prepared for a game and then played it in the right way."

Cone was a thoughtful pitcher throwing to a Hall of Fame catcher (Gary Carter), all the while paying close attention to the first baseman he called Mex. Hernandez provided essential advice not only on situational strategy, but on how to approach certain batters, as well. As needed, he'd cheer, wheedle, or will his pitcher to the next out. "He'd get in my face, with that look and intensity, and whatever he was thinking was contagious," Cone said. "Sometimes, it was what he said; sometimes, it was that look he gave you; sometimes, it was just the way he swung the bat in the clubhouse preparing for the game. There was something about Mex. He had that intangible leadership quality that affected the entire team. After he left the Mets in the early '90s, I thought there was a big void in the Mets' clubhouse. In 1991, I switched from 44 to 17 so his presence would still be felt."[17]

According to the testimony of Hernandez himself, the differences in his St. Louis and New York personas were both perceived and actual. They were influenced by the people both above and next to him. They reflected the states of both his mind and his ballclubs. They were

predicated, as are every player's more mysterious contributions, on circumstances.

"Frank Cashen was the general manager of the Mets when I came to
New York from St. Louis," Hernandez explained in *Diamond Gems*. "He
would later say that he knew what kind of player I was but didn't know
if I was a leader. Neither did I. In St. Louis, I learned from Lou Brock,
who was our silent leader. Bob Gibson was our other leader, and he was
more inclined to get in your face. I was just trying to get my feet wet my
first few years with the Cards. And when [in 1979] I was the National
League's co-MVP with Willie Stargell, I didn't realize that I'd reached
that level where my teammates were looking up to me." Nor did Hernandez feel encouragement along those lines from Herzog. On the contrary,
he perceived, from Herzog's comments in the press, that the skipper
wasn't looking for leaders among the players because *he* was the leader
of the club.

By contrast, Cashen reached out to Hernandez and asked him to
assume the burden of dealing with the media, relieving the pressure on
young stars Darryl Strawberry and Dwight Gooden. "So," he recalled,
"as a veteran on a team of mostly young players, I immediately was
looked on to provide leadership. I grew into a verbal, emotional leader
as we evolved into a championship team."[18]

BY JAFFE'S BREAKTHROUGH CALCULATIONS, THE GAME'S GREATEST MANAGER, BY A SUB-
stantial piece, was Joe McCarthy, who guided the Yankees to seven world
championships in the 1930s and '40s. Marse Joe enjoyed a measure of
assistance from the likes of Babe Ruth, Lou Gehrig, Bill Dickey, Lefty
Gomez, Red Ruffing, Red Rolfe, Joe DiMaggio, and Phil Rizzuto, but
Jaffe's arithmetic told him that while the players most certainly made
the manager, as the old maxim tediously reminds us, there was an abun-
dance of data to demonstrate that it worked the other way, as well. "The
central theory of this book is that managers are primarily managers of
men, not of the game," Jaffe wrote,[19] and by *men*, he meant, specifically,

hitters and pitchers. Working with the Birnbaum Database, Jaffe evaluated a manager's impact by the statistical gains or deficits he oversaw from his players, sums derived from the differences between their actual production and the numbers those players were sabermetrically *expected* to deliver, according to the outcomes of surrounding seasons. Regarding McCarthy, the process (using a standard ratio of ten runs to one victory) revealed an extraordinary added-win value of 145. That, in light of total player ratings compiled by premier analyst Pete Palmer, is more than Ruth's, and more than Gehrig's and Mantle's combined.[20]

If you're looking for a rub, here's one: Ruth's and Gehrig's and Mantle's metrics don't include the kind of stuff for which McCarthy is receiving full credit—influencing players in an assisted, second-level, *environmental* fashion. Those fellows may or may not have contributed significantly in that capacity; but what is the chance, really, that the wisdom, counsel, and example of the great manager, gauged against that of the three great players, actually added up to 145–0? It simply isn't reasonable. In addition to the intuitive observation that great players are likely to have *some* favorable effect upon their teammates, Ruth and Gehrig happened to be great players who played on McCarthy's watch. McCarthy was a stickler for traditional ballplayer virtues and the critical mass of teamship they attained, producing in turn a singleness of purpose that would characterize his clubs. McCarthy's teams were reference material for the way the game is supposed to be played.

In that spirit, the first of his ten commandments was: "Nobody ever became a ballplayer by walking after a ball." Number seven: "Always run them out. You can never tell." Number eight: "Do not quit."[21] When a card table popped up in the Yankees' clubhouse, McCarthy overturned it. That sort of thing. Marse Joe expected his players to be shining citizens of the game, harder-sweating extensions of himself. And, to a famous extent, they were. When Yogi Berra first arrived in New York and neglected to run out a harmless ground ball with the appropriate fervor, it was DiMaggio who immediately approached him in the dugout, wondering what was the matter with the rookie's legs.

Self-policing was an inherent aspect of McCarthy's team culture, much as it was for the venerable Connie Mack, his much older contemporary. Branch Rickey described Mack as his "greatest friend in baseball," and regarding the tall gentleman's views on a player's accountability wrote, "He believed that no real discipline was obtained unless it was self-imposed and voluntary. Here was Mr. Mack's highest contribution to team morale. Every man was his own manager in his desire for knowledge and physical fitness. That was, and still is, the uncharted but everlasting influence of Mr. Mack's teachings. This is his immortality." [22]

Mack's legacy, Rickey was effectively saying, is the imperative that players advance team morale by their own initiative. They can do the same for team intelligence, team professionalism, and team energy. "This may sound surprising to those unfamiliar with baseball," wrote longtime third baseman Buddy Bell, "but in the big leagues, players learn more from each other than from their coaches." [23]

If fruitful, the lessons absorbed play out as indirect, second-level contributions from their source. Those, it bears repeating, are not cataloged or conspicuous, but rather concealed within the statistical dossiers of the players who've been gainfully influenced. And if the personal assistance were somehow, analytically, revealed, there would remain the virtual impossibility of isolating, comparing, scaling, and indexing—in general, *measuring*—its value.

To wit, DiMaggio might have earned himself some intangible points when he impressed upon Berra the advantages of running hard, but mightn't Bill Dickey, talking softly catcher to catcher, have imparted a similar lesson in some subtler way,[24] or Rizzuto's scrappy example have somehow accomplished the same effect? And what of the teammates who, in turn, might have gotten through to DiMaggio, Dickey, and Rizzuto? The fact is, McCarthy's rosters, by design, were chock-full of good actors; and so, for that matter, were the Major Leagues.

• • •

IN QUANTIFYING THE WIN VALUE OF McCARTHY AND OTHER MANAGERS, IT WAS NECESSARY for Jaffe to deviate from the metric of Win Shares (introduced by Bill James in 2001) and their prevalent adaptations, WAR (Wins Above Replacement, popularized by Fangraphs) and WARP (Wins Above Replacement Player, a function of *Baseball Prospectus*), none of which involves the kind of environmental intangibles that were central to the exploration of a manager's influence. A manager, of course, doesn't have his own on-base percentage or strikeout-to-walk ratio by which his performance can be assayed. Inherently, his bottom line can't be toted up without regard for his participation in the production of his players.

While Jaffe did a commendable job of validating this dynamic with numbers, the task is more troublesome when the principles are applied to the players themselves. When a ballplayer's season bears the fingerprints of a manager, there's typically only one possible match. But if that player has benefited from his association with teammates, the suspects number as many as twenty-four. Considering what it takes to reach the big leagues in the first place, it figures that most of the guys in the clubhouse bring some useful, infectious intangibles to the room. In that context, a player's relative level of teamship must be appraised through the device utilized by WAR and WARP—comparison WITH the standard of a neutral or replacement-level player. In a ballpark sort of way, it can be reckoned by what I'll call *WART:* Wins Above Replacement Teamship.

WART would not, could not, hold fast at a hard number, but rather would point nonspecifically to an approximate gauge of a player's intangible value. It's compiled anecdotally, with a tuned ear and keen appreciation.

Because of its countervailing nature, WART could not be stitched, like fielding and baserunning and perhaps even a smattering of small ball, into WAR or WARP. Then again, as a different strain of fruit, it needn't and shouldn't be. WAR submits a comprehensive statistical tabulation of a player's performance. It represents a significant proportion of the value he contributes to his ballclub. But not all of it. The rest remains more inscrutable, more elusive, more subjective.

Consequently, the player's whole value, his *performance-plus*, might be expressed as WAR + WART. As the dominant weight in that equation, WAR is a number. WART is not. Offering no empirical pretense, it's simply something: the uncalculated difference between the player he measures out to be and the player he actually *is*, in the grand scheme of winning games.

In lieu of an arithmetic expression, WART could, perhaps, be broadly denoted by the kind of label—minus, plus, or plus-plus, for instance— often used in scouting circles to describe the likes of speed and throwing arm. By acclamation, Derek Jeter would bring plus-plus WART to the table. Yadier Molina, the same, along with the likes of Chase Utley, Albert Pujols, and Michael Cuddyer. On the other hand, Manny Ramirez, an unhappy camper whom the Red Sox, in the throes of a furious pennant race, dealt away at the 2008 trading deadline in spite of his eleven straight All-Star selections and average of well over 100 RBIs in his eight Boston seasons,[25] would fall on the minus side. Alex Rodriguez is another whose full effect comes up short of his numbers; Joe Torre alluded to this in *The Yankee Years:* "I think when Alex came over he certainly changed just the feel of the club . . . you could see his focus was on individual stuff."[26] Other players—Brandon Phillips, for instance—are not so easily assessed, and strike at an essential fact of WART: Indistinct as it necessarily is, much is left to the eye of the critic.

And yet, for all of WART's ambiguity, a player's profile, lacking it, is simply missing something.

BECAUSE CATCHERS, LIKE MANAGERS, HAVE TRADITIONALLY BEEN CRITIQUED ACCORDING to the conspicuous flow-of-game functions that put them on the spot, Mike Piazza's defensive skills were generally taken to task. He didn't throw out many base-stealers. That phase of his performance, so easy to see and tally, was, in effect, the equivalent of a manager's efficiency rate in sacrifices, double-switches, pitching changes, and the like. However, just as Chris Jaffe's research revealed broader, more important ways in which a manager makes a difference, so have contemporary studies shed light on far more meaningful criteria with which to measure a catcher's contribution behind the plate.

Any of countless factors—calling pitches, framing pitches, encouraging pitchers, correcting pitchers, calming pitchers, knowing hitters, setting targets, captaining the defense—might impact the whole of a catcher's defensive package more than his percentage of throwing out base-stealers does. The underlying statistic for that kind of analysis is catcher's ERA (CERA), which, historically, has been dismissed by critics for its obvious flaws, starting with the relative quality of the pitchers the catchers catch. But that drawback can be surmounted by what analyst Craig Wright called "matched plate appearances," which couch a catcher's ERA in the context of those of other catchers who have caught the same pitchers in similar circumstances. In a playing log as long as Piazza's, that sort of examination provides a generous sample size.

"It is reasonable to estimate that in the career sample of matched plate appearances of Mike Piazza . . . ," wrote Wright, "through his work with the pitchers in stopping the hitters, . . . he prevented 344 base runners and helped pick up 265 more outs. And if we assume quite reasonably that his influence was approximately at that level for all the plate appearances that Piazza was behind the plate in his career, it becomes 758 base runners and 584 outs for his career. That's a lot of defensive value, and those positives are far, far more valuable than the negative of what was surrendered to the opposition's running game by his weak arm."[27]

A method comparable to matched plate appearances was used by another respected researcher, Tom Tango, who referred to it as With-Or-Without-You (WOWY). A *Baseball Prospectus* writer, Max Marchi, applied the WOWY principles to his 2012 study of catchers' effects on their pitching staffs, and his results paralleled Wright's in at least one salient respect. Piazza tied for third with Javy Lopez, behind only defensive stalwarts Tony Pena and Mike Scioscia, in total runs prevented.[28]

The two studies revealed no particular, observable, or secret skill in Piazza. He was simply shown to be very good at getting the most out of his pitchers. Other recent, more focused analyses have zeroed in on the art of framing pitches—that is, a catcher's talent for presenting a pitch to an umpire as a strike—and assigned comparative metrics for that contribution. The results show that, by framing alone, a catcher can generate an extra win or more per season, a significant value-added when considered against the background of WAR, by which the standard for an All-Star is four to five wins. (In recent years, the catchers most proficient at framing include the likes of Brian McCann, Russell Martin, Yadier Molina, Jose Molina, David Ross, and Ryan Hanigan.)[29] In the main, though, a catcher's capacity for getting the most out of his pitching staff remains largely social, something tantamount to good all-around managing. It's teamship a tad more recognizable than most.

"That catcher is way, way, way important," said Dusty Baker, who, while known as a hitters' manager,[30] doesn't sound like one on the subject of catchers. "That part of the game is big-time underrated. The catcher is my general on the field. His number-one job is to get the most out of that pitcher. The pitching coach is the defensive coordinator and the catcher is like the middle linebacker calling the plays. Guys like Charlie O'Brien, Paul Bako—guys whose numbers don't equate to much, but the way they control the game, or the tempo of the game—they're worth their weight in gold.

"Now, as a hitter you try to figure out who's in charge of this equation. When [Baker was batting and] Johnny Bench was catching and [an unimposing pitcher such as] Frank Pastore was on the mound, I was thinking with Johnny Bench because Frank Pastore wasn't really in the equation. Then when I had Tom Seaver on the mound and John Stearns catching in New York, then John Stearns isn't in the equation, Tom Seaver is. Then when Tom Seaver got traded to the Reds [and Bench was behind the plate], now I'm messed up, because I've got two guys there who know about game-calling."

Bench, as it happened, was whiling time away one afternoon in Baker's clubhouse at Great American Ball Park, discussing the working relationship of catchers and pitchers, when the topic brought him, in fact, to Pastore, who at the time of the story was a promising youngster emboldened by a temporarily winning record. On the evening in question, Bench gave the sign, Pastore shook him off, Bench gave the sign again, and Pastore shook him off once more, at which point Bench called time, marched to the mound, and instructed the willful pitcher, "Don't you *ever* shake me off again." The Hall of Famer had a similar experience with Gary Nolan, who, unlike Pastore, had earned the right to call at least some of his own pitches but tended to abuse the privilege. "A lot of times," recalled Bench, "he'd shake me off and I'd come back with the same sign because he just had a rocking-chair head. It wasn't my ego. If I had a guy who was trying to learn to pitch and started to think too much, I knew he'd be in trouble."

SEAVER, OF COURSE, WAS THE ANTITHESIS OF THAT TYPE, ESPECIALLY BY THE TIME HE arrived in Cincinnati with three Cy Young Awards under his belt. When Bench first visited Seaver on the mound, it was to ask whether he preferred the ball returned with a hard or soft throw. Seaver advised him to never come out there again.

"Guys like Seaver, they knew how to pitch.[31] But I still had to pace the game by cleaning the batter's box or somehow slowing the tempo down so he could rethink what he's doing. You go into the four corners for a minute and just give them time to take a deep breath. Catchers have to control pitchers psychologically."

That artful task varies from pitcher to pitcher. "There's three types of ids," Bench explained. "You've got the guy who you've got to tell who you are and what city you're in. There are other guys who have to really work on mechanics. And then there are guys who you've really got to stay on and pace him and control the game without him knowing it." Bench, for example, through his pitch calling and targets, would often make sure that certain hitters never got a strike to whack at. "I might pitch around two guys, and then you hear, well, so-and-so walked five batters. Yeah, so what? *I* walked four of them. Controlling the game was something we did."

While Bench, regardless of the intangibles, would still have been a state-of-the-art catcher and arguably the best all around that the game has known, his descendant in Cincinnati, Ryan Hanigan, undrafted and underwhelming out of Massachusetts, would quite possibly have not been a Major Leaguer without a handsome WART. "He carries around the brain of the ballclub in his duffel bag," is how Reds broadcaster Jeff Brantley has summed up Hanigan many times. As his teammates bounced about the Reds' clubhouse in various stages of banter and preparedness three hours before a particular night game, Hanigan sat at his locker reflecting on his complicated craft, all the while clutching a white notebook containing scouting reports on the Houston Astros.

"It boils down to being able to relate to each pitcher's different personality," said the ruddy New Englander, son of an FBI agent. "You can't approach everyone the same way. Different guys need to be pushed, different guys need to be helped along a little bit, different guys have different ways of getting to where they're comfortable and successful. When they're going well, what are the factors that allow them to have success? You've got to see where a guy's at, where his demeanor is, where his focus level is, his confidence, and react accordingly. There's some psychology to it. Everybody's got different buttons to push. I try to be that guy for them."

In Hanigan's view, the button-pushing is not incidental to his job; it's the first priority. If the pregame schedule calls for a hitters' meeting and a pitchers' meeting at the same time, he attends the latter. At those, his double-sided mission is to become as familiar as possible with the pitchers he catches and as familiar, also, with the strategies specific to the lineup they're about to face. The objective, on both counts, is twenty-seven outs of rapport. It remains for the pitchers to make the pitches, but, for that challenging task, Hanigan's hefty WART is at their disposal.

"Catcher is not the kind of position where you're seeking credit," he said, "but pitchers understand what we do. Being on the same page, getting into a rhythm depending on what the hitters are doing, is everything. That's what winning baseball games is: doing *that* as many times as you can. When things are clicking, keep it rolling. We're directing the pitchers, for the most part. If a pitcher wants to throw a pitch, that's fine, but at the same time the end-all is really understanding what the scouting report is, and we're the ones who go through that."

In these advanced days of baseball reconnaissance, scouting reports are not necessarily confined to the opposing team. Hanigan catalogs umpires, as well, seeking a working knowledge of their respective strike zones. This intelligence, however, is not put to the purpose of finagling strike calls, subtly maneuvering his catcher's mitt into the perimeter of the zone after the ball is received. Rather, Hanigan's aim is to make certain that he doesn't *lose* strikes by allowing the mitt to drift *out* of the zone. To give the ump a clearer and surely appreciated view, he also sets up in an unusually low catching stance.

"I don't think you're going to *work* the umpire necessarily," remarked the veteran whom Bill James alluded to as perhaps the most underrated player in baseball.[32] "I wouldn't put it that way. They're like the cops. You don't have any leverage. All you can do is put your point of view across in a nonconfrontational way. A lot of times they're pretty receptive to that. You're never going to sway them too much one way or the other, but you can definitely get on a page with them to where they're not going to fuck you. And that's all you can really ask for."

Having come to terms with the umpire's predilections, Hanigan will make certain that his battery mate is in the loop. At the same time, though, he will not allow the nuances of the strike zone to supersede the considerations of the pitcher. If a certain umpire is known to be generous in the upper reaches of the zone and the pitcher on duty is uncomfortable working there, Hangian won't ask him to. "You don't want to take your pitcher out of his game," he said.

When he asserts his wisdom with young pitchers, and does so in an agreeable, benevolent way, Hanigan, wittingly or not, is passing forward some of the methods he picked up in the minor leagues from the likes of periodic big-leaguer Corky Miller, whose manifest WARTness not only makes him an obvious managerial prospect but extended his playing career by several seasons. And when he defers to a sagacious pitcher on the order of Bronson Arroyo, Hanigan is, at the same time, honoring the guidance Arroyo embraced when he threw to Jason Varitek—the inspiration for James's exploration of "Catcher Pride Points"[33]—with the Boston Red Sox. For his part, Varitek had allowed himself to be informed by such astute pitchers as Pedro Martinez, Tim Wakefield, and Bret Saberhagen, and became a cagier catcher for the experience. It's a perpetual, edifying cycle.

"I really think a catcher can make a big difference, and the younger the player, the bigger the impression," said Arroyo, who requested Hanigan as his personal catcher in 2009 and subsequently stayed the course.[34] "I didn't know the American League when I got to Boston, and Varitek would talk about small things that I wouldn't have faith in doing otherwise: 'Listen, since the last time we played, Posada's starting to creep up on the plate two or three inches closer than he usually does because he's having trouble getting to the ball on the outer half. So, let's jam him here.' The less you know and the less experience you have against other hitters, you might not be sure how you want to approach getting them out. If you have a guy behind the plate who's telling you, 'I know you can beat Mark Teixeira on the inner half with two strikes, I've done it time and time again with different hitters,' you take his word, you believe it, you trust in him, and you go and do it."

In turn, Arroyo has shared his acquired savvy—many have called it *artistry*, and have noted that the wispy-thin, soft-tossing, angle-changing, ball-bending right-hander depends upon it more profoundly than any other pitcher in the game—with such younger teammates as Johnny Cueto and Mike Leake. Of course, the passing along of an idea doesn't necessarily make it a *good* idea, or even well received, but it stimulates a ballclub's exchange of information and extends, beyond the manager and coaches, its wellspring of influence. It sprinkles manager value around the roster.

In effect, that's what environmental intangibles amount to: Players reaching corners of the clubhouse that the manager can't. Diligent catchers do it specifically. Veteran leaders do it broadly. Good teammates do it gratuitously. And good teams prosper from all of the above.

Perhaps there's no better example than the famously brainy Baltimore teams managed by Earl Weaver. It was as though, from Opening Day to the end of September, Weaver and his strong-minded men were in a perpetual state of coming to an understanding. "Weaver's teams kept improving all season long," wrote Jaffe. "You cannot produce a similarly impressive table for any other manager."[35]

All the while, the Orioles consistently outperformed their sabermetric expectations. While mainstream modern analysis, for lack of a better explanation, commonly attributes such overachievement to good fortune, Jaffe's research assigned at least some of it—sometimes a lot— to the manager. "One season's results . . . tell you more about luck and random happenstance, but over a period of time the signal to noise ratio improves dramatically," he pointed out in an article for *Hardball Times*. "For example, it turns out that Earl Weaver's teams were lucky pretty much every year he was in Baltimore. Funny how that works."[36]

Then again, Weaver's teams were Brooks Robinson's teams, Frank Robinson's teams, Jim Palmer's teams, Don Baylor's teams, Davey Johnson's teams, Eddie Murray's teams, Rick Dempsey's teams, Cal Ripken's teams. They were teams with model players, winning pitchers, sharp catchers, and various managers across the field, all feeding off the Hall of Famer in the dugout. They were skilled, symbiotic, make-each-other-better teams with plenty of gestalt and heavy concentrations of monster WART.

Funny how *that* works, as well.

ELEVEN

ORGANIZATION OF THE YEAR

TOWARD THE END OF MARCH, ABOUT A WEEK BEFORE THE 2012 REGULAR SEASON BEGAN, the Reds were playing an exhibition game one afternoon at the complex of the Milwaukee Brewers while their Triple-A and Double-A affiliates stayed home in Goodyear and divided up for informal scrimmages. Maximizing his practice time, Joey Votto doubled up as a designated hitter in both of the intrasquad affairs, shuttling between the practice fields to get his rips in.

It was vintage Votto, the earnest first baseman intent on redefining Major-League preparation. Informed by his copious personalized scouting, he comes to bat with a plan for every conceivable pitcher, count, or circumstance. He doesn't talk much to teammates because he doesn't want to use up the emotional energy required for any workday, game or not. Soaking himself in the science of readiness, Votto goes so far as to study the example of a *pitcher,* Roy Halladay. His is a full-time, full-tilt mission to be the best player in the game, and has been, it seems, since he was a kid. When he was sixteen, the elite amateur team he played on supplied batting gloves and the coach became suspicious when, several times a week, Votto would request a new pair. Finally, he told Joey he could have a fresh set only if he returned the old one. A day or so later, Votto handed the coach two bloodied gloves with holes in the palms. The teenager was so determined to play pro ball, and so certain that he would, that he refused to use a metal bat, even as college recruiters turned out in number and requested that he do so.[1] After winning the MVP award in 2010, Votto still considered himself a work in progress, a fellow on his way to bigger things. Taking seriously—as he takes everything (in spite of my wife's repeated suggestions that he lighten up a little)—the advice and example of Albert Pujols, with whom he shared an agent (Dan Lozano), he hunkered down defensively in 2011 and carried home his first Gold Glove Award. He also scored 101 runs, drove in 103, and led the National League in doubles, walks, and on-base percentage.

By that time, plenty of influential people were floating Votto as the National League's best player, and Walt Jocketty had no objections. Jocketty, however, was more impressed by the personal forces that fed the Canadian's talent. Those forces—a raging ambition supported strategically by a gifted, dedicated, untiring intellect—represented a powerhouse combination. Votto, it seemed, could *think* his way to 300, and let his state-of-the-art swing take over from there. Some of his most distinct, fundamental assets were not only sustainable, but uncommonly nourishing. In terms of discipline and drive, Jocketty compared his solemn star to the two players who, to the GM, had always embodied those qualities: Pujols and Mark McGwire. It wasn't unusual for Votto to seek out Jocketty with questions about Pujols's habits and approach. All things considered, Votto—an unimpeachable citizen and model employee who, before leaving the clubhouse after virtually every game, will make a point of asking Reds publicity director Rob Butcher if he's needed for any interviews[2]—was the rare sort of low-risk, little-worry superstar whom a small-market club might, under the right confluence of conditions, dare to heavily invest in, long-term.

In Cincinnati, the conditions clamored for proactivity. After the division title of 2010, Jocketty had perhaps trusted excessively in the culture he'd created. Perhaps he undervalued the teamship contributions of Orlando Cabrera and thought, mistakenly, that they could be approximated by Edgar Renteria. Perhaps, for all the raising of consciousness the organization had accomplished, he lost sight of the essential, propitiously fitting collection of *talent*—a chemistry of *physical* assets—that a winning roster requires. Perhaps the pieces he needed simply weren't available at a price he could pay. At any rate, his winter acquisitions for the 2011 season amounted to the likes of Fred Lewis, Jeremy Hermida, Dontrelle Willis, and Brian Barton, none of whom altered the landscape in the NL Central. He placed too much on the dicey, aging shoulders of Scott Rolen. He surrounded Votto with too little. He overshot on Edinson Volquez. His pitching staff, aside from Bronson Arroyo, had been a hopeful assortment of wings and prayers, and Arroyo was weakened by mononucleosis. He didn't provide Baker with a compelling alternative to Drew Stubbs as the leadoff hitter. He didn't take advantage of the rich farm system that the Reds had developed. He didn't keep up with the Brewers or Cardinals.

And now, with the approach of 2012, daylight was fading. Jay Bruce had signed a six-year contract the year before, Johnny Cueto had hopped on for four more years at around the same time, and the young pitching staff as a whole was on the rise; but Votto was two years from free agency, and Brandon Phillips only one. Time was of the essence. With the blessing of owner Bob Castellini, Jocketty went to work.

In mid-December, instructed by his passivity of the previous season and recognizing that even in 2010 the Reds had been overmatched against teams with ace pitching at the top of the rotation, he traded Volquez and three of the Reds' top prospects (Yonder Alonso, Yasmani Grandal, and Brad Boxberger) to San Diego for the Padres' youthful workhorse, Mat Latos. A week later, understanding that the free-agency departure of Francisco Cordero had left the bullpen a little short, he traded three more promising players (Travis Wood, Dave Sappelt, and Ronald Torreyes) to the Cubs for left-handed stopper Sean Marshall.

In mid-January, he brought in former Phillies closer Ryan Madson as a free agent. In early February, he signed Ryan Ludwick as a good egg and much-needed power bat in the outfield. On the first day of April, he swapped Rolen's ostensible backup at third base, home-run-hitting Juan Francisco, to the Braves for young reliever J. J. Hoover. By that point, the bullpen had become a theme, and the emphasis on it was hardly co-incidental. On the contrary, it was part of Cincinnati's plan to develop a no-holes pitching staff to work arm-and-glove with the same kind of de-fense. The emphasis on pitching was so thorough that the Reds created a position for a minor-league *catching* coordinator, and turned it over to Rick Sweet, their highly successful manager at the Triple-A level.[3]

And yet, all of that, it turned out, was but a prelude to the head-spinning announcement concerning the twenty-eight-year-old fixture batting third in the Cincinnati order. For his part, Votto was taken aback by the Reds' unexpected offer, which, technically, was an extension onto the two years for which he was already signed. A *ten-year* extension. For *$225 million*.

When, at the age of eighteen, he had signed his first contract with the Reds for less than the slot value placed on his second-round position in the draft, Votto's soft bargaining had resulted in a hard time given him by his coach back home. Votto was embarrassed, and vowed to make up the shortfall, which was about $300,000. This deal, obviously, took care of that. It was his deep desire, also, to become the highest-paid Canadian player, and this took care of that, too. In fact, it made him his country's highest-paid *athlete*. The money impressed him. But the *term* of the con-tract floored him: the longest in the game's history. Votto would be forty when the agreement expired, and that was without the option year. His thirties were already paid for, and they were still a year and half away.

The day after Lozano passed along Cincinnati's bold overture, the handsome slugger walked up to Jocketty at the Reds' training facility, extended his hand, and said, "Really?"[4] It was a greeting of apprecia-tion, not acceptance—Votto was sincerely moved by the Reds' outra-geous commitment—but the acceptance would follow in a matter of days, after he had talked to Castellini and Rolen and his mother and the old coach who had given him what for ten years earlier. Once the deal was done, Votto approached Hal McCoy, the longtime Reds beat writer for the *Dayton Daily News,* and said, according to McCoy, "Hal, you've seen all the greats—Johnny Bench, Pete Rose, Tony Perez, Barry Larkin, Frank Robinson. . . . Let me know if I ever get out of line."[5]

So startling was the contract that, before the signing day was over, critics around the country were chiming in about its game-changing potential. "This deal," wrote Dave Cameron of *Fangraphs,* "is going to have lasting repercussions on the sport. Not only does it suggest that the Reds are going to remain competitive in the NL Central going forward, but it also resets the price expectations for every pre-free-agent player in the sport."[6] And yet, when Buster Olney queried Major-League scouts and executives for their takes, he found mostly cynicism.[7]

"It is nuts," one said.

"What was their alternative?" countered another. "If he were to leave, it would crush the franchise."

"This is absolute insanity," declared a third.

The apprehension circulated even in Cincinnati, which knew, all too well, the perils of a modestly funded franchise with a debilitating indebtedness to a lavishly paid player. The nine-year, $116 million investment in Ken Griffey, Jr., which had all the markings of a premium value at the time, had coincided with the club's miseries over the first decade of the century.[8] In the press conference announcing the Votto transaction, on Opening Day eve, Castellini spoke directly to that skepticism.

"What we are doing will not be to the financial detriment to our team in the future," the owner assured the reporters. ". . . Make no mistake, we understand we need more than Joey. . . . The team and franchise has the capability and capacity of meeting its financial challenges even as a small-market team. Is it risky? No doubt. That's the environment we live in."[9]

Two weeks later, to less hullaballoo but a comparable level of unlikelihood, the Reds wrapped up Phillips for another six years at $72.5 million.

• • •

AS UNCHARACTERISTICALLY AUDACIOUS AS THEY WERE IN RATCHETING UP THEIR ROSTER, the Reds, even with Votto and Phillips in the fold, managed to keep their payroll in its familiar ballpark. According to the tables compiled by *USA Today,* the obligations taken on for 2012 bumped it only from $75 million to $82 million. Both figures ranked tenth in the National League. This was in dramatic contrast, for instance, to the team that would visit Great American on Opening Day.

The Miami Marlins, feeling flush with the completion of $515 million Marlins Park and eager to fill it, had swum with the sharks in the off-season. First, they pledged four years and $10 million to the game's most colorful manager, pulling off a creative trade to bring in Ozzie Guillen from the Chicago White Sox. Then, filling in around their presiding star, former batting champion Hanley Ramirez, they committed $191 million to the signing of three high-profile free agents: reliever Heath Bell, starting pitcher Mark Buehrle, and former Mets shortstop Jose Reyes, whose celebrated arrival would nudge Ramirez over to third base. For 2012, the Marlins' player budget more than doubled, from $57 million in 2011 to $118 million; from thirteenth in the league to second, behind the Phillies.

The move of Ramirez to third was a matter of some concern, insofar as his teamship had never kept pace with his talent. In 2010, manager Fredi Gonzalez had yanked him from a game for jogging after a ball that he'd booted, his apparent lack of effort enabling two runs to score—this, it should be noted, after he had fouled a pitch off his ankle. In 2011, manager Jack McKeon benched him for being late to a meeting.[10] Against that background, some wondered how receptive Ramirez would be to a position switch that amounted to a defensive demotion.

Publicly, as it turned out, there was little complaint on the player's part. In the bottom of the ninth inning of the rubber game of the opening series, however, there was this: The game was tied, with one out, when Cincinnati's Drew Stubbs knocked a high-bouncing ball toward third. Ramirez immediately started forward, a false move that prevented him from making the play. Ryan Hanigan followed with a single, and when Stubbs sprinted to third, the throw eluded Ramirez. Heath Bell, the pitcher, hustled over to pick up the ball before it rolled into the photo well and allowed Stubbs to score. Scott Rolen, pinch-hitting, then struck a hard grounder to Ramirez's right. He stopped it but, not having properly positioned his feet, was unable to field it cleanly and prevent Stubbs from rushing home with the winning run. Ramirez had been charged with no errors in the inning, but he had failed to make three pressing plays that decided the game's outcome.

And so it would go for the Marlins. Their gaudy reconfiguration, which projected statistically to eighty-eight wins,[11] simply didn't work. By the end of July, Miami was fourteen and a half games out of first place and Ramirez had been traded to the Dodgers. Holdovers Omar Infante, Anibal Sanchez, and Gaby Sanchez were also gone by the trading deadline. When the disastrous season ended, Bell was dealt to Arizona. Shortly thereafter, Reyes and Buehrle were sent to Toronto.

Meanwhile, the Reds' third baseman, steeped in the nuances of the position and staggered by seventeen hard years of playing it, was, in the context of Ramirez, a fellow of an entirely different ilk. Rolen no longer commanded the kind of salary and attention that Ramirez had cut out for himself, but respect within the ballclub was another matter. The Reds were still counting on him to lead by presence and even bat cleanup. By the middle of May, however, when he was hitting .174 and, to no one's surprise, went on the disabled list yet again with shoulder pain, it was evident that too much had been asked of him.

Rolen's replacement was Todd Frazier, a spirited rookie from New Jersey and former hero of the Little League World Series champs representing Toms River.[12] Back then, Frazier was a freckled, 105-pound leadoff man who started the title game against Japan with a home run and ended it on the mound. He was also the quarterback of a U.S. champion Pop Warner football team, winner of the NFL Punt, Pass & Kick competition, and later, at Toms River South High School, a fearless six-foot-three center on the basketball squad. The Reds made Frazier a first-round draft choice out of Rutgers, and his minor-league managers had subsequently attributed any manner of virtue and victory to his leadership, enthusiasm, work ethic, and periodic hot streaks with the bat. In Cincinnati, he was quick to gain the approval of his teammates, as well, and they happily went along when he led them in song and dance before important ballgames.

On the first night of a series in New York against the Mets, Frazier ripped two home runs. A week later, at home, he beat the Braves with a ninth-inning walkoff shot. After the obligatory on-field, pie-in-the-face interview, teammates chanted his name in the clubhouse. Around that time, Cincinnati happened to put together a six-game winning streak, then another one three weeks later, sweeping the Indians and Mets in mid-June to open up a four-game division lead over Pittsburgh, with the Cardinals closely following. Having missed the sort of jocular, loosen-up personality that Cabrera gave them in 2010, the Reds were getting rejuvenation from a good-time rookie.

They were taking heart, also, from a tightly constructed pitching staff led by Johnny Cueto, whose sweep-completing victory over New York extended his record to 8–3 and shrank his earned run average to 2.38. Cueto had doggedly established himself among the top rank of National League starters, and suddenly, with Latos on board and Arroyo regaining his old form, the Cincinnati rotation, as a whole, had clambered into the upper reaches. None of the five starters had missed an assignment—Arroyo, a thirteen-year-veteran, had never missed one *in his life*—and the starters were well supported by a deepened bullpen, led by the lightning left-hander, Aroldis Chapman.

The original winter plan had been for Chapman to occupy a starting spot, but that was dashed by spring-training injuries to relievers Nick Masset, Bill Bray, and the free-agent closer, Madson, who, in spite of the considerable expenditure, would never make an appearance for Cincinnati. Chapman assumed the setup role he had previously occupied, but when he established a club record by not allowing a run in his first twenty-four appearances—for that matter, rarely allowing contact—he was promoted, inevitably, to closer. For the most part, he fared spectacularly, even historically, well, striking out nearly two batters per inning with a frightening fastball that often exceeded 100 miles an hour. After he hit a wall in June, giving up deciding home runs in consecutive outings against Cleveland and Minnesota, the normally stolid Cuban celebrated a save against the Brewers by turning two somersaults as he came off the mound. For Chapman, adventure was always close at hand, though often far from the playing field. There were traffic violations, a bizarre incident involving an exotic dancer who was tied up and allegedly robbed in Chapman's hotel room, and a *more* bizarre incident in which he was sued by a Cuban American who attributed his imprisonment to false statements from the flamethrower. Baker, at least, could advise him on the issue of somersaults, and did.

His questionable gymnastics notwithstanding, Chapman was voted onto the National League All-Star team by the players. Jay Bruce was chosen by the coaches, and Votto, not surprisingly—he led all of baseball in OPS by more than fifty points—was a fan selection. The Reds and others *were* quite surprised, however, when old nemesis Tony La Russa, manager of the NL side, passed over Phillips and Cueto, whose ERA was now down to 2.26, when filling out his bench and pitching staff. Those two, of course, were central figures in the infamous brawl between the Reds and Cardinals two years earlier.[13]

At the break, the Reds, in spite of sweeping the Padres in San Diego to end the season's unofficial first half, had fallen a game behind the sizzling Pittsburgh Pirates, although they still led St. Louis by a game and a half. The second half started with a home series against the Cardinals, which, of course, implied drama. This time, though—this *year*, now that it had some traction—the arrangement of the set simply wasn't the same. No one had forgotten that the Redbirds were the defending world champions, or that there was something special in their DNA, but with La Russa retired and Pujols in the American League, the cloak of the underdog had been removed from Cincinnati's shoulders. What's more, there was a rapidly escalating point of view that, in the psychologically relevant matter of the league's premier figure, Pujols had already been succeeded.

"Joey Votto," stated Jonah Keri at one particular juncture in June, when the Reds began to have their way, "staked his claim as the best player in the world."[14]

Sabermetricians were deeply impressed with Votto's relentless eye and the soaring on-base percentages it produced, but his profile as a hitter far exceeded just that. His power involved not just home runs yanked to right, but extra-base blows of all types, to all fields, a good many of them delivered with his hands choked up two inches from the knob of the bat to protect the plate with two strikes. Votto was the uncommon slugger perfectly pleased with a well-executed single, the unusual lefty who waited eagerly for a southpaw's *curveball*. What separated him from other leaders in the field, and made him so fascinating to the correspondents, was his holistic approach to hitting, from fitness to cage work, diet to swing, video to circumstance, theory to practice.

While gushing over Votto on his baseball blog, David Schoenfield called attention to the remarkable nature of the discerning Red's OPS+, a statistic that recasts a player's OPS in the context of his league and ballpark. That brought Ted Williams, considered by many to be the greatest pure hitter of all time, into the discussion. "I may look silly for saying this," Schoenfield wrote, "but that's kind of who Votto is right now: Ted Williams."[15]

It's perhaps no coincidence that Votto, not unlike Mike Piazza, grew up reading and memorizing Williams's famous book, *The Science of Hitting.* By his sixth big-league season, it seemed that he might be ready to write his own. He was certainly not lacking concepts and guiding ideas, such as "reframing the challenge," as he put it to Buster Olney. "I've stopped caring about runs and RBIs," he said, sounding not much different from a contemporary, calculating analyst. "I care more about how high a percentage of productive at-bats I can have, how consistently tough and competitive I can be for the opposing pitcher. . . . If you can find a way to frame the fight to be patient as a challenge in and of itself, that can be more satisfying than catching a ball the right way and shooting it through the gap or out of the ballpark."

As might be expected, Votto's meticulous study of video and scouting reports amounts to more than a simple absorption of data. He uses it as an X-ray of a pitcher's head, examining not just velocity and movement but patterns, tendencies, and perhaps most important, intended locations. On the bench, watching other hitters, Votto calls out pitch sequences with uncanny accuracy. Carrying that knowledge to the plate, he changes his approach according to the balls and strikes on the board, all of it under the calculated assumption that the pitcher does, too. As the count progresses, he adjusts not only his strategy, but also his expectations.

This learnedness is an object of considerable admiration to the players around him. But even so, the particulars are not easily transferred. "Votto could be a great hitting resource for his teammates," observed Olney, "but it's almost as if his language is a personalized Latin, something that others can't understand. . . .

"There are many ways to define how great a hitter Votto is. . . . For the SABR set, there's this: Using the advanced metric Adjusted OPS-plus . . . Votto rates as the offensive equal of Hank Aaron and Joe DiMaggio and is just a tick better than Frank Robinson. But maybe the best way to describe Votto is that he's baseball's most cerebral hitter, the Einstein of the batter's box." [16]

For all his private focus and detached intellectualism, the Reds' franchise player is not insensitive to the value of reaching out. At one juncture during Frazier's rookie year, on an evening when the game was proceeding without them, Votto plopped down next to the young third baseman and apologized for not having taken the time to get to know him better. The frank visit continued at length, eventually prompting Frazier to say, "Joe, since we're speaking the truth here, you're a little different. But I respect you ten times more for coming up and talking to me." [17]

Gradually and purposefully, though seldom loudly, Votto raised his mode of influence from tacit to vocal. His dugout conversations would often involve his buddy, Jay Bruce, and follow their plate appearances. Occasionally, he delivered his message on the field. In the tenth inning of one midseason game in 2012, for example, after he doubled and Bruce walked, the former MVP observed that Bruce was not being held at first base and implored him to extend his leadoff in the interest of preventing a double play.

Meanwhile, his methods and makeup remain on display to teammates and other hitters, just as theirs are to him. Votto considers great hitters, especially, to be invaluable resources, through observation and dialogue. His mantra—never give away an at-bat—derives not only from some consuming motivation deep within, but also from discussions with Pujols and Pete Rose. Pujols spoke to him once about entering every plate appearance as though it were the last of his career, and Votto has carried that to the extreme: He often steps out of the batter's box and asks himself if this might be the last *pitch* he ever sees. It reinforces his extraordinary readiness.[18] Rose's contribution occurred early in Votto's career when the Canadian was standing in the on-deck circle at Great American Ball Park. From his box seat, Rose engaged him, having recognized a kindred spirit at the plate.

"Pete kept an eye on me," said Votto, who would soon begin exchanging text messages with Rose on the subject of hitting, "and the one piece of advice he gave me was, 'When you get the second hit, get the third hit. And when you get the third hit, get the fourth hit. And when you get the fourth hit, get the fifth hit.' That really stuck with me, because it's a genuine challenge when you're tired, or you're sick, or the score is mismatched, or you're facing a tough pitcher, or you're not in a good mood that day. . . . So when I have that at-bat when the score is 10-0, yeah, I usually check in with myself and make sure I'm in a prime place to hit and I'm ready to go and I'm not about to give away this at-bat."[19]

In that respect, Votto's principal hitting model was Barry Bonds, a recognition of Bonds's patience, selectivity, and singular talent for taking advantage of the rare pitch that strayed into his wheelhouse. Joe Morgan was also famous for his plate discipline, and Votto has capitalized on Morgan's presence as a front-office operative for the Reds. An avid basketball fan, he has picked up on Kobe Bryant's intensity, relentlessness, and disdain for excuses. He carries on a running conversation with Canadian-raised point guard Steve Nash. Knowing that Jonny Gomes was a former Tampa Bay Ray, he cross-examined his teammate about Carl Crawford's work ethic and daily regimen.[20] He understands, almost as well as he understands pitchers, that teammates and athletes can make each other better.

Out of the All-Star break, and out of character, Votto went hitless in the first two games of the St. Louis series, both of which were won suspensefully by Cincinnati. Failure at the plate was always vexing to Votto, but this time his concern ran a little deeper. He had felt some irregularity in his left knee since sliding into third base in San Francisco on June 29, and hadn't delivered a home run since then. The Reds had suggested an MRI, but the steely player waved that off. Now, though, having found himself unable to execute the game plans he so assiduously charted, he was rethinking the situation. Nevertheless, Votto was in the lineup for the Sunday evening finale against the Cardinals—he toughed out a single and double—and the night went well for Cincinnati, evolving, in fact, as a subtle ode to Dusty Baker.

The stubborn Reds manager, choosing, often in contradistinction to the prevailing sabermetric wisdom, to be informed by an intuition honed from all that he had observed and experienced, was an object of epidemic second-guessing. On this occasion, the daily critics protested his decision to start the brittle Rolen, who had come off the disabled list in June, for a second straight game. Rolen would deliver a tie-breaking, two-run single in the eighth inning. To many, it seemed inadvisable, also, that Baker should insert Chris Heisey in center field. Heisey went three for four. To most, it seemed downright foolish that he let Bailey, whose career had suffered from a history of sudden self-destruction, bat for himself in the bottom of the seventh inning of a 2-2 game. Bailey singled.

When Matt Holliday and Carlos Beltran started the St. Louis eighth with base hits, Baker stuck with Bailey, who struck out Lance Berkman, then stayed in to face Yadier Molina, who had already homered. Molina flew out. David Freese grounded out. In the bottom of the eighth, Rolen put Cincinnati in position for a stirring sweep. Chapman struck out the side in the ninth. The Reds, winners of six in a row, were back in first place, all by themselves.

On such a triumphant occasion for the franchise in general and its embattled manager in particular, there was, however, one unfortunate caveat. Joey Votto wouldn't play again for more than seven weeks. The belated MRI revealed a torn meniscus that would require immediate surgery.

THE DISABLING OF VOTTO COST THE REDS MORE THAN JUST THEIR BEST HITTER. Jocketty's roster reconstruction had placed a low priority on handedness, leaving Votto and Bruce as the only lefty swingers in the lineup. Two days later, when Bruce got a day off against Arizona's Trevor Bauer, Cincinnati became the first team since 2005 to start nine right-handed batters against a right-handed pitcher. Cueto and four relievers cobbled a shutout—Chapman's save left him with an unthinkable twenty-three strikeouts over a stretch of nine and a third innings (this following the rough patch, during which many of Baker's critics clamored for Chapman to be stripped of his role)—but the Reds could manage only a split of the series. Their division lead was reduced to half a game over Pittsburgh, with the Cardinals trailing by five.

With Rolen back at third base, Frazier was seeing considerable time at first in Votto's stead. It was with this configuration that the Reds, to the astonishment of most, proceeded, after the final Arizona victory, to win nine more in a row. After a loss to Edinson Volquez and the Padres, they clicked off another five straight. Ludwick, Phillips, Frazier, and Rolen—playing probably more than he should have—all stepped up significantly. The starting pitchers, pushing each other with their conditioning and results, rolled on without missing a single turn. Teeming with teamship, Baker's men won eleven straight against division opponents; won *twenty-two of twenty-five games* all together, sixteen of nineteen without their MVP.

When the unlikely rally finally wound down with a victory over Pittsburgh on August 4—the winning run that night was scored when Rolen clubbed a ball off the center-field wall and slid headfirst into third base with a triple, then came home on a chopper to the mound—Cincinnati led St. Louis by a healthy eight games (the fading Pirates were actually still in second place) with a run differential of seventy-six. The Cardinals' spread was 107, the largest in the major leagues. The Reds were maxing out.

Votto was on track to return to the lineup on August 14, but that plan was dashed when he suffered a setback a couple of days before and underwent follow-up surgery for floating bone chips. The club gritted through an arduous stretch of thirty-four games in thirty-four days from late July to late August, its lead holding firm. Frazier reached base in twenty-two consecutive outings. Ludwick, with an inspired OPS of 1.051 in Votto's absence, laid claim to the cleanup spot. Cueto was leading the league in ERA. Chapman closed out a tight win with a 103-mile-an-hour missile and saved another ten days later by fanning Chase Utley at 102. It was the first season since the Big Red Machine tore up the sport in 1976 that a Cincinnati team won its eightieth game in August.

By the time Baker could once again write his best player into the batting order, it was September fifth and the Reds were twenty-nine games over 500, eight and a half ahead of the Cardinals. When Votto went on the DL, they had stood twelve over and a single game in front. The crisis had been routed, plausibility defied. A week later, as if to prove they could win even *with* their main man, they hit season highs of thirty over and eleven and a half in front. The organization was indisputably back.

Ludwick's contribution entailed more than his twenty-six home runs and eighty RBIs in fewer than 500 at-bats. He and reliever Sam LeCure (whose mustache, named Cornelius, my daughter followed on Twitter) were the fraternal forces behind the Cup, a token incentive to win whatever series happened to be at hand.[21] The gimmick originated when, playing the Cleveland Indians in June for the Ohio Cup, the Reds won three games in Cincinnati but couldn't take one more in Cleveland to carry home the spoils. Irritated by that, the players conjured an imaginary, generic version of the Cup and played every opponent for it (without the opponent's knowledge, of course) until catcher Devin Mesoraco wandered into an antique shop in Bellevue, Kentucky, and spotted just the right ticket for fifty bucks. The Windy City Cup, or Cheesesteak Cup, or whatever it needed to be for the series in question, would occupy a prominent place in the clubhouse until two of three games had been won or lost. Ludwick and LeCure, as it happened, were also leading figures in a hearty in-house brotherhood, if that's the proper term for a band of coworkers who referred to each other using the various forms of male sibling—brother, half brother, stepbrother, brother-in-law, big brother, little brother, soul brother, and so on, with the emphasis, quite loudly, always on the *brother*. In any event, the family implications, however jocular, seemed just about right for a team managed by a champion of the human connection.[22]

Dusty Baker came honestly by his devotion to baseball's interpersonal side. He was schooled in the ways of the game not only by Aaron, his Atlanta teammate and mentor, but also by opposing luminaries whom he would visit on the road: Willie Mays and Bobby Bonds in San Francisco, Ernie Banks in Chicago, Willie Stargell in Pittsburgh, Joe Morgan and Pete Rose in Cincinnati. If, as a manager, he seemed at times excessively patient with struggling players, it was in part because Tommy Lasorda was that way with him when he labored through his first year in Los Angeles. If he seemed stubbornly loyal to the methods of a previous generation, perhaps it was because they'd served him with more victories than any of his contemporary skippers, with the exception of Detroit's Jim Leyland.

Among Baker's credits, his teams had a history of playing well in September. When that point approached in 2012, Arroyo wondered aloud how his manager, whose two-year contract was set to expire after the season, might be allowed to get away from Cincinnati. "It's weird, man, that he hasn't been extended yet, because this guy is so good," the funky pitcher told *USA Today*. "He may be [sixty-three], but he's just as hip as a thirty-year-old. People want to discount those types of things, but for the same reason he can go out to a jazz club and hang out after a game and mix it up with people, is the same reason he's close to the ballplayers. There's no wall with him."[23]

As the month progressed, however, the contract became a secondary concern for Baker. He wasn't feeling particularly well on the evening of September 18 when, in Chicago, he notched his three-thousandth win as a manager. The next day, noting an irregular heartbeat, he left Wrigley Field before the game started and checked into a hospital. Two days later, the sweep of the Cubs complete, he was in the process of being released when he suffered what was described as a ministroke. Baker stayed in Chicago while the Reds returned home and, behind Latos, clinched the NL Central by shutting out the Dodgers. A week later, he was watching on television when Homer Bailey, commanding the game with control, confidence, and a cooperative catcher (Ryan Hanigan), threw a no-hitter in Pittsburgh, Cincinnati's first in twenty-four years.[24]

It wasn't until the regular season's final three-game set against the Cardinals that the Reds' manager was back in the dugout with the team he had so thoughtfully nurtured. By winning two of the three, St. Louis earned itself a place in the playoffs as the National League's second wild-card. By losing two, Cincinnati finished with ninety-seven victories, one fewer than the Washington Nationals, who had the most in all of baseball.

YOU COULD SAY THAT THE SAN FRANCISCO GIANTS HAD A LOT TO DO WITH WHAT THE REDS had become. Even after Jocketty's retooling and the division title in 2010—certainly, painfully, in 2011—it was obvious that, whether in the regular season or postseason, the Reds were no match for teams like the

Phillies (Halladay, Lee, Hamels, Oswalt) and Giants (Lincecum, Cain, Vogelsong, Bumgarner) that could lay multiple aces on the table. San Francisco, of course, had won the 2010 World Series with bottomless pitching, and had designs on doing the same in 2012, opening the play-offs with a pair of home games against the Reds. But Cincinnati's trade for Mat Latos had shifted the turf by a shiver. The maturity of Homer Bailey had narrowed the gap a bit further. And the rise of Johnny Cueto had signaled a whole new ballgame.

Having hit the big leagues at the age of twenty-two as an emotional, bantam-sized, bullet-throwing, inconsistent ace-in-waiting, Cueto had been transformed by an aggressive conditioning program, effectual guidance from pitching coach Bryan Price, and a prudent willingness to evolve. Curiously, his strikeout pace had dropped since his rookie season, but so had his walk and home run rates, the last dipping to an almost freakish level for Great American Ball Park. Counterintuitively, his control had improved even as his repertoire rounded out and his windup turned elaborately wacky, involving a rhythmic hip rotation that twisted him in the direction of second base before the pitch. Oldsters were reminded of the entertaining Luis Tiant. Meanwhile, Cueto excelled at pitching's little things: holding runners, provoking double plays, and fielding his position. In consecutive seasons, the wild-haired Dominican had challenged for the ERA title of the National League, turning in a combined 2.55, all the while pitching in a smallish home stadium notoriously friendly to fly-ball hitters. In 2012, his nineteen wins marked the most a Red had produced since 1988. His thirty-three starts led the league and a rotation that, remarkably, never missed a turn, and held the bad ones to a minimum. It was only the eighth time in Major-League history that five pitchers on one team had made at least thirty starts. Between them and the league's best bullpen, Cincinnati's unheralded pitchers crafted a 3.34 ERA. Washington led the NL at 3.33. When this figure was adjusted for ballpark conditions (ERA+), the Reds were the best in the league by a considerable margin.

It was a far cry from 2010, when, upon winning their division and stepping into the postseason against Philadelphia, they had served up Edinson Volquez as the foil for Roy Halladay's no-hitter. This time, when the Giants opened with Matt Cain, the Reds could submit Cueto as a peer. And with that air of worthiness, Cueto whiffed the Giants' leadoff hitter, Angel Pagan, with his sixth pitch of the playoffs.

After his eighth, he walked off the mound and flailed his arms in a gesture more of disgust than pain. Cincinnati's bulletproof rotation had taken a shot in the side.

The injury was described variously as an issue with Cueto's back or lat. More definitively, it was a serious strain on the Reds' staff. After Sam LeCure answered the immediate emergency, finishing the first inning and grinding through the second, Baker turned reluctantly to Latos, who had already thrown a bullpen session in preparation for his scheduled start in game three. The rotation was off, but at least the game was in good hands. Latos surrendered just a run in four innings, Phillips and Bruce homered, and the Reds chalked up their first playoff victory in twenty-two years. The second came the next night, with Arroyo yielding just one hit in seven shutout innings and Hanigan, his catcher of choice, driving in three runs.[25]

The final three games would be played at Great American, and the home team had to win but one of them. Homer Bailey was given the game-three start originally meant for Latos and held up his end, allowing only a harmless single and a hitless run over seven innings. The Reds put a run across in the first, but it was all Ryan Vogelsong would permit in his five innings.

San Francisco had still managed but one hit when Posey singled to lead off the tenth against Jonathan Broxton. Pence followed with another. After a couple of strikeouts, Hanigan uncharacteristically misplayed a fastball from Broxton, the runners advancing. As if that weren't curious enough, implausibility then cuffed Cincinnati a second time. Joaquin Arias bounced a ball toward third that Rolen had to play on an in-between hop he couldn't quite handle. After a momentary bobble, he made a strong recovering throw to first, but it wasn't in time to prevent the error or go-ahead run. When the Reds succumbed to Sergio Romo in the bottom of the inning, they found themselves confronting a fourth game and the scenario they'd hoped to avoid: They had to cover, once again, for Cueto.

The opportunity fell to Mike Leake. He neglected to seize it. The day's best pitching was delivered in long relief by San Francisco's two-time Cy Young winner, Tim Lincecum. The Giants had forced a fifth game.

Latos, positioned now to be the series savior, started it for Cincinnati and appeared equal to the occasion until blindsided by six runs in the fifth inning, four of them coming home on a grand slam by Posey. By the ninth, with two outs, the Reds had hacked the 6-0 deficit down to 6-3, with a pair of runners on base. At the plate, as the potential tying run, stood Rolen. When Romo struck him out swinging, San Francisco had completed its dumbfounding comeback.

It would be the last cut of Rolen's career.

"I got everything I needed from him, playing beside him," Votto reflected later. "I tell you what: He changed my path as a player. He was a shining example of the kind of player I want to be."[26]

Four days after the Reds' season ended so cruelly, Baker signed on to manage them for two more tries.

And in December, for what it was worth, *Baseball America* named them Organization of the Year.

TWELVE

GOD'S PARTICLE

THE REINVENTION OF THE REDS, WHILE GENERALLY SUCCESSFUL—WITH TWO DIVISION titles in three years, you could call it that, in spite of the crushing conclusion to their 2012 season—did not distinguish them from their competitors. Culturally, they were approaching the game much as the Cardinals, the Phillies, and the Giants did on their routes to championships. For all of the retro aspects, it was a hot philosophy, and a pragmatic one. The emphasis on teamship coupled smartly with the playing style toward which the sport seemed to be trending.

"We're seeing the game go through a renaissance right now," said Bill Bavasi, the Reds' executive overseer of scouting and player development, in an interview with the *New York Times*. ". . . [A] premium is going to be placed on speed, on range and on doing all the little skills that were so important in baseball until all of a sudden, you started seeing 70 home runs and guys getting on base and waiting for bombs."[1]

For Cincinnati, the whole business has amounted to intangibles bundling, packaging the situational with the environmental. Under Jocketty, the Reds have been devoted not only to their critical mass of character, but, notwithstanding their homer-popping ballpark, to deep pitching and daunting defense. The defense, in turn, is wedded to swiftness.[2]

It has all worked in concert: After a protracted down period in drafting and development, the organization has stocked up on both the quality players it needs and the player qualities it values. So doing, the Reds have developed an identity and prospered by it, as their sharp improvement in the annual standings would attest.

Be that as it may, Cincinnati still hasn't won a postseason series since 1990.[3]

Of course, there's no downloadable formula for that. A short series can be madly haphazard, taking on a life and capriciousness known to mock the 162 games that went before. The right stuff can seize the day, as it does the season, but that abstraction comes in countless forms.

The fact is, baseball, in the long haul or short, can't be mastered through a single, superior theme. For all the ways to succeed—pitching, power, speed, defense, balance, chemistry, experience, numbers, judgment, fundamentals, spending—the separator is not the particular approach, per se, but the steadfast commitment to a couple or few that pull in the same direction. It's a working, thriving organizational culture, rigorously applied.

And capped, in the consummate scenario, by a little something extra when the final rounds arrive.

PRIOR TO THE FOURTH GAME OF THE 2012 WORLD SERIES, GREGOR BLANCO, A PUNCHLESS twenty-eight-year-old whom the San Francisco Giants had handed left field when Melky Cabrera, batting .346 at the time, was suspended after testing positive for high levels of testosterone, walked up to his fellow Venezuelan, Giants second baseman Marco Scutaro, and told him, flat out, that he (Scutaro) was about to have a great night. It was not an outrageous prediction. Scutaro had been named the MVP of the League Championship Series in honor of batting .500 against the Cardinals and had, in fact, perpetrated magic from the moment he arrived by trade in late July, turning in a preposterous .362 average for the remainder of the regular season.

As it developed that chilly late October evening in Detroit, Scutaro had only a single to his name when the game went into the tenth inning, but it was he who came to the plate with two outs and Ryan Theriot on second base. To nudge the odds a bit, the San Francisco players spread themselves around in lucky places, Blanco's being the batting cages. And, as they all fully expected, Scutaro delivered the single to center that, after Sergio Romo struck out three straight Tigers in the bottom of the inning, completed the Giants' astonishing sweep.

That fateful episode testified explicitly to the unconventional but hardly accidental force of nature that the Giants became to win their second world championship in three seasons. The particulars included:

Scutaro. At age thirty-six, with eleven workmanlike years behind him, Scutaro was precisely the type of competent, understated, irreproachable professional with whom the Giants' general manager, Brian Sabean, liked to fortify his teams. To make certain he had the right man, Sabean, renowned for his emphasis on scouting, flew to Colorado to watch Scutaro play for the Rockies. Four days after dealing for the savvy infielder, Sabean applied the same criteria to the acquisition of outfielder Hunter Pence.

Blanco. Statistically, there was very little to recommend Blanco as an everyday outfielder. The year before, he had batted .201 *in Triple-A*. But he ran well, fielded his position, was a vibrant teammate, and so satisfied the Giants that, when Cabrera's suspension was up, they stuck with Blanco and told the better hitter that he was not welcome back—an act of integrity that flattered the franchise. Blanco simply fit the culture. The premonition he conveyed to Scutaro was, in substance, a bolstering sense of assurance, a flash of confidence in both teammate and team. That confidence was tantamount to expectation, a bracing, empowering state of mind that had become fundamental to the San Francisco organization.

Theriot. It was Theriot's place that Scutaro took in the Giants' lineup. Theriot's place on the *team,* however, was not negotiable. Although he'd been a starting middle infielder for most of his career, he approached his modified task with the zeal of a happy role player. "Theriot," wrote Jeff Passan of *Yahoo Sports,* "is one of those fighters and scrappers and gamers and grinders, someone whose talent never quite has dovetailed with his playing time. Managers like having him around anyway. The same thing happened to him last year, when St. Louis traded for Rafael Furcal midseason. Rather than complain his way off the roster, Theriot won a World Series with the Cardinals."[4] In San Francisco, he was the guy who orchestrated the goofy celebrations the Giants undertook in the dugout before ballgames, basically bouncing around like schoolkids and pelting each other with ice, gum, sunflower seeds, energy bars, and whatever absurd artillery happened to be handy. Between Theriot's mini-riots and Pence's impassioned motivational speeches, the Giants built up an emotional store that kept them charged through six elimination games. They'd been cornered into winning three straight against not only the Reds, but the Cardinals, as well, with enough left over to rout the Tigers.

Although they'd finished in the upper half of the National League in runs scored, the Giants, for the season, had rung up the fewest home runs in the majors. That profiled them, offensively, as a resourceful team, relying less on muscle than execution, and lent an air of the preternatural to their ascendency. When they swept Detroit—shrinking not a whit in the face of Miguel Cabrera, Prince Fielder, and Justin Verlander, and completing an unforeseeable seven-game winning streak in which they outscored the Cardinals and Tigers by a cumulative 36-7, with four shutouts—the pundits rallied to explain a crowning that so contravened the empirical standards. The Giants' competitive camaraderie was as vivid as their inauspicious lineup, their will as prominent as their pitching, and around the nation the keyword was chemistry.

"The Giants struck the right balance to create the perfect clubhouse mix," declared Jon Heyman of cbssports.com. "There's little doubt the chemistry was special."[5]

"[Giants manager Bruce] Bochy asks three simple things of his players," pointed out Richard Justice of mlb.com. "Respect the game. Compete. Be a good teammate."[6]

"They wore their intangibles of fighters and scrappers, gamers and grinders, like they meant more than just words," added Passan. "They embraced their ability to defy defeat and couldn't explain it but for the sort of survivalism needed to advance in October.[7]

"Belief is a tricky beast. Brian Sabean, for example, never has believed in all of the principles that guide baseball's sabermetric revolution, leaving him among a small minority of general managers whose emphasis on scouting is far greater than numbers-based analysis. Accordingly, he has been cast as a Luddite, a nincompoop, stubborn, inefficient and all sorts of other labels that even if they're true can't take away that he has built two World Series champions in three years, and none of his peers can say that. . . . Sabean, fifty-six, believed in Gregor Blanco enough that when Melky Cabrera's suspension ended, he stuck with his punch-hitting, slick-fielding left fielder instead of one whose presence could ruin what the Giants perceived as peerless clubhouse chemistry. While sports chemistry's formula is something like winning + winning = good, the Giants adhered to the idea that this is a different group, a special one."

Trusting what he'd observed, Passan understood that San Francisco's chemistry, as a product of its culture, ran deeper than pep talks, dugout stunts, and kumbaya. To Sabean, Bochy, and the players in whom they both placed their confidence, being a Giant, much like being a Cardinal, was a system of standards. Of *expectation*.

Of the regulars who constituted the Giants' basic lineup in 2012, only Posey—as an everyday player to build around, it doesn't get any better than a catcher capable of winning the MVP award, as Posey did—remained from the title team of two years before. But the system, like the pitching, was still in place. The expectation of winning hadn't been traded or released.

"There appears to be a direct correlation between what people expect and what really happens," noted Elwood Chapman in *Life Is an Attitude!*[8]

Joe Torre witnessed exactly that while managing his championship Yankees in 1996. He marveled at their mettle as his unyielding players reeled off improbable comeback victories in a dramatic postseason. "As this pattern continued," Torre wrote, "we began to *expect* to win games in late innings. The more we *saw* ourselves as resilient, the more resilient we became. It was one of those instances of mind over body: Believing that something is possible makes it possible."[9]

Needless to say, the believing gets easier when the precedents pile up. But it can also be acquired by other means, including irrepressible confidence and third-party persuasion. Norman Vincent Peale, the clergyman who famously preached positivity, waxed at length about the power of expectation, his go-to tale being one he repeated from popular Chicago sportswriter Hugh Fullerton.

"One story which I have never forgotten," remarked Peale in *The Power of Positive Thinking,* "concerned Josh O'Reilly, one-time manager of the San Antonio Club of the Texas league. O'Reilly had a roster of great players. . . . But the club fell into a slump and lost seventeen of the first twenty games. The players simply couldn't hit anything, and each began to accuse the other of being a 'jinx' to the team. Playing the Dallas Club, a rather poor team that year, only one San Antonio player got a hit, and that, strangely enough, was the pitcher. . . . Josh O'Reilly knew that he had an aggregation of stars and he realized that their trouble was simply that they were thinking wrong. They didn't expect to get a hit. They didn't expect to win. . . . Their mental pattern was not one of expectation but of doubt. This negative mental process inhibited them, froze their muscles, threw them off their timing, and there was no free flow of easy power through the team.

"It so happened that a preacher named Schlater was popular in that neighborhood at that time. He claimed to be a faith healer and apparently was getting some astounding results. . . . O'Reilly asked each player to lend him his two best bats. Then he asked the members of the team to stay in the clubhouse until he returned. He put the bats in a wheelbarrow and went off with them. He was gone for an hour. He returned jubilantly to tell the players that Schlater, the preacher, had blessed the bats and that these bats now contained a power that could not be overcome. The players were astounded and delighted. The next day they overwhelmed Dallas, getting thirty-seven base hits and twenty runs. They hammered their way through the league to a championship, and Hugh Fullerton said that for years in the Southwest a player would pay a large sum for a 'Schlater bat.' Regardless of Schlater's personal power, the fact remains that something tremendous happened in the minds of those ball-players. Their thought pattern was changed. They began thinking in terms of expectation, not doubt. They expected hits, runs, victories, and they got them." [10]

From the tenth inning of game three against the Reds, and especially after game four against the Cardinals, the 2012 Giants were swinging Schlater bats. They stepped to the plate and took to the field with a discernible sense of good things about to happen. They had, along with considerable pitching and Buster Posey, an abiding self-perception as winners. The challenge at hand, however stiff, was never quite beyond the scope of their confidence or capability. When all was settled, the Giants, once again, had demonstrated what works in October.

At least, what has *been known* to work. The postseason prescription is a fluid one, adapting to the landscape. In the golden times when the 154- or 162-game champion of the National League would advance directly to meet the 154- or 162-game champion of the American, the World Series well served the purpose of anointing the best team of all; or, at any rate, the more opportunistic of the top two. As the leagues expanded and, starting in 1969, the postseason followed suit, the odds gradually loosened their support of the most accomplished clubs. By the twenty-first century, with the field of qualifiers dramatically widened (from a pair in 1968 to ten in 2012) and the short series further defining the exercise, the best-team model had been so subverted that World Series champions were averaging five fewer regular-season victories than they had when the matchup was set by the summer-long pennant races.

This escalating trend was discussed at length in a blog by Joe Posnanski, renowned for discussing baseball matters at length. As he explained, "Here's another way to look at it: From 1903 through 1968, the team with the best record in baseball won the World Series a little more than 50% of the time. When four teams made the playoffs, the team with the best record in baseball won the World Series 28% of the time (7 out of 25). Since 1995, the team with the best record has won the World Series 17% of the time (3 out of 18) and one of those winners, the 2007 Red Sox, actually tied for the best record." [11]

The new postseason paradigm was, in effect, what Oakland general manager Billy Beane, Mr. Moneyball himself, was grousing about when he muttered, "My shit doesn't work in the playoffs. My job is to get us to the playoffs. What happens after that is fucking luck." [12]

Luck, no doubt, plays its part in the game, and the smaller the sample size, the greater the chance that chance will carry the day, sabotaging the statistical likelihoods. But the Giants, grasping that, had expressly chosen not to build their organization upon the percentages. In a postseason climate drifting away from cold probability, they had consistently and systematically erred on the side of culture—one steeped in pitching, it should be noted.

"When [San Francisco] players arrive in the big leagues, they already understand what it means to wear the Giants uniform," wrote Richard Justice. "In short, the Giants are a model franchise."

A model *modern* franchise, he might have added, old school as they are.

PRESUMABLY, PAT RILEY, THE GREAT BASKETBALL COACH, WAS SPEAKING MOSTLY OF HIS own sport when he said, "Feelings of significance happen when a team's energy takes on a life of its own." [13] And yet, couldn't Riley's comment also be applied to the San Francisco Giants of 2012? Or the indomitable St. Louis Cardinals the year before? Or the unimposing Giants of 2010?

Doesn't a baseball team radiate an energy and answer to it? In baseball, are the likes of enthusiasm, attitude, commitment, collectivism, confidence, and chemistry of no consequential account, seeing as how the players, after all, take turns; seeing as how, in baseball, the outcomes are simply strike or ball, safe or out, end of story, all of it flowing into tidy units of three, four, nine, twenty-seven, 300 . . . ; seeing as how, in baseball, the numbers speak for themselves?

These were questions I hoped to surround in the taming of this book. I wished to reveal, through baseball, that the sort of vitalities Riley was getting at—the power of collective purpose, the efficacy of teamship— were actually sustaining verities. Facts of life. The charge, in effect, was to magnify baseball and character in the same stroke.

In this pursuit, basketball weighed in more than once. In the summer of 2008, just as the Reds were trading Griffey and Dunn, reconfiguring themselves, and making me watch, our younger daughter attended a coed camp called Point Guard College. Fortunately, she took good notes. They weren't about just ballhandling, seeing the floor, and managing the tempo; they also hammered home such themes as body language, tone of voice, eye contact, encouragement, effort, spirit, *making other people better.* "If you're not making people better," Emily wrote in her camp journal, "you're not doing your job. Not just by example. By saying things. Tell them what they need to do, not what they should have done. Say two positive things a minute."

"Demand enthusiasm."

"Exude confidence when things aren't going well."

"Look like you agree with the coach. Act like you have confidence in your teammates. 93 percent of communication is non-verbal."

"Don't underestimate getting excited."

"Don't roll your eyes when a teammate makes a turnover. Look at them and say it's OK."

"Hustle is contagious."

For one illuminating week, the point guard was profiled as a source of energy, a conduit of culture, a purveyor of self-esteem. If one dribbles without purpose or vision, the campers were taught, she discourages her teammates from cutting, hustling, playing the game for all it's worth; she makes them *worse*. If he neglects to come to the aid of a teammate trapped by the press, he fails the guy and possibly embarrasses him. By contrast, if a player shouts help to a fellow defender, he enhances his teammate's physical tools by lending an extra pair of eyes. If she delivers the ball to a shooter in perfect position and rhythm, she pumps up her teammate's percentage and point total, makes her demonstrably *better*.

"Pass in stride. Create opportunities. Make people on the team feel like you have a special interest in getting them the ball. Make them play harder because you're looking at them, counting on them, trusting in them."

The point guard, in other words, embodies the essence of intangibles, both situational and environmental. To a degree that is roundly recognized, they're his job description. They represent a considerable slice of his contribution. They rack up second-level statistics. They raise boats.

That said, a basketball team is hardly best served by a roster full of floor leaders. The effect of a point guard's precise, timely passing is largely lost on a teammate who can't catch and shoot. His magic on the fast break goes poof in the absence of a teammate who can start one with a rebound. The infectiousness of his enthusiasm is of little consequence to a teammate who supplies his own. Players need to be completed. They need partners.

And so it is in baseball. Just as a dozen Jason Kidds would not be likely to collaborate on an NBA title, neither would twenty-five Ecksteins storm the pennant. After the first, each additional Eckstein would offer diminishing returns and, in fact, lower the value of the original. Intangibles are not like total bases; they don't just stack up gainfully. They don't report straight to the scoreboard. Like garlic, they are stirred into the sauce. Like yeast, they are baked into the loaf.

Nevertheless, as covert as those contributions tend to be, the likes of Branch Rickey, Pat Gillick, John Schuerholz, Joe Maddon, Joe Morgan, Scott Rolen, Tony La Russa, Bill James, Bronson Arroyo, Chipper Jones, Earl Weaver, Whitey Herzog, Dusty Baker, Joe Torre, Derek Jeter, Pete Rose, Terry Pendleton, Carlos Pena, Chase Utley, Kevin Millar, Jonny Gomes, Ryan Hanigan, Brooks Robinson, Jackie Robinson, Albert Pujols, Marco Scutaro, and Norman Vincent Peale, among others, have made it manifestly clear that the sort of teamship qualities associated with a true, crackerjack point guard—the supportiveness, the toughness, the accountability, the moxie, and so on—are vital to the winning baseball player, and to the winning baseball team. Oftentimes, they are what's at work, beneath the surface, when the game is at its breathtaking, memory-making best.

On the flip side, when contemporary teams have made an extravagant talent grab in the off-season, it has, on occasion—the Marlins (Jose Reyes, Mark Buehrle, Carlos Zambrano) of 2012, the Angels (Josh Hamilton, on top of Albert Pujols and C. J. Wilson the year before) of 2013—failed abysmally. That's not to say that those teams have added the wrong types of players. But recent world champs have gone about things quite differently. Clubs like the Giants and Cardinals have attested that an economical balance of the quantitative and qualitative, hand in hand, can outproduce payroll. It stands to reason, given the marketplace and its confederation with the measurable, that two quarts of WART come cheaper than half a gallon of OPS, and their chemical accents might provide just the right touch. The less perceptible assets are more likely to slip past the arbitrator and retain their low profiles in free agency, rendering them financially viable to the discerning employer. They're a source of positive arbitrage, a market inefficiency, a cost-effective option to bolster a ballclub that has the tools to hit and pitch.

Interviewed by a Boston blog, Bill James, the most eminent of sabermetricians, stated emphatically that he is also a respecter of the abstract and undocumented. "It is one thing," he said, "to build an analytical paradigm that leaves out leadership, hustle, focus, intensity, courage and self-confidence; it is a very, very different thing to say that leadership, hustle, courage and self-confidence do not exist or do not play a role on real-world baseball teams. The people who think that way . . . not to be rude, but they're children. They may be 40-year-old children, they may be 70-year-old children, but their thinking is immature." [14]

No doubt, the popularity of fantasy baseball, in step with proliferating research and its vast availability, has cast the game in a statistical radiance, which in turn lends a sense of understanding and an air of authority to those viewing it in that light. And their perspectives are widely supportable, particularly if one credits the caveat that luck can explain away the discrepancies.

To that end, luck's presence in the game is irrefutable. One batter catches a fastball flush and whistles it into the glove of the left fielder; the next is overmatched by the same pitch, makes partial contact on an awkward swing, and deposits it safely thirty feet shorter. An apparent double down the line finds an irregularity in the wall and rolls away for an extra base. An umpire ends a rally by calling strike three on a late curve that never reaches the corner. Two runs score when a fly ball aligns itself with the sun. Grounders carom capriciously, sneak through holes, or linger too long for lack of authority. A scorching line drive doubles up a helpless runner. A surefire triple loses ninety feet when it bounces over the fence. The wind changes abruptly. A cleat gets caught in the grass. A bullpen is blown up by a game that won't end. An ace starter slams a car door on his hand.

For hitters, luck is typically gauged by BABIP, the rationale being that if fair contact is made and the ball doesn't leave the park, the hitter is at the mercy of its proximity to the defense; a shot in the gap, for example, is but a fortuitous variation of a screaming out. But was it entirely luck that allowed Rod Carew, perhaps the greatest bat-handler of his time, to post a .408 BABIP in 1977? [15] Was it largely good fortune that enabled Wade Boggs, a five-time batting champion, to compile a .396 BABIP in 1985? Was Boggs simply kidding himself when he explained it as follows?

"Defenses didn't know how to play me. I drove Yankees shortstop Wayne Tolleson nuts. We had a four-game series, and before the final game, Tolleson called me over and said, 'I have to ask you a question. Do you watch me?' I said, 'Wherever you go.' He said, 'It seems like if I move to the right to the hole, you hit it up the middle, but if I move to the middle, you hit it in the hole.' I said, 'You finally figured me out.' The best was [former Twins manager] Ray Miller. He told me that he figured me out and that I had no chance of getting a hit that day. I asked, 'What are you going to do?' He said, 'You'll see.' We were in Minnesota, and when I came to bat, while the pitcher waited for a sign, the second baseman and shortstop were behind second base, one behind the other. When the pitcher wound up, one of them would run to his position, and the other would stand there. I went 5-for-5 that night. I'd just hit it into the position of the one who didn't move."[16]

It's generally conceded that certain hitters—very good ones, for instance, and guys who produce a high percentage of line drives[17]—can repeatedly generate higher BABIPs than most players. Luck is cited in the outliers, the seasons that deviate dramatically from a player's standard range. By that reasoning, though, was it also luck when Roger Maris's home runs leaped from sixteen to thirty-nine to sixty-one before falling back to thirty-three when he was age twenty-seven? Or when Hank Greenberg once hit fifty-eight, exceeding his second-best season by fourteen? Big years happen. When a hitter avoids more defenders than ever before, must it be luck?

The fact is that while sabermetrics do a stunning job of cataloging the great game and luck plays an obligatory part in its personal and collective outcomes, there remains much to be accounted for. Baseball teems with subtlety, humanity, and phenomena.

"The baseball memoir we're still waiting for," remarked David Leonhardt in a 2009 book review for the *New York Times*, "is the one that treats the recent information revolution not as a sign of cultural decay but as something worthy of thoughtful challenge."[18]

That challenge, however thoughtful, is issued here not toward the

integrity or relevance of baseball's elaborate analytics, but to their final-
ity and jurisdiction. It contends, simply, that the game can't be contained
by calculus. Needless to say, that's not an original position. It's endorsed
by most of the industry and the devout majority of color commentators.
Character and passion and intensity—all the performance-enhancing
qualities that constitute teamship—have ennobled the sport since it
began taking chunks out of our pastures and towns. We seek from baseball, and recognize in it, more than sliding triples and isolated slugging
percentages; a glimpse, perhaps, of life's secrets, revealed in the moment
and matchup; of the human soul, lunging at curveballs and crashing into
walls. America looks into a mirror and sees a line drive heading into
green space, outfielders chasing, infielders lining up, runners circling,
lights blazing, umpires poised, managers frozen, fans on their feet, teammates straining over the dugout rails.

To identify so closely with the game, and to revel as we do in that
connection, is to confer upon baseball an immanent worth; to trust that
transcendent ideals are somehow in play, even if they can be seen only
conceptually and validated only testimonially. It's to exercise faith in the
intangible. In that respect, devotees of the pastime are not unlike the
theoretical physicists who, for nearly half a century before its confirmation in 2013, could neither substantiate nor surrender their belief in the
existence of the Higgs boson, the so-called God's particle. Without the
Higgs particle, the order of their universe—the nature of its very mass—
remained unacceptably unexplained, intolerably nonsensical.

What order—what satisfactory *meaning*—can there be to a baseball
world in which a struggling rookie benefits not a bit from the encouraging words of the veteran who drapes his arm around the kid's shoulders;
in which Jeter's professionalism serves none but him; in which there is
no underlying reward for hustle, no implicit edge for enthusiasm, no
second-level payoff for sacrifice; in which there is no place for the ambient contributions of Eckstein, Scutaro, or the aging, battered Rolen;
in which shared purpose serves *no* purpose? What gratification would
baseball impart without the handiwork of Rose's will or Hinske's wis-

dom; without the championship destinies of the Giants in 2012 or the Mets in 1969; without big effects from the little things; without the One Great Scorer's commendation for playing the game the right way? In baseball, the intangibles are God's particle.

There is no Large Hadron Collider to accelerate the sport's essence and nail down the linear weight of moxie. There have been no falling apples, no eurekas in the bathtub, no thrilling epiphanies in the quest to properly honor the people who play well with others, and to certify the difference they make. All the same, if one keeps watching, listening, reading, believing, the confirmation is continuous, the faith easily kept. You come to *know*. Teamship, in tandem with the culture that cultivates it, is not merely advantageous to the cause of winning; it's indispensable.[19]

You come to know, also, that baseball is a proving ground of human merit, if a little light on the proving. But in the pleasing absence of clinical certainty, the mysterious will endure. The balance of tools and toughness, OBP and makeup, scouts and stats, bat speed and heartbeat, science and art, arm strength and expectation, individualism and *e pluribus unum,* will never be reduced to a pithy algorithm.

The game, thank goodness, is bigger than that.

ACKNOWLEDGMENTS

I'D LIKE TO ACKNOWLEDGE AND THANK THE NUMEROUS BASEBALL FOLKS WHO NOT ONLY consented to discuss the subject of intangibles, but did so with enthusiasm, insight, and genuine interest, all the while providing a validation that was not unappreciated. Of special note, among those, were John Schuerholz, Pat Gillick, Dusty Baker, Joe Maddon, Andrew Friedman, Bronson Arroyo, Carlos Pena, Joe Torre, Charlie Manuel, Gene Tenace, Ryan Hanigan, Jonny Gomes, Johnny Bench, Tony La Russa, Mike Radcliff, Kevin Millar, David Ortiz, Lance Berkman, Brandon Phillips, Chipper Jones, Rick Sweet, J. P. Ricciardi, Ken Ravizza, Wayne Krivsky, Tim Naehring, Hep Cronin, Jim Thome, Rocco Baldelli, David Ross, and Cody Ross.

Thanks to Rob Butcher and the Reds for providing access; also Brad Hainje of the Braves, Mike Herman of the Twins, and Rich Vaughn of the Rays; to Baseball-reference.com for being awesome; and to journalistic buddies who helped out with interviewing: Dennis Tuttle, Marc Lancaster, Jeff Wallner, and C. Trent Rosecrans.

As always, my estimable agent, David Black, made it happen.

I'm grateful that my editor, Thomas LeBien, stuck with the book through a change of publishing houses, believed in it steadfastly, read it wisely, and improved it deftly; and that, when change came again, Bob Bender, just the right guy, took up the baton for the homestretch.

I'm grateful, too, that while all this was going on, Martie stuck with *me*. What a wife.

NOTES

CHAPTER 1

1. Bill Felber, *The Book on the Book,* 175. "Defying the decade's previous pattern," Felber continued, the '99 Reds did all that winning "... (and came within a playoff game of reaching the postseason) on a payroll that should have supported 78 victories."

2. In an arranged bargain, the Chicago Cubs selected Hamilton in the Rule 5 draft, then sold him to the Reds for $100,000. The Rule 5 draft is a provision that enables teams to select minor-league players who have been with an organization for a certain period of time (in Hamilton's case, since he was drafted at the age of eighteen, four years) for $50,000, with the caveat that they must be placed on the acquiring team's twenty-five-man Major-League roster for the entire season that follows the draft. If the selected player is removed from the twenty-five-man roster, he must be offered back to the original franchise for $25,000.

3. Jayson Stark, "It's a changing of the guard with Reds," espn.com, March 17, 2009.

4. While a scenario of that sort can challenge a manager, Dusty Baker had at least been there before, having dealt with Barry Bonds in San Francisco. "Guys didn't really care about Barry being off by himself," Baker said, "because, whatever he did, his numbers far exceeded the distraction. I got to

the point where I'd say, 'Barry, I know you don't stretch, but just don't distract the other guys by not stretching in front of them.' So he stayed inside. But if I told him to stay inside, he'd come out and stretch. I think Barry wanted a lot of people to think he didn't work out. He did a lot of his stuff away from the field, much like Dick Allen. Griffey was different. I didn't see him work as hard as Barry. Grif was more of a natural. The thing I see about greatness is they're all different."

5. Kevin Kaduk (Duk), "J. P. Ricciardi does not think very highly of Adam Dunn," yahoo.com, June 19, 2008.

6. Ben Reiter, "Where's the Love?" *Sports Illustrated*, March 23, 2009, 78.

CHAPTER 2

1. Branch Rickey, "Goodby to Some Old Baseball Ideas," *Life,* August 2, 1954.

2. Roth was a Canadian with a background in hockey statistics. Gawking at his baseball minutiae, Rickey said, "Mr. Roth, that's like telling me how many nudges of the nose it would take someone to push a peanut up Pike's Peak." John Monteleone, editor, *Branch Rickey's Little Blue Book,* 218.

3. Rickey, "Goodby to Some Old Baseball Ideas," *Life.*

4. Lee Lowenfish, *Branch Rickey,* 71. Rickey's insistence on the team mentality was such that in 1940 he traded Joe Medwick, a future Hall of Fame outfielder only twenty-eight years old, in part because Medwick was the type of player who, in his own words, was in the game for "base hits and buckerinos." Lowenfish, 301.

5. Branch Rickey with Robert Riger, *The American Diamond,* 16.

6. Monteleone, *Branch Rickey's Little Blue Book,* 4.

7. Independent of mainstream recordkeeping, teams, of course, maintain their own statistics, often customizing them according to the organizational points of emphasis. On an ESPN baseball telecast, Bobby Valentine remarked that former Dodgers manager Tommy Lasorda kept a journal he called the "yellow pages," in which was documented every small play that made a difference in a ball game. One of his coaches, Joe Ferguson, was responsible for the in-game updating.

8. Joe Torre with Henry Dreher, *Joe Torre's Ground Rules for Winners,* 250.

9. Tim McCarver with Jim Moskovitz and Danny Peary, *Tim McCarver's Diamond Gems,* Kindle edition.

10. Joe Morgan and David Falkner, *Joe Morgan: A Life in Baseball,* 259.

11. Ibid., 54.

12. Craig Wright, "Baseball's Best Batting Coach," *A Page from Baseball's Past,* June 15, 2012. Along the same lines, Pete Runnels, whose offensive production jumped noticeably after he was traded from the Washington Sena-

tors to the Red Sox, with whom he won two batting titles, recognized Ted Williams for his part in that, letting it be known that he learned more about hitting from Williams than he did from the rest of the global population combined. Bill James, *The New Bill James Historical Abstract,* 511.

13. Sean McAdam, "Strong work ethic defines Varitek," espn.com, February 16, 2005.

14. McCarver, *Tim McCarver's Diamond Gems.*

15. Max Marchi, "The Stats Go Marching In: The Hidden Helpers of the Pitching Staff," *Baseball Prospectus,* March 9, 2012. Based on 5,000 plate appearances approximating a catcher's full season, the highest annual total of runs prevented was credited to Jose Molina with 38. For a career, the standard was Tony Pena with 248. Concerning the method involved in his calculations, Marchi wrote, "Suffice it to say that a With-Or-Without-You approach has been used here."

16. One of those was gifted shortstop Garry Templeton, whom Herzog once pulled down the dugout steps after Templeton tugged at his crotch as a salute to hometown fans who booed his loafing. After the season, Templeton was traded to San Diego in a six-player deal that brought Ozzie Smith to St. Louis in his place.

17. Whitey Herzog and Kevin Horrigan, *White Rat: A Life in Baseball,* 139. Completing the thought, Herzog wrote: "[A]nd so I figured I'd end my career as a general manager. I had the team I wanted, and if I couldn't win with it, I didn't want to have to fire myself. . . . I flew back to St. Pete and looked over my team. The thing that impressed me the most was that they were the hardest-working bunch of players I'd ever seen."

18. Matt Klaassen, "King of the Little Things 2009," *FanGraphs,* November 9, 2009. Other sources touching upon intangibles and the like include *Hardball Times, Baseball Prospectus,* and various Bill James publications.

19. James, *The New Bill James Historical Baseball Abstract,* 479. Later, when discussing Jackie Robinson on page 502, James wrote, "Never underestimate the power of intelligence, particularly when that intelligence is combined with athletic ability, determination, and a formidable competitive instinct."

20. Joshua Fisher, "It's Okay to Be Mystified by Linear Weights," *Hardball Times,* March 9, 2010.

21. James, *The New Bill James Historical Baseball Abstract,* 546. In discussing Darrell Evans, whom he called "in my opinion, the most underrated player in baseball history," James wrote, "Undocumented skills (leadership, defense, heads-up play) tend to be forgotten over time. Everything else deteriorates faster than the numbers."

22. Sheldon Hirsch and Alan Hirsch, *The Beauty of Short Hops: How Chance*

and Circumstance Confound the Moneyball Approach to Baseball. Hirsch and Hirsch also wrote, "The problem that animated Bill James's revolution was colossal ignorance pervading the baseball world. He helped cure it. The problem he inadvertently ushered in was excessive faith in a particular path to knowledge and insufficient appreciation of how much can never be quantified. James has acknowledged a problematic aspect of the revolution he wrought. Before resurfacing in the Red Sox front office, he spent years in relative seclusion, disheartened by the direction things had taken."

23. I posed some questions like those to the reflective members of a baseball forum I frequent called Redszone. Among the many discerning responses was this one from a woman posting under the name vaticanplum:

I usually roll my eyes when people talk about the benefits or drawbacks of "intangibles." My sense is that a lot of people who are drawn to baseball more than other sport—myself included—are pulled in that direction because baseball is so measurable. Each movement is very calculated, and you can see stats take shape in real time to a degree that you can't in other sports. I find great comfort in this. I often feel that baseball is my measurable compass within a completely intangible, unexpected world.

At the same time, I am a hypocrite, because my interest in the sport and my teams [is] rooted in the personal. I still get inordinately attached to certain players, and most of the time I can't even tell you why. I cry over baseball several times a week. No joke. So [while] I would never belittle my very real interest in the way the sport works, and this interest sustains me whether my team is good or bad—because there are always numbers to crunch—it's crazy for me to try to admit that the personal side isn't a huge factor.

24. Joe Torre and Tom Verducci, *The Yankee Years,* 340.

25. For the nine consecutive years (1998–2006) in which Torre's Yankees won the American League East title, along with five AL pennants and three World Series championships, there was something about them that indeed didn't quite "make sense," according to contemporary analytics. Each of those seasons, the Yankees, often emphatically, exceeded the victory total that, by the calculus of the Pythagorean Theory, would have been appropriate for their run differential. In the book *Mind Game* (chapter by Jim Baker and Clifford J. Corcoran, page 134), that anomalous feat was described as "akin to defying gravity." Some analysts would attribute the discrepancy, in large part, to the redoubtable New York bullpen led by Mariano Rivera, bullpens being instrumental in winning an uncommon percentage of close games, which, in turn, messes with the predictability of run differential. Torre, however, while fully appreciating the contributions of his relief pitchers, consistently ascribed his club's extraordinary gift for winning to such qualities as toughness, expectation, and heart. Either way, as pointed

out in *Mind Game,* "there is something exceptional occurring when a team consistently exceeds its Pythagorean record." Steven Goldman, editor, and the writers of Baseball Prospectus, *Mind Game.*

CHAPTER 3

1. Michael Lewis, *Moneyball,* 294.
2. Ibid., 290. "The Club of people who made their living just off the field of play—GMs and scouts, along with some of the noisier members of the Women's Auxiliary, the writers and commentators—flipped out. Not at me, mind you: at *Billy Beane.*"
3. Bill Shanks, *Scout's Honor,* 186. Quoting Gillick: "I think really if you want to say the foundation from where all this came from . . . the philosophy and the style would go back right to Baltimore. A lot of credit would have to go to Harry [Dalton]."
4. Jayson Stark, *Worth the Wait: Tales of the 2008 Phillies,* Kindle edition.
5. Like Griffey and Johnson, Rodriguez, in his prime, looked to be a certain Hall of Famer. His legacy, however, was dramatically altered by subsequent complications involving PEDs and the Biogenesis scandal, which resulted in his suspension for the 2014 season.
6. Bill Felber, *The Book on the Book,* 166.
7. Well, Bret Boone's 141 RBIs certainly played a part, as did Edgar Martinez's 116 and Mike Cameron's 110, not to mention Ichiro Suzuki's 242 hits, John Olerud's .401 on-base percentage, and four starting pitchers—Jamie Moyer (20-6), Freddy Garcia (18-6), Paul Abbott (17-4), and Aaron Sele (15-5)—going a remarkable 70-21 between them. What's more, according to Gillick, "We fundamentally executed better than any team I ever had."
8. It may or may not be coincidence that, since Gillick left Toronto in 1994 after five division titles and two World Series championships over a nine-year period ending in '93, the Blue Jays haven't been to the playoffs; and that, after Gillick left Baltimore in 1998 after a wildcard and a division title in his first two of three years there, ending a spell of twelve seasons without a playoff appearance, the Orioles suffered thirteen consecutive losing records; and that, since his four years in Seattle concluded in 2003, the Mariners, like the Blue Jays, have not experienced the postseason.
9. Stark, *Worth the Wait.*
10. Jayson Stark, "It's a Changing of the Guard with Reds," espn.com, March 17, 2009.
11. Cliff Floyd had a similar relationship with young outfielder B. J. Upton, urging him specifically on matters of hustle. Floyd told Marc Lancaster of the *Tampa Tribune,* "It's not about getting on him about this; it's about

running a ball out. That's the easiest thing you can possibly do. I'm on him as hard as you can be on him. It's a shame to be labeled as a guy like that when that's not who he's about." Marc Lancaster, "Floyd vows to get Upton in gear," *Tampa Tribune* blog, August 18, 2008.

12. Jonah Keri, *The Extra 2%*, 108.

13. In his autobiography, Gibson wrote of the Cardinals, "The team concept manifested itself conspicuously on the field. McCarver has said that the '67 Cardinals were the most remarkable team he has ever been associated with because we never made a mental mistake. We never threw to the wrong base and we always took advantage of every inch the opponent would give us. When it came to intangibles—execution, resourcefulness, sacrifice, etc.—we were the equal of any team in modern baseball." Bob Gibson with Lonnie Wheeler, *Stranger to the Game*, 132.

14. To Rickey, a player's enthusiasm for the game was comparable in importance to his throwing arm. There was, for example, this scouting report on Dick Groat, a future MVP and batting champion: "The best thing about Groat is his disposition, his desire to play and win." John Monteleone, editor, *Branch Rickey's Little Blue Book*, 5.

15. Ken Ravizza and Tom Hanson, *Heads-Up Baseball*.

16. Maddon has been described as possibly "the most relentlessly positive person on the planet." Joe Henderson, "Character counts in Rays' clubhouse," *Tampa Tribune* blog, February 17, 2009.

17. "I call it the lead bull theory," said Maddon. "If you've ever read *Centennial*, by Michener, he talks about when the Indians need to kill a bunch of buffalo. They would find the lead buffalo in the herd and start him toward the cliff. They'd just start running and running and by the time the lead buffalo gets there it's too late for him to stop, he's over the side, and the rest of the group follows him. The Indians stand on the bottom and skin about a thousand buffalo. So you've got to get the lead bull running in the right direction."

18. Keri, *The Extra 2%*. Over that period, Eliot and Ken Ravizza both served the Rays as sports psychologists. Said Eliot, "Everybody talks about five-tool players. The guys that are the best are six-tool players—guys with five tools, but also the mental game."

19. Marc Lancaster, "Melees Show Rays' United Front," *Tampa Tribune*, June 8, 2008.

20. Keri, *The Extra 2%*.

21. To assist in the crunching of numbers, the Rays hired analysts from *Baseball Prospectus*, a leading advocate of sabermetrics. Statistical research directed the club toward its emphasis on defense, the result being that, when 2008 was said and done, Tampa Bay had increased its victory total by

thirty-one while actually scoring eight fewer runs than the year before. The reconstituted Rays, however, had permitted an astonishing 273 fewer.

22. Stark, *Worth the Wait.*

23. Tom Verducci, "Dear America, Wish You Were Here," *Sports Illustrated,* November 3, 2008.

CHAPTER 4

1. The Yomiuri Giants of Japan's Central League endorse this school of thought in a code of conduct they issue to their players, known as the Gaijin Ten Commandments. The tenth of these states, "Do not disturb the harmony of the team." In the same spirit, Rule 6 stipulates, "Do not severely tease your teammates." Robert Whiting, *You Gotta Have Wa,* 84, 85

    The Bible imparts a similar message, saying that "six things doth the Lord hate . . . [including] he that soweth discord among brethren." Proverbs 6:16–19 (King James Version).

2. Andrew Oswald, Eugenio Proto, and Daniel Sgroi, "A New Happiness Equation: Worker + Happiness = Improved Productivity," Warwick University Economics Department. Further quoting: "If happiness in the workplace brings increased returns to productivity, then human resource departments, business managers and the architects of promotion policies will want to consider the implications."

3. Branch Rickey with Robert Riger, *The American Diamond,* 39.

4. Larry Senn and Jim Hart, *Winning Teams—Winning Cultures,* 187. Vision, wrote the authors, "provides the fuel, motivation and energy needed to win in a competitive marketplace. . . . A vision is much more than just a goal or picture of a future; it evokes a strong feeling. It is the feeling, not the goal, which inspires high energy and commitment."

5. David Eckstein with Greg Brown, *Have Heart,* 40.

6. Whitey Herzog and Kevin Horrigan, *White Rat: A Life in Baseball,* 139.

7. Joe Torre with Henry Dreher, *Joe Torre's Ground Rules for Winners,* 53, 260.

8. C. Trent Rosecrans, "Talking with Bill James: Part I," CNATI.com, March 19, 2010.

9. Peter Senge, *The Fifth Discipline: The Art and Practice of the Learning Organization,* 249. Senge was founder of the Center for Organizational Learning at the Sloan School of Management, MIT.

10. Tim McCarver with Jim Moskovitz and Danny Peary, *Tim McCarver's Diamond Gems,* Kindle edition.

11. Bob Gibson and Reggie Jackson with Lonnie Wheeler, *Sixty Feet, Six Inches,* 184–87.

12. Bob Gibson with Lonnie Wheeler, *Stranger to the Game,* 101.
13. Torre with Dreher, *Joe Torre's Ground Rules for Winners,* 42. In St. Louis, Torre joined up with Gibson, Tim McCarver, and Dal Maxvill to form an informal dinner club, featuring fine wine and serious baseball talk.
14. Thomas Boswell, *Why Time Begins on Opening Day,* 291.
15. Ibid., 24–25.
16. Bob Hertzel, *The Big Red Machine,* 75–76.
17. Daniel Coyle, *The Talent Code,* Kindle edition.
18. Hertzel, *The Big Red Machine,* 7–8.
19. The question that became so revealing to McPherson was, in fact, virtually the same one asked of all prospects by famous baseball scout (and later executive) Bill Lajoie, when he met with them in their kitchens and living rooms. Lajoie called it his "Magic Question": What are you going to do in your life? If the young man was sufficiently talented and his answer demonstrated not only that he *identified* himself as a ballplayer but also his desire to be a good one and confidence that he would—that, for instance, his plan was to become an All-Star—Lajoie had a draft choice on his hands. Anup Sinha and Bill Lajoie, *Character Is Not a Statistic,* 269.
20. McPherson's conclusions square with those of clinical psychologist Charles Garfield, whose study of high achievers showed that "the single most powerful predictor of success in the long run is commitment." Eric Bronson, editor, *Baseball and Philosophy,* 212.

CHAPTER 5

1. Jayson Stark, "It's a Changing of the Guard with Reds," espn.com, March 17, 2009.
2. Votto took a rehab stint with the Reds' Class A affiliate in nearby Dayton, Ohio. While he was there, he spotted a flaw in the swing of Byron Wiley, a left-handed-hitting outfielder for the Dayton team, and discussed it with him. Wiley, who said he watched every cut Votto took in batting practice, had been struggling along with a .212 average. After the session with Votto, he promptly went on a tear, batting at greater than a .400 clip over the next sixteen games, with seven home runs—three in one game.
3. Phillips was not the only creative Red inclined toward histrionics and trickery. On May 25 of that year (2009), against the Astros, a game in which Jerry Hairston was filling in for Phillips at second base, Houston's Jeff Keppinger ripped a double to left center that should have scored the runner at first, Kaz Matsui. However, as Matsui approached second base, Hairston and shortstop Alex Gonzalez pantomimed a double play, causing Matsui to come to a full stop. He quickly continued on and reached third, eventually scoring.

4. Mark Sheldon, "Baker: 'This is Embarrassing,'" *MLBlogs Network*, July 29, 2009.

5. One of Rolen's best attributes as a Gold Glove third baseman was the remarkably consistent accuracy of his throws across the diamond. When he took infield practice, he made certain to position his feet properly for every throw and execute it with the same energy that would be required to retire a swift batter at first base.

6. Paul Daugherty, "'Need Ya on Third, Brucie,' Has Become Reds' Mantra," *Cincinnati Enquirer,* March 10, 2011. Quoting further: "First to third with less than two outs is a huge play," Rolen would say to Bruce. "That turns everything around and all it is, is effort."

7. Tyler Kepner, "Investment in Rolen Is Paying Off for the Reds," *New York Times,* June 1, 2010. The first paragraph came from an accompanying *New York Times* blog by Kepner, "First-Place Reds Follow Scott Rolen's Lead," *New York Times* blog, June 2, 2010.

8. To better appreciate the empirical perspectives that I knew would vigorously challenge the case for intangibles, I engaged in a protracted email dialogue with an operative steeped in good sense and analytics. This was an individual who worked thoughtfully in Major League Baseball for a couple of decades and preferred not to involve his name in this discussion. He was extraordinarily helpful.

9. "We are constantly looking for holy grails of meaning," wrote my analytic confidant, adding that specific conclusions should not be leaped to on the basis of general trends. "The point is not to kid ourselves that the way to weigh an apple is to pick up an apple tree."

10. Bronson Arroyo was also at his best down the stretch, and in fact held the Reds' staff together for much of the season. Aaron Harang, their Opening Day starter, won only six games in 2009. The game two starter, Edinson Volquez, won four, and never pitched after sustaining an elbow injury on June 1.

11. Rick Bozich, "Bailey's Split Decision Has Foes Dazzled," *Louisville Courier-Journal,* June 17, 2009.

12. Also coincidentally or not, Louisville's starting pitchers had put up an 11–18 record before Lehr joined the club, and had gone 32–14 afterward. Louisville manager Rick Sweet credited Lehr with helping future Reds pitcher Sam LeCure in much the same way he had benefited Bailey.

CHAPTER 6

1. Susannah Cahalan, "How Jeter Put A-Rod in the Yankees' 'Snubhouse,'" *New York Post,* April 25, 2011. According to the story, Cashman wasn't the

only one who made that request of Jeter: "Don Mattingly, then the hitting coach and former captain, tried to intervene, citing his own unfriendly history with teammate Wade Boggs. 'I faked it with Boggs,' he told Jeter. 'And you have to fake it with Alex.'"

   When he signed pitcher C. C. Sabathia prior to the 2009 season, Cashman implied that Jeter's leadership was not quite all-inclusive. "We need somebody to bring us together," he told the large left-hander. Jayson Stark, "Four remain pride of the Yankees," espn.com, November 4, 2009.

2. In their book *Mental Toughness: A Champion's State of Mind,* authors Karl Kuehl, John Kuehl, and Casey Tefertiller write, "The championship Yankee teams of the late 1990s placed high value on what might be called teamsmanship, the collective responsibility of performing together as a cohesive unit and not showing up teammates." My unrelated (though not dissimilar) use of "teamship" is applied a bit more comprehensively, as an umbrella term for the sum of intangible qualities that make up an ideal teammate and materially enhance a player's value to his ballclub.

3. Branch Rickey with Robert Riger, *The American Diamond,* 97.

4. Scutaro's heady play was reminiscent of one executed by George Brett in game one of the 1980 American League Championship Series. Kansas City led the Yankees, 3-2, in the top of the eighth inning when Bob Watson hammered a ball off the left-field wall and Willie Randolph attempted to score from first base. The throw from left fielder Willie Wilson carried beyond the Royals' relay man, shortstop U. L. Washington, but Brett, the third baseman, was in the right place to back it up. His throw to catcher Darrell Porter nailed Randolph and preserved the lead that Kansas City would maintain. The next day, Brett's three-run homer off Goose Gossage completed the Royals' sweep.

5. Rick Weinberg, "Jeter's backhand flip rescues Yankees," espn.com, July 23, 2004.

6. Tim McCarver with Jim Moskovitz and Danny Peary, *Tim McCarver's Diamond Gems,* Kindle edition.

7. Lawrence S. Ritter, *The Glory of Their Times,* 210. Though he recognized the error of his ways and, in fact, became fast friends with Roush, Neale had obviously disqualified himself as a ballplayer's ballplayer. He was, as it turned out, in the wrong sport altogether. More than half a century later, Neale was inducted into the Pro Football Hall of Fame for his success in coaching the Philadelphia Eagles.

8. "The essence of the performance value is accountability," wrote Larry Senn and Jim Hart. "Individuals may be accountable, but do all team members feel accountable for each other's success?" Senn and Hart, *Winning Teams—Winning Cultures,* 143.

9. Thomas Boswell, *Why Time Begins on Opening Day,* 290.
10. Helping out can, of course, take countless forms. For Pete Rose, it meant, among other things, switching from left field to third base four weeks into the 1975 season, so that the Reds could make a place in the lineup for George Foster, who would lead the National League in home runs twice and RBIs three times over the next four years. Rose had been an MVP in left field. He also moved willingly from second base after winning the Rookie of the Year award at that position, and from right field after claiming two batting titles from there.
11. Nearly a century before digitally monitored fitness centers turned up in every hotel and strip mall, Honus Wagner cross-trained in the off-season with ice skating, hockey, basketball, lifting, and tossing around Indian clubs. Wagner emphasized the conditioning of the legs, a lesson taken to heart by younger teammate Max Carey, who became a Hall of Fame base-stealer. Craig Wright, "The Aging of Honus Wagner," *The Hardball Times Baseball Annual 2009.*
12. Boswell, *Why Time Begins on Opening Day,* 228.
13. McCarver with Moskovitz and Peary, *Tim McCarver's Diamond Gems.*
14. Thomas Boswell, *How Life Imitates the World Series,* 215.
15. Moxie, however, must be a fairly newfangled word. There's no mention of it in the seventeen-pound, 3,350-page *Webster's New International,* unabridged, published in 1934.
16. Honus Wagner's grasp of fundamentals was so secure that his manager, Fred Clarke, left the operation of the Pittsburgh infield to the Flying Dutchman. From his shortstop position, Wagner was given the responsibility for such tasks as setting up the bunt defense, positioning the other players, and calling the pickoff plays. Wright, "The Aging of Honus Wagner," *The Hardball Times Baseball Annual 2009.*
17. Malcolm Gladwell, "The Physical Genius," *The New Yorker,* August 2, 1999. "What sets physical geniuses apart from other people, then," wrote Gladwell, "is not merely being able to do something but knowing what to do—their capacity to pick up on subtle patterns that others generally miss. This is what we mean when we say that great athletes have a 'feel' for the game, or that they 'see' the court or the field or the ice in a special way. Wayne Gretzky, in a 1981 game against the St. Louis Blues, stood behind the St. Louis goal, laid the puck across the blade of his stick, then bounced it off the back of the goalie in front of him and into the net. Gretzky's genius at that moment lay in seeing a scoring possibility where no one had seen one before. 'People talk about skating, puck-handling, and shooting,' Gretzky told an interviewer some years later, 'but the whole sport is angles and caroms, forgetting the straight direction the puck is going, calculating

where it will be diverted, factoring in all the interruptions.' . . . When he sends a pass to what to the rest of us appears an empty space on the ice, and when a teammate magically appears in that space to collect the puck, he has in reality simply summoned up from his bank account of knowledge the fact that in a particular situation, someone is likely to be in a particular spot, and if he is not there now he will be there presently."

18. Omar Vizquel, the snappy shortstop, was another who made hay with histrionics. He would often pretend to field a ball that was actually out of his reach, confusing the baserunner and occasionally tricking one out of an extra base. Chuck Knoblauch pulled the same act in the 1991 World Series, causing Lonnie Smith to slow down, stumble, and come up a base short of scoring a critical run. Jason Varitek was known to work the ruse the other way. He would stand casually at home plate, apparently out of the action, as he awaited an incoming throw from the outfield, then snatch the ball at the last instant and tag the unsuspecting runner.

19. Ty Cobb made such a meticulous study of catchers giving signals that at one point, while watching White Sox catcher Ray Schalk, he called seventeen straight pitches.

20. Craig Wright, "Beauty Bancroft," *A Page from Baseball's Past,* September 16, 2013.

21. Jackie Robinson made it his mission to prod Brooklyn pitcher Don Newcombe, whom he found excessively easygoing on the mound. This provided ballast on a club captained by Reese, a kindly, sympathetic teammate.

22. Joe Morgan and David Falkner, *Joe Morgan: A Life in Baseball,* 73.

23. Ibid., 232.

24. Ibid., 94–95.

25. Bench, for instance, would note that Don Sutton drew his glove farther back for a curve than he did for a fastball. Morgan might describe a pitcher's pickoff move or an outfielder's throwing arm.

26. Tyler Kepner, "Jeter's Intangibles Hard to Quantify," *New York Times,* February 25, 2003.

27. Jane M. Von Bergen, "Strength in Mixed Numbers: Miniteams Make Whole Team Better," *Philadelphia Inquirer,* October 31, 2009.

28. Bob Nightengale, "Monster Deal Gives Albert Pujols 'Extra Chip on My Shoulder,'" *USA Today,* April 3, 2012.

29. Jeter's persona struck such a chord with Colorado's superstar shortstop, Troy Tulowitzki, that Tulowitzki chose to wear his number two.

30. And so iconic is Jeter's name that the Fire Joe Morgan Glossary (firejoemorgan.com) playfully defines the term "True Yankee" this way: "A leader. A guy who's full of intangible qualities that help him triumph—with class.

Derek Jeter. A guy who has a certain look in his eye, like he knows what it means to don the pinstripes with some motherfletching pride. Bernie. Mantle. Joe D. Jeter. . . . A winner. *Derek Jeter."*

31. Michael Silver, "Is Ray Lewis the Greatest Gridiron Leader Ever?" yahoo .com, January 3, 2013.

32. Bob Gibson with Lonnie Wheeler, *Stranger to the Game,* 166.

33. Maury Allen, *Jackie Robinson: A Life Remembered,* 238.

34. Joe Posnanski, "3000 Words About Derek Jeter," *Joe Blogs,* July 7, 2011.

35. Gary Mack and David Casstevens, *Mind Gym: An Athlete's Guide to Inner Excellence,* 191.

36. Pele, the soccer icon, held enthusiasm in similar esteem. "Enthusiasm," he said, "is everything. It must be taut and vibrating, like a guitar string." Henry Ford was a fan, as well, remarking that, "Enthusiasm is the sparkle in your eyes, the swing in your gait, the grip of your hand, the irresistible surge of will and energy to execute your ideas."

37. In an unpublished essay, Annie DeMario, a converted Jeter fan, described his passion this way: "It is a rare player who seems almost elated just to be on the field sometimes, but will then turn around and rip up his face diving into the stands to catch a foul ball or rip up his kidney diving into the out-field to catch a fly ball. Such a player can survive only when his pure, initial love of baseball filters undiluted through the rough years of rookie ball, the transience of daily major league life, and the ugliness of the business side of the sport. . . . This is infectious."

38. Jerry Crasnick, "Jeter Hitting Monumental Heights," espn.com, September 4, 2009.

39. Posnanski, "3000 Words About Derek Jeter," *Joe Blogs,* July 7, 2011.

CHAPTER 7

1. "I'm sure some organizations thought Scott Rolen was overpaid," said one baseball official, "both when the Reds traded for him and when they gave him an extension."

2. Albert Chen, "Feel the Glove," *Sports Illustrated,* March 1, 2010. The quote: "The story of teams falling back in love with defense doesn't begin in 2009, when the four most improved teams in the AL—the Mariners, Yankees, Rangers and Tigers—were also the most improved teams in de-fensive efficiency, as measured by *Baseball Prospectus.* Nor does it begin in 2008, when the Rays went from worst to first in the American League East primarily because they improved at almost every position defensively. The story begins in 2004 at baseball's trade deadline, when the Red Sox,

in the midst of a three-month .500 funk, unloaded Boston icon Nomar Garciaparra in a trade that netted them a Gold Glove shortstop (Orlando Cabrera), a Gold Glove first baseman (Doug Mientkiewicz) and an above-average outfielder (Dave Roberts)."

3. Jerry Crasnick, "Phillips Packs a Ton of Fun into His Game," espn.com, July 20, 2010.

4. Jodie Valade, "Orlando Cabrera is the Cleveland Indians' Voice of Experience (and winning)," *The Plain Dealer,* May 9, 2011.

5. The difference in the Reds was noted by Bronson Arroyo, who said, "A lot of guys in here are starting to feel something they've never felt before. The attention to detail. Without question, there's an upgrade this year, and it's growing."

6. Gomes was playing on a more regular basis than he ever had, and it deepened his impact. "To have a guy like him, I've always found it to be unbelievably important," said Bronson Arroyo. "That stuff bleeds off, without question. You're getting better team chemistry, you're getting guys who care more about other guys—maybe they'll go after that ball with a little bit extra and dive or smash into a wall for a guy, maybe because of what goes on in the locker room. It's a bad Catch-22 in the fact that if you take a guy with a great personality like that but he cannot produce on the field, people don't respect it. But if they *do,* then it becomes this momentum and it just won't stop. Fortunately for us, Jonny's gotten off to a good start."

7. After Arroyo had beaten St. Louis in a complete-game effort, his eclectic, inauspicious stuff was described by Cardinals outfielder Colby Rasmus as "doo-doo" and "a bunch of slop." Joe Strauss, "Digesting a Lost Series, Division Lead," *St. Louis Post-Dispatch,* May 16, 2010.

8. Paul Daugherty, "Anyone Still Questioning Reds' Trade for Scott Rolen?" *Cincinnati Enquirer,* May 19, 2010. "The general manager and owner had concluded the home clubhouse was a mess," continued Daugherty. "'The culture,' as Jocketty called it, was aimless. There were players who wanted to win. They didn't know how. Rolen knew."

9. C. Trent Rosecrans, "Thinking Out Loud," CNATI.com, May 19, 2010.

10. Matthew Futterman, "Baseball's New Best Enemies," *Wall Street Journal,* September 3, 2010.

11. John Fay, "Aroldis Chapman Gets First Win as Reds Sweep Brewers," *Cincinnati Enquirer,* September 1, 2010.

12. The Reds' fourth Gold Glove fielder, Orlando Cabrera, left the game in the fifth inning with a minor injury.

13. Michael Lewis, *Moneyball,* 275.

14. For that matter, so was Minnesota's, and yet, the Twins had an extensive

modern history of meeting the same fate as the A's, overachieving in the regular season and falling short in the post. Under old-school manager Ron Gardenhire, the Twins, recognized throughout the industry as a franchise devoted to character—perhaps the least dependent upon sabermetric analysis—secured six division titles in a nine-year period, but won only one playoff series during that stretch. That one came at the expense of Oakland in 2002, a compelling clash of small-market teams with polar-opposite approaches. "I like the human element and I like the heart way better than I like numbers," said Gardenhire. "And that's what I'll always stay with." Joe Kay, "Extra Base Can Translate into Higher Place," Associated Press, May 18, 2010.

Chris Jaffe, "Scioscia and Gardenhire . . . So Far," *Hardball Times,* April 12, 2010, Gardenhire ranked twenty-fifth all time in the ability to maximize the production of his players.

15. Andy Altman-Ohr, "Unknown Hero Helps Make Giants World Series Champions," Jweekly.com, November 4, 2010. Concerning Goldfarb's input on the signing of Aubrey Huff: "'There were a few things in his statistical background, the scouting reports and intangibles we knew about him that made us think he could bounce back from a relatively, for him, poor 2009 season,' Goldfarb said. In January, the Giants signed Huff for what proved to be a bargain, $3 million for one season (he had made $8 million in 2009). All the thirty-three-year-old first baseman did was go on to lead the team with 26 home runs and 86 RBIs, while also adding leadership and clubhouse chemistry."

16. See Henry Schulman, "Aaron Rowand: The (Broken) Face of the Franchise," *San Francisco Chronicle,* May 11, 2010.

17. Jayson Stark, "Welcome to The Information Age," espn.com, August 30, 2011. The story expounded: "The Giants are run by Brian Sabean, a GM who is more old school than new age, a GM who started as a scout, believes in scouts and surrounds himself with great scouting minds. So in an age in which many teams are firing or de-emphasizing scouts in favor of computer data and video, the Giants prepared for last October by using their best scouts to gather great information every possible way it could be gathered. . . . They also took their advance scout, Steve Balboni, off the road and brought him to San Francisco with fellow scout Joe Lefebvre to break down video, travel with the team and answer questions from players and the coaching staff. A third group, led by video-operations coordinator Danny Martin, put together an exhaustive package of video-augmented statistical data. . . . It was the perfect storm of tremendous preparation and near-perfect execution."

CHAPTER 8

1. Bill Shanks, *Scout's Honor*, 145, 153.
2. John Schuerholz with Larry Guest, *Built to Win*, 20; also on Sanders, page 19: "The Braves were just a platform of sorts for him to demonstrate his athletic prowess. A lot of people in our clubhouse felt that way and didn't sense he was committed to this team. He liked to promote 'Prime Time' as his nickname. Around our offices, he was more often referred to as 'Ego Man.'" And from Bobby Cox, same page: "'Deion was for one thing—himself. He couldn't care less about the team.'"
3. "I met with Bobby and John Schuerholz in December of 1990," said Terry Pendleton. "I was a little concerned because I didn't feel like our manager and general manager were on the same page [in St. Louis], and it trickled downhill. My biggest concern in signing with Atlanta was that I wanted to make sure we were on the same page trying to win. I sat down with them and I felt that presence right away."
4. When it was published in 2003, *Moneyball* tapped the baton for the lively scouts-versus-stats overture that would play on so controversially.
5. *Moneyball* advanced a departure from this premise. "For Billy [Beane and his assistants in the Oakland front office], a young player is not what he looks like, or what he might become, but *what he has done,*" wrote Michael Lewis. ". . . The scouts even have a catch phrase for what Billy and Paul [DePodesta] are up to: 'performance scouting.' 'Performance scouting,' in scouting circles, is an insult. It directly contradicts the baseball man's view that a young player is what you can see him doing in your mind's eye. It argues that most of what's important about a baseball player, maybe even including his character, can be found in his statistics." Michael Lewis, *Moneyball*, 38.
6. In an interview with Rich Lederer of *Baseball Analysts,* Paul DePodesta, head of scouting and player development for the New York Mets and former assistant to Billy Beane, had this to say about a player's enthusiasm for the game: "It can be really difficult for me to warm up to a player who has a low motor. . . . I prefer guys who play with energy and appear to really enjoy being out there. The minor leagues can be a real grind . . . so I worry about guys who don't seem to have that passion. That said, that passion isn't always illuminated by a player bouncing around the diamond." Lederer, "Q&A: Paul DePodesta," baseballanalysts.com, June 18, 2009.
7. Shanks, *Scout's Honor*, 242.
8. "Look," said Bobby Cox, articulating the premium he and the Braves placed on a prospect's makeup, regardless of his talent level, "there are guys who

went number one in the draft that I didn't want our guys to pick at number one because of character."

9. In the preface, Shanks offered a strong hint of how the Braves' emphasis on makeup differentiated their sensibilities from those of less traditional teams, such as Oakland: "Then I heard about a book by Michael Lewis called *Moneyball.* It focused on the Oakland A's and their reliance on computer technology in shaping [their] major-league roster and farm system. Several people in the Braves' organization warned me not to read it. 'It'll get your blood boiling,' they warned. 'They just do things differently than we do.'" Shanks, *Scout's Honor,* ii.

10. Ibid., 350.

11. Ibid., 58.

12. Ibid.,144.

13. Jim Bowden, "Chipper Jones sends a message," espn.com, June 8, 2011.

14. Pendleton on Maddux, Glavine, and Smoltz: "Those three guys, and even Steve Avery—those guys made each other. They made each other better. If Maddux threw a three-hitter, Glavine tried to back it with a two-hitter. They tried to beat each other in golf. If they go in to use the restroom, they're trying to out-pee each other. There's a lot of friendship there, but trust me, every one of them wanted to be better than the others every hour of the day."

15. The only other player to average .300 or higher as both a left- and a right-handed hitter was Frankie Frisch, who retired in 1937.

16. In the words of Frank Wren, who in 2007 succeeded Schuerholz as Atlanta's general manager, Jones provided "the greatest value to the organization that picked him . . . he's spent his whole career with one organization and had a Hall of Fame career." Jayson Stark, "The many feats of Chipper Jones," espn.com, September 26, 2012.

17. Ben Lindbergh, "The Whole Ball Player," *Baseball Prospectus,* April 13, 2012.

18. "I never used to sign a boy," said Campanis, "unless I could look in his face and see what I wanted to see: drive, determination, maturity, whatever. . . . Some scout would give me a report on a boy and I'd say, 'Tell me about his face,' or, 'Does he have the good face?'" Kevin Kerrane, *Dollar Sign on the Muscle,* 101.

19. Ibid., 116.

20. The tests conducted by McLaughlin were precursors to the Athletic Motivation Inventory (AMI) workups developed in 1969 by psychologists and administered by the Major League Scouting Bureau to assess a prospect's confidence, determination, mental toughness, and so on. The AMI tests, in

turn, were supplanted by the Athletic Success Profile (ASP), which measures eleven personal characteristics: drive, aggressiveness, endurance, leadership, self-confidence, emotional control, mental toughness, coachability, conscientiousness, responsibility, and trust.

21. Lindbergh, "The Whole Ball Player," *Baseball Prospectus*.

22. In late 1960, after a protracted power struggle between McLaughlin and Baltimore general manager Paul Richards, McLaughlin was fired and went to work in Cincinnati. Before returning to the Orioles in 1966, he helped build the Big Red Machine—whose first World Series, in 1970, resulted in a loss to Baltimore—by overseeing the drafts of Johnny Bench, Bernie Carbo, and Hal McRae.

23. While watching Robinson take infield practice one afternoon, Lou Gorman noticed that the great third baseman, considered perhaps the best fielder the game has ever seen at that position, was not uncommonly agile, nor possessed of an exceptional arm. Curious, Gorman pulled Robinson's scouting files and saw that, indeed, he had not been graded particularly high on physical skills but had received top marks in all the categories of makeup. "He had that great makeup and intensity to make himself a Hall of Fame player," said Gorman. Shanks, *Scout's Honor*, 172.

24. "We . . . knew [Murray] had very high drive, and we knew it was masked by something called emotional control," Ritterpusch remarked in a television interview. "Now, we really didn't realize how important emotional control would be in Eddie's career, but of course that's one of the things that enabled him to be a selective hitter and hit over .400 with the bases loaded." *The Orioles Warehouse*, "Inside the Orioles' heads," May 29, 2004. Ritterpusch's interview occurred on the "Take Me Out to the Ballgame" show on the Mid-Atlantic Sports Network.

25. Mike Stadler, *The Psychology of Baseball*, 109.

26. Mark Armour and Malcolm Allen, editors, *Pitching, Defense, and Three-Run Homers: The 1970 Baltimore Orioles*.

27. Baseball-reference.com.

28. John Monteleone, editor, *Branch Rickey's Little Blue Book*, 107, 58.

29. "A scout," said Rickey, "will enthusiastically tell me about a player: I'm telling you, 'He can hit a ball a "fur piece." . . . Branch, he loves to play.' Invariably, the scout tacks it on. Sometimes I think it has to be tacked on. It's a sad commentary on a man who is physically and materially set up for a great career in this game and has no showmanship in the field of desire to enjoy it, to want to play. . . . So there is that extra thing to look for in a prospective player." Ibid., 56.

30. Kerrane, *Dollar Sign on the Muscle*, 131.

31. Ibid., 135.

32. Ibid., 136.

33. Ibid.

34. Ibid., 238.

35. Shanks, *Scout's Honor*, 363.

36. In recent years, team after team, when replacing its general manager, has opted for a young respecter of both approaches, marrying the objective and subjective. In 2011 alone, five teams—the Cubs, Red Sox, Astros, Angels, and Padres—moved in that direction. Meanwhile, broad-based organizations such as the Rays, Red Sox, Cardinals, Giants, Phillies, Indians, and Angels have established a modern standard in that respect.

37. Ben Lindbergh, "Overthinking It," *Baseball Prospectus,* December 20, 2011.

38. The acronym TINSTAAPP was coined by Gary Huckabay, the founder of *Baseball Prospectus* and the previously unmentioned member of the "Great Debate" panel assembled by *Baseball America.*

39. What Ryan *doesn't* want to hear about is a prospect's changeup. "We're drafting a guy in the first round with a tremendous *changeup*? Number one, if you don't have a fastball to set up the changeup, it's worthless," he said. "As soon as you start hearing a guy talking about a changeup too much in the pitcher's description, you might as well turn the page. And about the same can be said about a curveball."

40. Kerrane, *Dollar Sign,* 160, 99. Jim Baumer, one of the Phillies' chief scouts and for a while their director of scouting and minor-league operations, was especially preoccupied with meanness in a pitching prospect. Wrote Kerrane on page 261: "*Meek* and *puss* were the most damning words in his reports."

    On page 275, Kerrane described how Baumer, when he was director of scouting for the Milwaukee Brewers, had dismissed a scout named Gary Nickels. "He never played pro baseball himself, so it's hard for him to size up a player's intangibles: dedication or teachability or toughness. A lot of young scouts have that problem."

41. John Burden, an area scout for the Los Angeles Angels of Anaheim, takes a similar approach. "We do a lot of research with coaches, teammates, opponents," Burden said. "We go in the house on any top-round kid and visit with the family. We talk to coaches, high school kids, meet with counselors, I may speak with athletic directors. I've caught myself even talking to umpires. How did that kid react when you missed a call? With us, it's a major part of it."

    Concerning the benefits of a scout consulting with numerous sources about a player, there's also this, as paraphrased from Anup Sinha and Bill Lajoie, *Character Is Not a Statistic* (32): Approaching the first Major-

League draft, which took place in 1965, the Cincinnati Reds were strongly considering Michigan teenager Bernie Carbo but were troubled by a remark from Carbo's high school coach, who suggested that Carbo lacked discipline and commitment. However, Lajoie, then a rookie scout, learned from his conversations with locals that the baseball coach was also the football coach, and he was upset with Carbo for quitting the football team in his senior year. Carbo thus became the Reds' first-ever draft choice, one round ahead of Johnny Bench.

42. Sinha and Lajoie, *Character Is Not a Statistic,* 78.

CHAPTER 9

1. Three weeks later, Phillips would make an even flashier play against an even faster runner, ranging to his left to charge a grounder from Houston speedster Jason Bourgeois and, without time to do anything else, flipping the ball between his legs to Votto for the out. Jayson Stark called it the "most inventive play of the year by far." Stark, "Month of May Delivered the Unexpected," espn.com, May 31, 2011.

2. Mark Sheldon, "Baker Still Seeing Red Over Rain Delay," mlb.com, April 23, 2011.

3. Bernie Miklasz, "Never a Dull Moment with Cards," *St. Louis Post-Dispatch,* May 2, 2011.

4. Bernie Miklasz, "Cards Look Like Runaway Winners," *St. Louis Post-Dispatch,* May 3, 2010.

5. Williams, for example, was a flat .500 pitcher over eleven years in San Diego and Toronto. After being dealt to the Cardinals at the 2001 trading deadline, he was 45–22 for them over four seasons. Pitching for four teams in nine seasons before coming to St. Louis, Suppan had never won more than ten games. In his three seasons with the Cardinals (2004–06), he won sixteen, sixteen, and twelve. Pitching for the Reds at the prime ages of twenty-seven and twenty-eight, Lohse was 9–17 with a 4.58 ERA. In five subsequent seasons with the Cardinals (2008–12), he was 55–35, 3.90.

6. John Perrotto, "New Blood, Same Result," *Baseball Prospectus,* May 10, 2010.

7. Rob Neyer, "Kyle Lohse Can't Get Work Because . . . Well, Just Because," sbnation.com, February 26, 2013.

8. Bryan Burwell, "Cardinals' Sideshow Is Quite an Event," *St. Louis Post-Dispatch,* August 29, 2009.

9. "Step aside, Yankees–Red Sox and Giants-Dodgers," wrote David Schoenfield on his espn.com blog. "There is a new most-heated rivalry in baseball. The Cincinnati Reds and St. Louis Cardinals are no longer just NL Central

rivals: They are officially blood enemies. . . . Those two [others] just don't have the animosity and dislike that fuels every Reds-Cardinals game these days." Schoenfield, "Reds-Cardinals Baseball's Best Rivalry," espn.com, May 16, 2011.

10. Bernie Miklasz, "Bernie Bytes: A Jillion Thoughts on Cards-Reds," *St. Louis Post-Dispatch,* May 16, 2011.

11. Mark Sheldon, "Reds Fall in 19 After Mistakes, Missed Chances," mlb .com, May 26, 2011.

12. The self-destruction of Volquez played out in sharp contrast to the attention to detail—and consequently the career path—of Johnny Cueto, his pal and fellow Dominican. In a duel with Clayton Kershaw, Cueto helped preserve a 3-2 victory and sweep of the Dodgers by slipping behind Matt Kemp as Kemp backtracked to first base after hitting a pop-fly single.

13. After Gomes played an important role in the surprising success of the Oakland A's in 2012, A's pitcher Brandon McCarthy, known for his uncommon (for a player) attention to sabermetrics, sang his praises while speaking at the SABR Analytics Conference. McCarthy's sentiments were reported in Jay Jaffe, "A Stathead Reconsiders His Position on Chemistry," si.com, March 14, 2013:

> McCarthy surprised the audience by asserting that had Brandon Inge and Jonny Gomes—a duo that combined for a modest 2.8 Wins Above Replacement Player—not been part of the team, the A's would have finished 2012 with 70 wins instead of 94, the difference being those players' efforts "behind closed doors." Elaborating to *AZCentral.com*'s Nick Piecoro afterward, McCarthy explained: "It sounds stupid, but if you have a rookie that comes up and rookies are filled with self-doubt, filled with worry, and now you're in the big leagues and you come to a team where nobody makes you feel welcome. . . . You don't feel kind of free and like you can do what you do. But if you have a guy like Jonny Gomes or Brandon Inge or someone who just comes up and is just kind of (BS-ing) with you and it just sort of loosens you up and then everyone else can kind of get in the mix. I know it sounds really stupid, but it's kind of like being an artist where the more comfortable you feel, usually your better work comes out. . . . It goes for veterans and everybody . . . there's a whole trickle down effect to it that's impossible to quantify but it does exist in there."

14. Jerry Crasnick, "Lance Berkman Again a Hitting Machine," espn.com, May 5, 2011.

15. Joe Strauss, "Rasmus Drama Remains Hot Topic," *St. Louis Post-Dispatch,* July 17, 2011.

16. From 1991, the year Schuerholz took over as general manager, through

2004, Atlanta outperformed its Pythagorean expectation on ten occasions (by a total of thirty-six wins) and fell short of it only twice (by a total of four wins). Twice, it was a wash. Those years, the Braves won 104 and 106 games.

17. The epic comeback of the '51 Giants covered a greater deficit than St. Louis's did in 2011, but required more time.

18. Jayson Stark, "Cardinals complete impossible dream," espn.com, October 29, 2011.

19. Howard Bryant, "In victory and defeat," espn.com, October 29, 2011.

CHAPTER 10

1. Chris Jaffe, *Evaluating Baseball's Managers: A History and Analysis of Performance in the Major Leagues, 1876–2008*, 27. By Jaffe's extensive, deeply considered criteria, La Russa trailed only Joe McCarthy, the great Yankees skipper of the thirties and forties. A sampling of other ranks: 4 Walter Alston, 5 John McGraw, 7 Earl Weaver, 11 Bobby Cox, 13t Dick Williams, 13t Sparky Anderson, 19 Casey Stengel, 21 Joe Torre, 23 Ron Gardenhire, 24 Whitey Herzog, 25 Davey Johnson, 28 Bobby Valentine, 30 Bruce Bochy.

2. Howard Bryant, "The Revolutionary," espn.com, July 26, 2009. Wrote Bryant, "The Moneyball way also diminishes the field manager's organizational influence while it increases the power and profile of the general manager position—a job that was once largely invisible. In the 140-year history of Major League Baseball, the office of field manager has never held less power than it does now, in the wake of Moneyball."

3. Examining Dusty Baker's tenure with the Giants, author Leonard Koppett wrote that Baker "was as close to perfect as one could find. . . . What made him truly exceptional were his people-person skills. He could establish and maintain a rapport with every player. . . . He was a people person to the core." Koppett, *The Man in the Dugout*, 316–21.

4. Gary Huckabay, Chris Kahrl, and Dave Pease, *Baseball Prospectus, 2003 Edition*, 491–92. Noted the authors, "Players seem to play better under Baker than under other managers. Much better. During the Dusty Baker era, Giant position players have a remarkable record for career years, career peaks, and career turnarounds. Player after player has joined the Giants and immediately begun exceeding all reasonable expectations at the plate."

5. Jaffe, *Evaluating Baseball's Managers*, 248.

6. Ibid., 11.

7. Ibid., 1.

8. Bob Gibson with Lonnie Wheeler, *Stranger to the Game,* 65.

9. Ibid., 101.

10. Hank Aaron with Lonnie Wheeler, *I Had a Hammer,* 71.

11. Max Marchi, "The Hidden Helpers of the Pitching Staff," *Baseball Prospectus,* March 9, 2012.

12. Jaffe, *Evaluating Baseball's Managers,* 14.

13. "A lot of my work is what guys do to get ready for the next pitch," explained Ravizza. "Control your emotions. Body language is huge. Watch a pitcher. If he's out there stalking, if a pitcher shows vulnerability, hitters are like sharks. They smell blood. Letting go of the body language sounds so simple, but it's so difficult to do. Just the way you walk back to the dugout; how you carry yourself. If a guy's shoulders are slouched and there's drama out there, that can pull other people down, no question."

14. In Herzog's view, Templeton "had troubles all year [1981] long, dogging it on us and complaining all the time." Whitey Herzog and Kevin Horrigan, *White Rat,* 135.

15. Ibid., 16.

16. Ibid., 148–51.

17. Tim McCarver with Jim Moskovitz and Danny Peary, *Tim McCarver's Diamond Gems,* Kindle edition.

18. Ibid.

19. Jaffe, *Evaluating Baseball's Managers,* 1.

20. Ibid., 29.

21. See baseball-almanac.com.

22. Branch Rickey with Robert Riger, *The American Diamond,* 32.

23. Buddy Bell and Nick Vahle, *Smart Baseball,* 34.

24. In fact, according to Yogi, he became a great catcher only because "Bill Dickey learned me all of his experiences." And according to Bill James in *The Bill James Gold Mine 2009,* page 167, Dickey ranked number one all-time in a contrived category called Catcher Pride Points. To arrive at those, James tallied a number of items (catching a no-hitter, catching a Cy Young Award winner, catching a staff that leads the league in ERA, catching for a team that wins a World Series, etc.) in which catchers are likely to take unusual satisfaction. "Dickey took the lead in converting from an outfielder to a catcher not only Yogi, but also Elston Howard," wrote James. "If you combine that with the large number of rookie pitchers, it creates an argument that Dickey did have an unusual ability to work with others and to bring out the best in them, which is central to what we are trying to measure here."

25. As Ramirez fussed with the Boston front office, "Manny got to the point he wanted to get out of here and it got out of hand; we had to make a move,"

said former teammate David Ortiz. "The Manny case got to be a little bit of a black cloud in the clubhouse because he wasn't happy and the team wasn't happy. Look, I'm not pointing any fingers, but when something happens you can't have twenty-four good apples going bad because of one bad apple. I'm not saying my boy was a bad apple, but he wasn't happy. He was a huge part of this ballclub and he just wasn't happy, and it was affecting everybody."

That sentiment was amplified in remarks by reliever Jonathan Papelbon, in Chris Jones, "Jonathan Papelbon Grinds His Teeth," *Esquire,* May 7, 2009: "[Manny] was on a different train! . . . It just takes one guy to bring an entire team down, and that's exactly what was happening. . . . It's like cancer. That's what he was. Cancer. He had to go. . . . We got Jason Bay—Johnny Ballgame, plays the game right, plays through broken knees, runs out every ground ball—and it was like a breath of fresh air, man!"

26. Joe Torre and Tom Verducci, *The Yankee Years,* 241. In the five years before A-Rod took his act to New York in 2004, the Yankees had appeared in four World Series (and six in eight seasons). In the five years after his arrival, they made it to none. "And because Alex Rodriguez became a Yankee," the authors wrote on page 238, "the Yankees' clubhouse and the personality of the team, already sliding further from the O'Neill-Martinez-Brosius band of brothers comportment, would never be the same."

27. Craig Wright, "Piazza, Hall of Fame Catcher," *Hardball Times Baseball Annual, 2009.*

28. "Piazza," wrote Marchi in his analysis of a catcher's influence, "has always been considered a poor defensive catcher because of his inability to throw out basestealers. However, he . . . now emerges as one of the best ever at handling the pitching staff." Max Marchi, "The Hidden Helpers of the Pitching Staff," *Baseball Prospectus*, March 9, 2012.

29. Max Marchi, "Evaluating Catchers: Quantifying the Framing Pitches Skill," and "Evaluating Catchers: Framing Pitches, Part 2," *Baseball Prospectus,* June 10, 2011, and June 24, 2011.

30. A quickie example of Baker's aid to hitters: On May 7, 2013, the Reds, playing at home, trailed the Atlanta Braves, 4-3, with two outs in the bottom of the ninth and nobody on base. Pitching for Atlanta was Craig Kimbrel, the sensational closer who had saved eighty-eight games over the past two seasons. Batting for the Reds, as a pinch hitter, was Devin Mesoraco. With the count three-and-two, Kimbrel delivered a smoking low fastball that Mesoraco deposited over the fence in right-center field to tie the game. The next batter, Shin-Soo Choo, won it for Cincinnati with a home run to left-center. In the words of Mesoraco "Dusty always says with two strikes, look for the hardest pitch away and that's what it was." C. Trent Rosecrans,

"Reds Stun Braves with Back-to-Back Homers in 9th," *Cincinnati Enquirer,* May 8, 2013.

31. In *Tim McCarver's Diamond Gems,* Seaver credited Mets manager Gil Hodges with developing his approach as a pitcher. "From a professional standpoint," Seaver told McCarver, "he was the most important individual in my career. . . . He made me think differently as a pitcher and look ahead as I went through the batting order. For instance, I came to understand the importance of getting the eighth-place hitter out to end the eighth inning so that in the ninth inning, they wouldn't get to their fourth-place hitter with the tying run on base."

32. This was on the MLB Network early in 2013.

33. Bill James, *The Bill James Gold Mine 2009,* 163.

34. In John Erardi, "Ryan Hanigan: Receiver of Wisdom," *Cincinnati Enquirer,* October 4, 2012, Arroyo described his devotion to Hanigan as follows: "He's a thinker, man. He's not one-dimensional; he thinks outside the box. He can catch onto adjustments I'm making on the fly. It's nice to have a guy back there who you know isn't wondering why I'm making these weird calls. He's a guy that you can tell by his body language is saying, 'I see where you're going with this.' It builds a nice confidence about what we're doing out there."

35. Jaffe, *Evaluating Baseball's Managers,* 198.

36. Chris Jaffe, "Scioscia and Gardenhire . . . So Far," *Hardball Times,* April 12, 2010. A similar thing could be said of the Los Angeles Angels of Anaheim under Mike Scioscia. Starting in 2004, the Angels, along the way claiming five division titles in a span of six years, exceeded their Pythagorean projections for nine consecutive seasons. Scioscia's resourceful teams were characterized by their lack of home runs and walks, offset by an emphasis on contact and aggressive baserunning. (In Anaheim's minor-league system, an annual award was given to the player who advanced most often from first base to third on a single.) The small-ball tradition was reminiscent of the Los Angeles Dodgers clubs for which Scioscia caught in 1,395 games. The Angels typically featured a deep pitching staff and outstanding bullpen, as well, completing a profile of a team that would play close games and consistently grind them out. All the while, Scioscia, over his first ten seasons, compiled a distinguished record in what Jaffe called "managerial impact," ranking fourteenth all-time in "the algorithms that focus on getting players to perform their best."

Tom Verducci, "Party's Just Getting Started," *Sports Illustrated,* July 16, 2007, described the Angels' style as "an organization-wide culture of unselfishness." Its tenets were taken with uncommon seriousness. When Reggie Willits, a speedy, slap-hitting outfielder, occasionally muscled up and hit a ball over the fence in batting practice, Scioscia would make him run a lap around the ballpark. Willits completed his six-year career with zero home runs.

CHAPTER 11

1. Scott Radley, "How MVP-Candidate Joey Votto Honed His Skills in Hamilton," *Hamilton Spectator,* October 5, 2010. Concerning Votto's insistence on using wood bats, Radley wrote, "Still refusing [to use a metal bat] and maybe feeling he had a little something to prove, Votto stepped in and hit a ball . . . over the 400-foot fence, over a small field and right into the middle of a pond 500-and-something feet from the plate."
2. In the interest of being a good teammate, Votto hired a tutor in the offseason to teach him Spanish, so that he could converse with Aroldis Chapman.
3. "Better catching means better pitching for us," said Bill Bavasi, the Reds' director of player development. Mark Sheldon, "Reds make some changes to Minors staffs," mlb.com, November 29, 2011.
4. Bob Elliott, "Joey Votto: The Legend Begins," *Toronto Sun,* April 14, 2012.
5. Ibid.
6. Dave Cameron, "Joey Votto's Massive Extension Changes the Game," *Fangraphs,* April 2, 2012. In an attempt to judge the financial soundness of the controversial contract, Cameron projected Votto's WAR on a year-by-year basis for the duration of the deal. "If we start at $5 million per win and apply the 5% future inflation to these expected performances," he wrote, "we'd get a total of $249 million over the next 12 years, almost exactly what the Reds just signed Votto for."
7. Buster Olney, "The Crossroads for Joey Votto," espn.com, April 3, 2012.
8. Three of the Griffey seasons also included a sentimental $27 million deal for shortstop Barry Larkin at the age of thirty-seven, a gesture that would have been favorably received around town—Larkin was a native Cincinnatian and future Hall of Famer—if it had not precluded the signing of essential personnel that the Reds acutely lacked.
9. John Fay, "It's Official: Reds Sign Joey Votto to Long-Term Extension," *Cincinnati Enquirer,* April 5, 2012.
10. According to a story in the *Miami Herald,* Ramirez had also alienated some of his teammates by the volume of his music in the clubhouse, his perceived indifference to defeat, and his treatment of staff personnel. Manny Navarro, "Miami Marlins Teammates Have Mixed Reaction to Hanley Ramirez's Exit," *Miami Herald,* July 26, 2012.
11. That's according to PECOTA, which stands for Player Empirical Compari-

son and Optimization Test Algorithm. PECOTA is a popular metric devised by Nate Silver and *Baseball Prospectus* to predict upcoming performances from players and, by extension, teams.

12. The Toms River club—not surprisingly, in light of Frazier's rollicking personality—is said to be the first to bark in chorus to "Who Let the Dogs Out." Jeff Bradley, "Toms River's Todd Frazier Has to Be the Favorite to Win NL Rookie of the Year," *Newark Star-Ledger,* August 22, 2012.

13. "I don't understand that one," Baker said. "A snub like that looks bad." John Fay, "Reds Angered by Snub of Cueto, Phillips," *Cincinnati Enquirer,* July 1, 2012.

14. Jonah Keri, "The 30, Week 11: Seeing Red," *Grantland,* June 18, 2012.

15. David Schoenfield, "More on Joey Votto's Awesomeness," espn.com, June 18, 2012. "Votto's 204 OPS+ isn't necessarily unprecedented, . . ." Schoenfield went on. "I'm not discounting all those other seasons, but merely pointing [out] the difficult[y] of Votto doing this at a time when pitchers have regained control of the game. So far, of course, it's only been through 65 games. But what a stretch of hitting."

16. Buster Olney, "Thinking Inside the Box," *ESPN the Magazine,* March 19, 2013.

17. Ibid.

18. Richard Griffin, "Griffin: Spotlight Still Not Shining on Joey Votto and He Loves It," *Toronto Star,* July 10, 2012.

19. Jerry Crasnick, "Joey Votto Has a Razor-Like Focus," espn.com, May 22, 2013.

20. Buster Olney, video blog, espn.com, April 28, 2011.

21. Mark Sheldon, "Reds Aim to Drink from 'The Cup' Three More Times," mlb.com, October 5, 2012.

22. The eclectic dimensions of Dusty Baker's life served him well in the company of the clubhouse. In Cincinnati, he brought in wine—perhaps a red from the vineyard next to his solar-powered home in Sacramento—for his coaches, fished with Mat Latos, picked out shirts for Bronson Arroyo, conversed in Spanish with Johnny Cueto, and exchanged books with Homer Bailey. His stories covered lessons from Aaron and hanging out at Haight-Ashbury in the sixties. He held forth on, among other topics, Egyptian art, the Marine reserves, Bob Marley, the blues, and the therapeutic properties of Kauai, where he recovered from prostate cancer.

23. Bob Nightengale, "Reds' Dusty Baker in Limbo, But He's Not Worried," *USA Today,* August 15, 2012.

24. Jack Moore gave an account of Bailey's no-hitter in which he credited Hanigan for recognizing that the Pirates were chasing high fastballs. "If ever a start showcased the possibilities when pitcher and catcher have everything

working together, this was it," he wrote. "Hanigan formed a distinct plan, showed precise targets and used great receiving to get extra strikes for Bailey. And of course, Bailey perfectly executed the plan, using pinpoint control to keep Pirates hitters from making hard contact." Moore, "Homer Bailey and Ryan Hanigan No-hit Pittsburgh," *Fangraphs*, September 29, 2012.

25. Both of the Reds' victories in San Francisco involved situational small things that altered the games. With a Giants runner at first base in the first inning of game one, Cincinnati center fielder Drew Stubbs saved a run by hustling over to cut off a double in the gap by Gregor Blanco and hold the runner at third. Later, Blanco reached base on an infield hit. Rolen's throw skipped past Votto at first base, but Phillips, dashing into foul territory to back up the play, made a diving stop to keep Blanco from advancing into scoring position. The Reds gained an advantage in game two when San Francisco outfielder Hunter Pence missed the cutoff man on an ill-advised throw to home plate, allowing two runners to alertly advance. Both scored when Hanigan punched a single through an infield positioned close to cut off a run. Had the runners been at first and second and the infielders deployed in normal position, Hanigan's ball probably would have been an inning-ending double play.

26. John Fay, "Stunning Playoff Loss Lingered," *Cincinnati Enquirer,* December 7, 2012. The nature of the season's abrupt conclusion was hard for Votto to handle. "I couldn't even talk about it for a good bit," he told Fay. "I still haven't spoken about it. I have no interest in speaking about it. To have it in your grasp and have it fall through . . . it's partially why I'm wearing this beard right now, I'm going Rocky IV style. I'm really upset with the way the season ended."

CHAPTER 12

1. Tyler Kepner, "The Name and Speed to Revive the Steal," *New York Times,* May 5, 2012.

2. At the end of 2012, Cincinnati's top-rated prospect was Billy Hamilton, an absurdly fast switch-hitter who, as the Reds were taking the NL Central, was setting a minor-league record with 155 stolen bases in a season.

3. In 2013, the Reds reached the postseason for the third time in four seasons. However, in faltering at the finish line of the regular season, losing their final five games, they missed the opportunity for home-field advantage in the wildcard game. Traveling instead to Pittsburgh, they went down meekly. On that note, Dusty Baker was fired after six seasons as Cincinnati's manager.

4. Jeff Passan, "Giants' Cast of Characters Share Starring Role in World Series Triumph," *Yahoo Sports,* October 29, 2012.

5. Jon Heyman, "Giants Turned Out to Be Tougher, Smarter, Better Than Most Everyone Expected," cbssports.com, October 29, 2012.

6. Richard Justice, "Giants Flew Under the Radar to Their Title," mlb.com, October 29, 2012.

7. Passan, "Giants' Cast of Characters Share Starring Role in World Series Triumph," *Yahoo Sports.*

8. Elwood Chapman, *Life Is an Attitude!* 133.

9. Joe Torre with Henry Dreher, *Joe Torre's Ground Rules for Winners,* 156.

10. Norman Vincent Peale, *The Power of Positive Thinking,* Kindle edition.

11. Joe Posnanski, "It's All About October," joeposnanskiblogspot, October 29, 2012. "The Giants have now won two of three World Series," wrote Posnanski, "and they have done so in a thoroughly modern way. . . . It used to be that you wanted to build the best team. Now, though, you want to build the best October team."

12. Michael Lewis, *Moneyball,* 275.

13. John C. Maxwell, *Teamwork Makes the Dream Work,* 108. An example of Riley's insight would be the George Mason University program developed by coach Jim Larranaga, who brought together undervalued recruits from championship high school programs, counting on their commitment to winning. That energy carried an eleven seed to the Final Four in 2006.

    Similarly, former Butler University coach Brad Stevens, unable to compete for top-rated talent with the power-conference programs, based "the Butler way" on such core values as "humility, passion, unity, servanthood and thankfulness," those feelings of significance fostering consecutive trips to the NCAA title game in 2010 and 2011. Mike DeCourcy, "The 'Butler Way' of success will be much tougher to sustain in A-10," *The Sporting News,* May 2, 2012.

14. James T., "An Interview with Bill James," sonsofsamhorn.net, September 14, 2007.

15. The average BABIP falls in the vicinity of .300. Carew's career mark was .359, fifth-best all-time for players with at least 3,000 at-bats, according to waswatching.com. The top four are Ty Cobb, Shoeless Joe Jackson, Rogers Hornsby, and Joey Votto.

16. Tim McCarver with Jim Moskovitz and Danny Peary, *Tim McCarver's Diamond Gems,* Kindle edition.

17. In *Tim McCarver's Diamond Gems,* Warren Spahn provided a vivid symbol of Hank Aaron's surpassing ability to square up the baseball. "One year in the middle of June," he said, "Lew Burdette and I picked up one of his bats,

a bat that he had used all year since spring training. That bat wasn't broken; it wasn't even chipping—all of the marks were on the fat part of the bat, in one place. That's kind of scary, isn't it?"

18. David Leonhardt, "You Gotta Have Clutch," *New York Times,* October 22, 2009.

19. A blog in the *Harvard Business Review* cited a study in which 91 percent of corporate executives attested that "culture is as important as strategy for business success." Paul Meehan, Darrell Rigby, and Paul Rogers, "Creating and Sustaining a Winning Culture," *Harvard Business Review,* February 27, 2008.

 According to the survey, which was conducted by Bain & Company, 70 percent of the executives agreed that culture, in fact, "provides the greatest source of competitive advantage." Paul Rogers, Paul Meehan, and Scott Tanner, "Building a Winning Culture," Bain.com, August 25, 2006.

BIBLIOGRAPHY

Aaron, Hank, with Lonnie Wheeler. *I Had a Hammer.* New York: HarperCollins, 1991.

Allen, Maury. *Jackie Robinson: A Life Remembered.* New York: Franklin Watts, 1987.

Altman-Ohr, Andy. "Unknown Hero Helps Make Giants World Series Champions." Jweekly.com, November 4, 2010.

Armour, Mark, and Malcolm Allen, editors. *Pitching, Defense, and Three-Run Homers: The 1970 Baltimore Orioles.* Lincoln: University of Nebraska Press, 2012.

Baseball-almanac.com.

Baseball-reference.com.

Bell, Buddy, and Neal Vahle. *Smart Baseball.* New York: St. Martin's Griffin, 2005.

Boswell, Thomas. *How Life Imitates the World Series.* New York: Penguin, 1982.

———. *Why Time Begins on Opening Day.* New York: Viking Penguin, 1985.

Bowden, Jim. "Chipper Jones Sends a Message." espn.com, June 8, 2011.

Bozich, Rick. "Bailey's Split Decision Has Foes Dazzled." *Louisville Courier-Journal,* June 17, 2009.

Bradley, Jeff. "Toms River's Todd Frazier Has to Be the Favorite to Win NL Rookie of the Year." *Newark Star-Ledger,* August 22, 2012.

Bronson, Eric, editor. *Baseball and Philosophy.* Chicago: Open Court, 2004.

Bryant, Howard. "In Victory and Defeat." espn.com, October 29, 2011.

———. "The Revolutionary." espn.com, July 26, 2009.

Burwell, Bryan. "Cards' Sideshow Is Quite an Event." *St. Louis Post-Dispatch,* August 29, 2009.

Cahalan, Susannah. "How Jeter Put A-Rod in the Yankees' 'Snubhouse.'" *New York Post,* April 25, 2011.

Cameron, Dave. "Joey Votto's Massive Extension Changes the Game." *Fangraphs,* April 2, 2012.

Chapman, Elwood. *Life Is an Attitude!* Menlo Park, Calif.: Crisp Publications, 1992.

Chen, Albert. "Feel the Glove." *Sports Illustrated,* March 1, 2010.

Claire, Fred. *My 30 Years in Dodger Blue.* Champaign, Ill.: Sports Publishing, 2004.

Coyle, Daniel. *The Talent Code.* New York: Bantam Press, 2009.

Crasnick, Jerry. "Jeter Hitting Monumental Heights." espn.com, September 4, 2009.

———. "Joey Votto Has a Razor-like Focus." espn.com, May 22, 2013.

———. "Lance Berkman Again a Hitting Machine." espn.com, May 5, 2011.

———. "Phillips Packs a Ton of Fun into His Game." espn.com, July 20, 2010.

Daugherty, Paul. "Anyone Still Questioning Reds' Trade for Scott Rolen?" *Cincinnati Enquirer,* May 19, 2010.

———. "'Need Ya on Third, Brucie,' Has Become Reds' Mantra." *Cincinnati Enquirer,* March 10, 2011.

DeCourcy, Mike. "The 'Butler Way' of Success Will Be Much Harder to Sustain in A-10." *The Sporting News,* May 2, 2012.

Dorfman, H. A., and Karl Kuehl. *The Mental Game of Baseball.* Lanham, Md.: Taylor Trade Publishing, 2002.

Eckstein, David, with Greg Brown. *Have Heart.* Bothell, Wash.: Positively for Kids, 2003.

Elliott, Bob. "Joey Votto: The Legend Begins." *Toronto Sun,* April 14, 2012.

Erardi, John. "Ryan Hanigan: Receiver of Wisdom," *Cincinnati Enquirer,* October 4, 2012.

Fay, John. "Aroldis Chapman Gets First Win as Reds Sweep Brewers." *Cincinnati Enquirer,* September 1, 2010.

———. "It's Official: Reds Sign Joey Votto to Long-Term Extension." *Cincinnati Enquirer,* April 5, 2012.

———. "Reds Angered by Snub of Cueto, Phillips." *Cincinnati Enquirer,* July 1, 2012.

———. "Stunning Playoff Loss Lingered." *Cincinnati Enquirer,* December 7, 2012.

Felber, Bill. *The Book on the Book.* New York: St. Martin's Press, 2005.

Fisher, Joshua. "It's Okay to Be Mystified by Linear Weights." *Hardball Times,* March 9, 2010.

Futterman, Matthew. "Baseball's New Best Enemies." *Wall Street Journal,* September 3, 2010.

Gibson, Bob, with Lonnie Wheeler. *Stranger to the Game.* New York: Viking, 1994.

Gibson, Bob, and Reggie Jackson with Lonnie Wheeler. *Sixty Feet, Six Inches.* New York: Doubleday, 2009.

Gladwell, Malcolm. "The Physical Genius." *The New Yorker,* August 2, 1999.

Gola, Mark. *Baseball's Sixth Tool.* New York: McGraw-Hill, 2008.

Goldman, Steven, editor, and the writers of Baseball Prospectus. *Mind Game.* New York: Workman Publishing, 2005.

Greenberg, Eric Rolfe. *The Celebrant.* New York: Penguin, 1986.

Griffin, Richard. "Griffin: Spotlight Still Not Shining on Joey Votto and He Loves It." *Toronto Star,* July 10, 2012.

Henderson, Joe. "Character Counts In Rays Clubhouse." *Tampa Tribune* blog, February 17, 2009.

Hertzel, Bob. *The Big Red Machine.* Englewood Cliffs, N.J.: Prentice-Hall, 1976.

Herzog, Whitey, and Kevin Horrigan. *White Rat: A Life in Baseball.* New York: Perennial Library, 1988.

Heyman, Jon. "Giants Turned Out to Be Tougher, Smarter, Better Than Most Everyone Expected." cbssports.com, October 29, 2012.

Hirsch, Sheldon, and Alan Hirsch. *The Beauty of Short Hops: How Chance and Circumstance Confound the Moneyball Approach to Baseball.* Jefferson, N.C.: McFarland, 2011.

The Holy Bible. King James Version.

Huckabay, Gary, Chris Kahrl, and Dave Pease. *Baseball Prospectus, 2003 Edition.* Washington, D.C.: Brassey's Sports, 2003.

Jaffe, Chris. *Evaluating Baseball's Managers.* Jefferson, N.C.: McFarland, 2009.

———. "Scioscia and Gardenhire . . . So Far." *Hardball Times,* April 12. 2010.

Jaffe, Jay. "A Stathead Reconsiders His Position on Chemistry." si.com, March 14, 2013.

James, Bill. *The Bill James Gold Mine 2009.* Skokie, Ill.: ACTA Sports, 2009.

———. *The New Bill James Historical Abstract.* New York: Free Press, 2001.

Jones, Chris. "Jonathan Papelbon Grinds His Teeth." *Esquire,* May 7, 2009.

Justice, Richard. "Giants Flew Under the Radar to Their Title." mlb.com, October 29, 2012.

Kaduk, Kevin (Duk). "J. P. Ricciardi Does Not Think Very Highly of Adam Dunn." yahoo.com, June 19, 2008.

Kay, Joe. "Extra Base Can Translate into Higher Place." Associated Press, May 18, 2010.

Keese, Parton. *The Measure of Greatness.* Englewood Cliffs, N.J.: Prentice-Hall, 1981.

Kepner, Tyler. "First-Place Reds Follow Scott Rolen's Lead." *New York Times* blog, June 2, 2010.

———. "Investment in Rolen Is Paying Off for the Reds." *New York Times,* June 1, 2010.

———. Kepner, Tyler. "The Name and Speed to Revive the Steal." *New York Times,* May 5, 2012.

Keri, Jonah. *The Extra 2%.* New York: ESPN Books, 2011.

———. "The 30, Week 11: Seeing Red." *Grantland,* June 18, 2012.

Keri, Jonah, editor. *Baseball Between the Numbers.* New York: Basic Books, 2006.

Kerrane, Kevin. *Dollar Sign on the Muscle.* New York: Beaufort Books, 1984.

Koppett, Leonard. *The Man in the Dugout.* Philadelphia: Temple University Press, 2000.

Klaassen, Matt. "King of the Little Things 2009." *FanGraphs,* November 9, 2009.

Kuehl, Karl, John Kuehl, and Casey Tefertiller. *Mental Toughness: A Champion's State of Mind.* Lanham, Md.: Ivan R. Dee, 2005.

Kurkjian, Tim. "Herrera Short in Stature, Not Heart." *ESPN The Magazine,* June 13, 2009.

Lancaster, Marc. "Melees Show Rays' United Front." *Tampa Tribune,* June 8, 2008.

Lederer, Rich. "Q&A: Paul DePodesta." *Baseball Analysts,* June 18, 2009.

Leonhardt, David. "You Gotta Have Clutch." *New York Times,* October 22, 2009.

Lewis, Michael. *Moneyball.* New York: W. W. Norton, 2003.

Lindbergh, Ben. "Overthinking It." *Baseball Prospectus,* December 20, 2011.

———. "The Whole Ball Player." *Baseball Prospectus,* April 13, 2012.

Lowenfish, Lee. *Branch Rickey.* Lincoln: University of Nebraska Press, 2007.

Mack, Gary, and David Casstevens. *Mind Gym: An Athlete's Guide to Inner Excellence.* New York: McGraw-Hill, 2002.

Marchi, Max. "Evaluating Catchers: Quantifying the Framing Pitches Skill." *Baseball Prospectus,* June 10, 2011.

———. "Evaluating Catchers: Framing Pitches, Part 2." *Baseball Prospectus,* June 24, 2011.

———. "The Stats Go Marching In: The Hidden Helpers of the Pitching staff." *Baseball Prospectus,* March 9, 2012.

Maxwell, John C. *Teamwork Makes the Dream Work.* Nashville, Tenn.: J. Countryman, 2002.

McAdam, Sean. "Strong Work Ethic Defines Varitek." espn.com, February 16, 2005.

McCarver, Tim, with Jim Moskovitz and Danny Peary. *Tim McCarver's Diamond Gems.* New York: McGraw-Hill, 2008.

Meehan, Paul, Darrell Rigby, and Paul Rogers. "Creating and Sustaining a Winning Culture." *Harvard Business Review,* February 27, 2008.

Miklasz, Bernie. "Bernie Bytes: A Jillion Thoughts on Cards-Reds." *St. Louis Post-Dispatch,* May 16, 2011.

———. "Cards Look Like Runaway Winners." *St. Louis Post-Dispatch,* May 3, 2010.

———. "Never a Dull Moment with Cards." *St. Louis Post-Dispatch,* May 2, 2011.

Monteleone, John, editor. *Branch Rickey's Little Blue Book.* New York: Macmillan, 1995.

Moore, Jack. "Homer Bailey and Ryan Hanigan No-Hit Pittsburgh." *Fangraphs,* September 29, 2012.

Morgan, Joe, and David Falkner. *Joe Morgan: A Life in Baseball.* New York: W. W. Norton, 1993.

Navarro, Manny. "Miami Marlins Teammates Have Mixed Reaction to Hanley Ramirez's Exit." *Miami Herald,* July 26, 2012.

Neyer, Rob. "Kyle Lohse Can't Get Work Because . . . Well, Just Because." sbnation.com, February 26, 2013.

Nightengale, Bob. "Monster Deal Gives Albert Pujols 'Extra Chip on My Shoulder.'" *USA Today,* April 3, 2012.

———. "Reds' Dusty Baker in Limbo, But He's Not Worried." *USA Today,* August 15, 2012.

Okrent, Daniel. *Nine Innings.* New York: McGraw-Hill, 1985.

Olney, Buster. "Baseball's Strengthening Code of Conduct." espn.com, February 26, 2009.

———. "The Crossroads for Joey Votto." espn.com, April 3, 2012.

———. "Thinking Inside the Box." *ESPN the Magazine,* March 19, 2013.

———. Video blog. espn.com, April 28, 2011.

The Orioles Warehouse. "Inside the Orioles' Heads, part 2." May 29, 2004.

Oswald, Andrew, Eugenio Proto, and Daniel Sgroi. "A New Happiness Equation: Worker + Happiness = Improved Productivity," Bulletin no. 3. Coventry, UK: Warwick University, 2009–10.

Passan, Jeff. "Giants' Cast of Characters Share Starring Role in World Series Triumph." *Yahoo Sports,* October 29, 2012.

Peale, Norman Vincent. *The Power of Positive Thinking.* New York: Touchstone, 2003.

Perrotto, John. "New Blood, Same Result." *Baseball Prospectus,* May 10, 2010.

Posnanski, Joe. "It's All About October." joeposnanskiblogspot, October 29, 2012.

———. "3000 Words About Derek Jeter." *Joe Blogs,* July 7, 2011.

Radley, Scott. "How MVP-Candidate Joey Votto Honed His Skills in Hamilton." *Hamilton Spectator,* October 5, 2010.

Ravizza, Ken, and Tom Hanson. *Heads-Up Baseball.* New York: McGraw-Hill, 1998.

Reiter, Ben. "Where's the Love?" *Sports Illustrated*, March 23, 2009.

Rickey, Branch. "Goodby to some old baseball ideas." *Life,* August 2, 1954.

Rickey, Branch, with Robert Riger. *The American Diamond.* New York: Simon & Schuster, 1965.

Ritter, Lawrence. *The Glory of Their Times.* New York: Macmillan, 1966.

Rogers, Paul, Paul Meehan, and Scott Tanner. "Building a Winning Culture." Bain.com, August 25, 2006.

Rosecrans, C. Trent. "Little Things Lead to Reds' Win." CNATI.com, September 16, 2009.

———. "Reds Stun Braves with Back-to-Back Homers in 9th." *Cincinnati Enquirer,* May 8, 2013.

———. "Talking with Bill James, Part I." CNATI.com, March 19, 2010.

———. "Thinking Out Loud." CNATI.com, May 19, 2010.

Rosenberg, Michael. "Good Chemistry Part of the Science Behind Giants' World Series Title." sportsillustrated.cnn.com, October 29, 2012.

Schoenfield, David. "More on Joey Votto's Awesomeness." espn.com, June 18, 2012.

———. "Reds-Cardinals Baseball's Best Rivalry." espn.com, May 16, 2011.

Schuerholz, John, with Larry Guest. *Built to Win.* New York: Warner Books, 2006.

Schulman, Henry. "Aaron Rowand: The (Broken) Face of the Franchise." *San Francisco Chronicle,* May 11, 2010.

Schwarz, Alan. "The Great Debate." *Baseball America,* January 7, 2005.

———. *The Numbers Game.* New York: St. Martin's Griffin, 2004.

Senge, Peter. *The Fifth Discipline: The Art and Practice of the Learning Organization.* New York: Doubleday, 2006.

Senn, Larry, and Jim Hart. *Winning Teams—Winning Cultures.* Long Beach, Calif.: Leadership Press, 2006.

Shanks, Bill. *Scout's Honor.* New York: Sterling & Ross, 2005.

Shaughnessy, Dan. *Reversing the Curse.* Boston: Houghton Mifflin, 2005.

Sheldon, Mark. "Baker Still Seeing Red Over Rain Delay." mlb.com, April 23, 2011.

———. "Baker: 'This is Embarrassing.'" *MLBlogs Network,* July 29, 2009.

———. Sheldon, Mark. "Reds Aim to Drink from 'The Cup' Three More Times." mlb.com, October 5, 2012.

———. "Reds Fall in 19 After Mistakes, Missed Chances." mlb.com, May 26, 2011.

———. "Reds Make Some Changes to Minors Staffs." mlb.com, November 29, 2011.

Silver, Michael. "Is Ray Lewis the Greatest Gridiron Leader Ever?" yahoo.com, January 3, 2013.

Sinha, Anup, and Bill Lajoie. *Character Is Not a Statistic.* Bloomington, Ind.: Xlibris, 2010.

Stadler, Mike. *The Psychology of Baseball.* New York: Gotham Books, 2007.

Stark, Jayson. "Cardinals Complete Impossible Dream." espn.com, October 29, 2011.

———. "Four Remain Pride of the Yankees." espn.com, November 4, 2009.

———. "It's a Changing of the Guard with Reds." espn.com, March 17, 2009.

———. "The Many Feats of Chipper Jones." espn.com, September 26, 2012.

———. "Welcome to The Information Age." espn.com, August 30, 2011.

———. *Worth the Wait: Tales of the 2008 Phillies.* Chicago: Triumph Books, 2009.

Strauss, Joe. "Digesting a Lost Series, Division Lead." *St. Louis Post-Dispatch,* May 16, 2010.

———. "Rasmus Drama Remains Hot Topic." *St. Louis Post-Dispatch,* July 17, 2011.

T., James. "An Interview with Bill James." sonsofsamhorn.net, September 14, 2007.

Tango, Tom (Tangotiger). "Measuring the Immeasurable." Insidethebook.com, February 9, 2009.

Torre, Joe, with Henry Dreher. *Joe Torre's Ground Rules for Winners.* New York: Hyperion, 1999.

Torre, Joe, and Tom Verducci. *The Yankee Years.* New York: Doubleday, 2009.

Valade, Jodie. "Orlando Cabrera is the Cleveland Indians' Voice of Experience (and winning)." *The Plain Dealer,* May 9, 2011.

Verducci, Tom. "Dear America, Wish You Were Here." *Sports Illustrated,* November 3, 2008.

———. "Party's Just Getting Started." *Sports Illustrated,* July 16, 2007.

Weinberg, Rick. "Jeter's backhand flip rescues Yankees." espn.com, July 23, 2004.

Whiting, Robert. *You Gotta Have Wa.* New York: Vintage, 1989.

Wright, Craig. "The Aging of Honus Wagner." *The Hardball Times Baseball Annual 2009.*

——. "Baseball's Best Batting Coach." *A Page from Baseball's Past,* June 15, 2012.

——. "Beauty Bancroft." *A Page from Baseball's Past,* September 16, 2013.

——. "Piazza, Hall of Fame Catcher." *The Hardball Times Baseball Annual 2009.*

INDEX